what
God
allows

Ivor Shapiro

Doubleday

New York   London   Sydney

Auckland   Toronto

what God allows

The crisis of faith and conscience in one Catholic church

PUBLISHED BY DOUBLEDAY
a division of Bantam Doubleday Dell Publishing Group, Inc.
1540 Broadway, New York, New York 10036

DOUBLEDAY and the portrayal of an anchor with a dolphin
are trademarks of Doubleday, a division of Bantam
Doubleday Dell Publishing Group, Inc.

Library of Congress Cataloging-in-Publication Data

Shapiro, Ivor, 1953–
    What God allows: the crisis of faith and conscience in
one Catholic church / Ivor Shapiro.
        p.   cm.
    1. Catholic Church.   Pope (1978– : John Paul II).
Veritatis splendor.   2. Christian ethics—Papal
documents.   3. Catholics—New York (State)—Buffalo.
4. United States—Church history—20th century.
5. Catholic Church—Doctrines.   6. St. Paul's Church
(Kenmore, N.Y.)   I. Title.
BJ1249.S42   1996
282′.74797—dc20   95-48986
                                                                    CIP

ISBN 0-385-47293-5
Copyright © 1996 by Ivor Shapiro
All Rights Reserved
Printed in the United States of America
March 1996
First Edition

1   3   5   7   9   10   8   6   4   2

Book design by Claire Naylon Vaccaro

*Jesus said to Simon Peter: "You are
'Rock,' and on this rock I will
build my church, and the jaws of
death shall not prevail against it. . . ."*

—THE GOSPEL FOR THE
TWENTY-FIRST SUNDAY
IN ORDINARY TIME

*". . . I will give you the keys of the
kingdom of heaven; what you forbid
on earth shall be forbidden in
heaven, and what you allow on earth
shall be allowed in heaven."*

—MATTHEW 16:19
(REVISED ENGLISH BIBLE)

For Louise
who believed

Contents

Easter

On Tuesday, October 5, 1993, Pope John Paul II sent to the bishops of the world an encyclical letter called *Veritatis Splendor (The Splendor of Truth)*. The letter declared that moral truths are absolute and certain, and weighed in against those Catholic thinkers who stress individuals' freedom to make moral decisions based on their own consciences. In preparation for a lengthy 1995 encyclical that would denounce abortion, euthanasia, artificial contraception, capital punishment, and other aspects of a burgeoning "culture of death," *Veritatis* urged the world's bishops to make sure that teachings and practices in Catholic institutions conform to official doctrine.

In an ordinary American parish, the months leading up to and following *Veritatis* were an opportune time to test the firmness of Rome's grip on Roman Catholics. While theologians debated the encyclical's merits and authority, bishops proved slow to respond to its call to take charge of colleges and hospitals. But neither prelates nor scholars would have the final say on Catholics' freedom of conscience. That verdict would be delivered in the court of the local parish.

This is the true story of how that year went in the parish of St. Paul's, Kenmore, New York.

Easter

Darkness

Saturday night, but the Sabres are playing away tonight, and the War Me-morial Auditorium, the "Aud" to the crowds who would otherwise be mass-ing here, is deserted as a pink dusk falls over the Niagara frontier. On the shoreline of Lake Erie a handful of walkers, jackets bravely open over their sweaters, celebrate the apparent onset of spring, though the wind off the icy lake brings shivers as it makes its way north, under the I-190 thruway, past the ochre stone of City Hall, and up Delaware Avenue. Over to the right, Saturday-nighters are congregating at the Sports City Grill and Network, a nightspot "as dedicated to sports as the town of Buffalo," a monument to its owner, Jim Kelly, indefatigable quarterback of the NFL's most reliably al-most-but-not-quite team. Just ahead, high atop a Fleet Bank building, twin green Statues of Liberty flash solemnly in the dusk over an empty banking district. Beyond, to downtown's east side, cops of the 12th Precinct are readying themselves for whatever violence this night may bring.

As the lake wind dissipates to the left and right of Delaware, the crowds are moving into the theater district. Jethro Tull is playing at Shea's; they're doing *Fiddler on the Roof,* again, at the Pfeifer; at the Kleinhans Music Hall, pianist Angela Cheng joins the Philharmonic to play Grieg. The wind has become a breeze by the time it passes Cleveland Street, named for one of the two Buffalo-raised U.S. Presidents, and Millard Fillmore Hospital, named for the other. On Main Street, to the east, it's jazz at the Anchor Bar, where Buffalo-style chicken wings were invented; to the west, the serious drinking is just beginning near Buffalo State College.

Near the parkland site of the Pan-American Exposition of 1901, where President William McKinley was shot dead, the night air is almost still and almost warm. A mile and a half further north on Delaware, in the "village" of Kenmore, some five hundred adults and children stand in near-silence and near-total darkness as a fire is lit in a sand-filled brass bowl at the back of a neo-Gothic cruciform church. In the dark silence, a small child's voice echoes, "Light out! Why?" As if to answer, a disembodied amplified voice says: *Dear friends in Christ, on this most holy night, when our Lord Jesus Christ passed from death to life, the church invites her children throughout the world to come together in vigil and prayer. . . . May the light of Christ, rising in glory, dispel the darkness of our hearts and minds.*

In a quiet chaos of shuffling and squeezing, those in the rear vestibule light long thin candles off the paschal flame and make their way back to their seats. The Easter candle itself is carried slowly down the center aisle. Three times, from the balcony above, a tenor announces: *The light of Christ.* Three times, as the light spreads slowly from wick to wick and creeps up stone walls amid incense fumes to shine on teak rafters, low, untrained voices intone the response: *Thanks be to God.*

Tonight, the ancient ritual will be played out hundreds of thousands of times in cities and towns on every continent and in most languages. Here in the parish of St. Paul's, Kenmore, in the diocese of Buffalo in the ecclesiastical province of New York, they are not just celebrating the discovery of an empty tomb in first-century Palestine but welcoming eight newcomers. Four women, three men, and one pubescent girl stand with their families in the dark, holding lit candles. Monsignor Paul Whitney, pastor of St. Paul's Church, chants the *Exultet* in Gregorian style and occasionally crackly voice—*Rejoice, heavenly powers! Sing, choirs of angels! Exult, all creation around God's throne! Jesus Christ, our King, is risen!* . . . These eight are the Elect—before this great vigil ends two and a half hours from now, they will belong to the Roman Catholic Church. Among them stands Mike Merrill, a student of medicine, a reader of philosophy, and a habitual questioner of things both sacred and profane. Mike must shortly proclaim his acceptance of and belief in the church's creed. Born to Presbyterians but married to a Catholic, Mike has taken his preparation for baptism with great seriousness, but he is too ambivalent by nature to be comfortable around creeds. He wonders, half seriously, if he might set a record for the fastest time from baptism to excommunication.

Judy Nice, standing in the gloom between her husband and daughter, can, if she strains, just pick out the backs of the heads of the seven adults whom she led through the initiation process culminating tonight. As Director of Adult Sacraments at St. Paul's, her chief preoccupation had been the progress of Mike Merrill and the others toward membership in the church. *Had* been, that is, until she was obliged to face head-on the question of whether, in conscience, she could continue to teach the doctrines of the Catholic Church. Two aisles to her right, both hands clasped tight on his missalette, stands Dennis Hurley, who wrote the letter that made up Judy's mind—after Dennis himself had decided that he could no longer, in conscience, keep silent about what was being taught in the church's name.

O happy fault, sings Father Paul, his voice rising and falling sporadically in the ancient rhythm, *O necessary sin of Adam, which gained for us so great a Redeemer.* . . . Bernice Graff, standing among the eucharistic ministers, watches the two priests in the sanctuary and thinks how fine her son Paul would have looked among them; never mind, she knows he is here, lightly present in the air just above her right shoulder. And, over the other shoulder, another dead son, Bob, free at last of AIDS. . . . *The power of this holy night dispels all evil, washes guilt away, restores lost innocence, brings mourners joy.* . . .

Among the lectors, ready to deliver a prophecy from Isaiah, stands Dick Shaner with his wife, Jamie. An encounter with tragedy nearly six years ago began their evolution into pillars of the church, although agents provocateurs might seem more like it of late, with Jamie, especially, emerging as a critic both of universal Catholic doctrine and of local pastoral practice. A few feet away, Ken Monaco, a vociferous supporter of Pope John Paul II's recent blunt attacks on liberal theology and loose morality, stands with his wife and son. The short distance between Jamie and Ken tonight conceals the deep gulf between them, a division over nothing less than the meaning of being Catholic. Similar lines divide laypeople, in parishes and dioceses across America. On both sides, combatants see themselves as underdogs, with the liberals ranged against the might of Rome and the orthodox against the very culture of modern America; they share only the certainty that the outcome of this conflict will determine the future shape of Catholicism. And they are right in this, because, given the waning strength of the celibate priesthood, lay leaders like Judy and Bernice and the Shaners and the Monacos are their church's only practical hope of survival.

. . . *It casts out hatred, brings us peace, and humbles earthly pride.* . . . Several rows back, Ruthie Hemerlein, who has difficulty staying on her feet this long, sits down carefully, holding her lit candle. It was Ken Monaco who drove seventy-year-old Ruthie to church tonight, and she is as fond of him as she is of Judy Nice. As a divorcée and longtime opponent of Catholic fundamentalism, she shares Judy's profound antipathy toward religious autocracies; as a devotee of the Blessed Virgin and of the holy Rosary, she has much in common with Ken. The ideological war is far from her mind tonight. Despite the weakness of her knees, a strange sense of inner peace has filled Ruthie. Amid the night's many reminders of death and new life, the prospect of her own dying seems as close as the flame of the candle in her right hand. This is a bit odd because she has not felt ill lately, although a sea of diagnostic storms lies behind her—systemic lupus and breast cancer among them—and ahead, perhaps close, lies the port of last refuge. The inevitable solitude scares her as much as it always has, but the idea of death itself has lost its sting.

. . . *Night truly blest when heaven is wedded to earth and man is reconciled with God.* . . . Ruthie closes her eyes—better just to listen for a while, since she can see nothing from her seat but the backs of a couple who, unlike all the others, have asked for their names to be changed here for reasons that will become clear. Call them Dave and Claire Taylor. Like many in church tonight, Dave and Claire understand little about the ideological warfare between liberal and conservative Catholics, and care less; they just hope for an early end to the doctrinal arguments that have divided a segment of their parish's leadership core. In Dave and Claire's shared view, love and a sense of family are all that matter in the end. Ken, Jamie, and Judy have all heard Dave Taylor tell, more than once, about another dark night, during a time when love and harmony seemed far away. Claire had left him, and Dave had filled his lonely world with rage. On that other night, Dave had been visited by a scene from his childhood—the family at table, little Dave announcing he "hated" potato salad, his father saying, "No, son, you *dislike* potato salad. Only animals hate." And Dave had heard a voice in his head, saying as clearly as the pastor's chant here and now, "Well, either my father was wrong or I'm an animal. Because I do hate her."

But that was three years before this night, and two years before the summer of Dave's rejoicing.

Summer

Ordinary Time

August: At the Saturn Club on Delaware Avenue in Buffalo, a few miles south of St. Paul's, a portly saxophonist with an outrageous nose led his band in a sensuous "Unforgettable." As bride and groom swayed in their postnuptial dance, heads together, murmuring and exchanging quick kisses, as friends raised cameras and the groom's father stood next to a buffet table watching a Polaroid take shape—this one moment existed outside of time. It could have been any wedding, anywhere.

The bride's family was not, after all, entirely absent. One sister was maid of honor, the other among the bridesmaids, and if Claire had entertained any hope that her parents would surprise everyone and show up, she had kept it to herself. Claire, broad-shouldered, a short veil perched behind her like a dove's tail, glided down the long center aisle of St. Paul's on Dave's arm, a beaming Dave chattering as always in her ear. As a young flutist executed the Pachelbel Canon in slow-march time, Claire wore the careful happy-nervous smile of the universal bride. As they approached the altar step, she grinned toward the front pew on her right, where Dave's family had turned to watch them—trim, white-haired Mr. Taylor, a picture of serious dignity; Mrs. Taylor, big and smiling in pastel blue; a long line of sisters and sisters-in-law. She didn't even glance at the two front pews on her left.

There were perhaps six or seven dozen people in the church, and all but the groom's family party were white. That discrepancy largely accounted for the emptiness of the front pews on the bride's side—that and the fact that Dave had been married before. But now, the routines of Mass provided a calm river of alleluias and also-with-yous on which to sail after too much time spent arguing and hoping and worrying. Words from scripture floated by. Mr. Taylor, Sr., read from Romans, in a slightly quavery version of his practiced Baptist deacon's voice: *Nothing can come between us and the love of Christ* . . . The Gospel offered Beatitudes: *Happy are the peacemakers* . . . There being no chairs at hand, Dave and Claire were obliged to kneel for the homily, which placed their backs to the pulpit, but no matter: They heard little of the priest's paean to "the holy place of human relationship," because Dave was whispering in Claire's ear most of the time.

Behind them, Jamie Shaner's son Scott whispered, "When do they say, 'I do'?"

"Soon," Jamie answered. "Shhhhhh."

Claire and Dave, do you come here freely, and without reservation, to give yourselves to each other in marriage? The answers were inaudible to Scott, but then bride and groom were facing each other, and first Claire, then Dave, promised to be true until death. And when Dave planted a firm kiss on Claire's ready lips, everyone applauded and the folk ensemble sang—". . . *Come and see, come and be, be all you are, and all you can be. . . . Come and journey with me"*—and the flute sang too, and the August heat rose to challenge the high ceiling fans, and Mass went on.

Racial differences aside, there was much here that was foreign to the Baptist Taylor family—the statues and candles; the instructions to sit, to stand, to kneel; the rapid rote responses (*May the Lord accept the sacrifice at your hands for the praise and glory of his name, for our good and the good of all his church* . . .); the prayers for Pope and bishop; the invocation of Mary, the apostles, and all the saints. But after the prayer of consecration, you could watch goose bumps crossing the barriers of background as Dave's oldest brother, a professor of voice and musicology at Alabama State University, tall and muscular in black tie and tails, sang the Lord's Prayer, robust baritone rising to a crescendo—"*For thine is the Kingdom*"—who would guess he grabbed three hours' sleep this morning after driving north through the hot night?—"*and the power*"—his brow soaked with sweat—"*and the GLO-O-O-RY*"—the notes filling the high roof and bouncing back—"*for ever, and e-e-e-ver. Amen.*"

For thirty seconds after the final note died, there was utter silence in the church. Afterward the exchange of the peace (Dave and his mom hugging hugely while Claire kissed his dad), the bustle of communion (Dave's Protestant parents joining the line after a hesitation, an exchanged glance, a mutual shrug), the Alabama baritone's *Ave Maria* (in Latin, while papers were signed amid flashbulbs at the feet of Mary and Joseph), and the final blessings blurred into the recessional. Then, as the congregation filed past the reception line at the back of the church, the "HAWWWW-ha-HAAWWW-ha-HAWWW" of Dave's mighty laugh echoed down the nave and backs were slapped with mighty thuds, in the way that backs are slapped when a long and difficult task is finished.

Dave's father, like Dave himself, was married and divorced before meeting the woman of his dreams. He was twenty-five; his bride, Evelyn, was just sixteen. Dave's father, an upholsterer, would go on to be the first black president of his union local and, later, an insurance consultant. His wife wanted to become a nurse, and so she did, although she did not return to high school until the youngest of her eight children had entered kindergarten. Dave was the third, born in 1952.

As the '50s became the '60s, the East Side began to deteriorate. One night when Dave was eight, his father got into a dispute with gang members who were partying late in the house next door. Dave remembers his father yelling for his wife to call the police. The police took forever to arrive; the gang gathered outside the Taylor house; jeers and threats got louder and more graphic. Mr. Taylor assembled his two oldest sons and a nephew, armed himself with a steel rake, and tried to reason with the gang.

Little Dave heard his father say, "We don't want trouble." But when someone grabbed Dave's cousin and knocked him to the ground, Mr. Taylor hit the guy in the head with the business end of the rake. The youth went down, his buddies started retreating, and Dave's dad raised the rake again, aiming for the throat. But as he brought it down, the rake head flew off, and when a siren wailed at last in the street, the boy staggered to his feet and followed his retreating gang buddies.

Mr. Taylor says today that it was God who saved him from killing a young man that night. Dave himself says that his memories of that night remain a fundamental piece of his makeup. "That night," he says, "I discovered that my father was ready to die to protect his family."

From age seven or eight, Dave's weekends were spent at Shiloh Baptist on Cedar and Pine, where his dad was, and is, a deacon. Prayer meeting Friday night; Baptist Training Union on Saturday; Sunday School followed by church on the Lord's Day. At fourteen, Dave decided that being an usher was preferable to sitting in a pew for hours on end. The sermons continued at home—the evils of drink and drugs; the virtue of hard work. Dave's dad would tell the kids, "I do what I can for you, but I'm not going to take any bull crap." A common punishment for bull crap was cleaning the kitchen floor—"You got all that energy to burn, let's see you burn it"—and when it was done, it had to be as clean as Mom would have left it.

In grade school, the kids called scrawny Dave "Celery." At high school in the late '60s, he was known for his individualist yellow pants and weird hats. At the State University of New York at Buffalo, where he juggled science courses with a full-time job taking care of research animals, his grades declined until he dropped out. He was twenty-one when he married the first time, a step he now ascribes to foolish youth; the marriage collapsed within six months.

Dave was working as a nurse-technician at Children's Hospital while studying economics part-time when he met nurse Claire, six years his junior, in 1980. He liked her shy careful courtesy; she noticed him staying back after his shift to tend a large and seriously ill girl whose care was especially demanding. He was gentle, respectful, and funny: a new nurse on the ward would often be greeted by Dave donning stethoscope and Peter Sellers voice, announcing himself as "Dr Goombody" and asking strange questions about nonexistent procedures ("What? You didn't do a uneridisis?"). He also seemed unusually helpful—and not just to Claire, although he did seem, as they say, "interested." Still, Dave was cautious. His divorce finalized at last, his off-and-on relationship with a white woman finally went bust in '82, and after that he didn't want any more relationships for a while—certainly not with anyone white.

But one night, a heavy snowstorm left a group of nurses and aides stranded in Claire's apartment near the hospital, and while the others drifted off in hospital blankets, Dave and Claire talked for most of the night. Soon they were meeting for drinks after work. When Claire dropped Dave off after a drink at JJ's pub one night, he leaned over and said, nervous as a teenager, "Thanks for a wonderful time," and pecked her cheek before disappearing into the night. It was the first time Claire had been kissed by a black man. Before spring arrived, they were dating.

It would be many years before Claire's parents learned anything about their daughter's new man beyond the obvious: his race and his religion. But that was enough. There were no gang fights in Claire's childhood memories of the sedate, all-white, middle-class village of Kenmore. Her father had been a fighter pilot in World War II; his young betrothed, German-American and devoutly Catholic like him, had waited for him until peacetime. After they married, the groom found work as an engineer with Bell Aerospace and the bride's parents made space for the newlyweds in their family home. As children arrived (Claire being the third), they moved to larger houses, in Kenmore and then in suburban Williamsville.

Claire's parents were Catholics first and last. They allowed Claire to switch to public school to keep her younger brother company on the bus to kindergarten (there being no preschool class at the parochial school), and allowed her to stay because she seemed to thrive on the superior music and art classes. But Claire and her brother were dragged to catechism classes at church, taught to pray the Rosary, and hauled to Mass every Sunday and holy day. Claire's mom would say, "I had five children because that's how many God wanted me to have." When ten-year-old Claire was diagnosed as a diabetic, her parents concluded that they must have done something to deserve it, which is also what they concluded in the spring of April 1984, when Claire announced that Dave had moved in with her.

Claire, who had emerged from the scary diabetes episodes with a clear sense that God had protected her, never lost altogether this feeling of connection with her heavenly father. Long after leaving her parents' home, she continued to attend Mass weekly—at Newman students' centers while earning her nursing diploma and B.S., and then, after starting at Children's in 1980, at Blessed Sacrament near her apartment. But, faithful as she was, Claire felt untouched by her church's view that she was living in grave sin,

on at least two counts. She considered artificial birth control a simple necessity, if only because of her volatile blood sugar levels. As for sex before
marriage, it didn't seem like sin to her because, as she reasoned, there was a
"commitment" to make the relationship work.

Except that when push came to shove, there was more commitment on
Dave's side than hers, and when Dave started talking about making a future
together, Claire got spooked. She knew she loved Dave, but she wasn't
ready to make war with the world. Dave's response was to push harder, and
meanwhile he had taken steps to shorten the distance between them. He
had decided to embrace Catholicism.

Dave hadn't regularly attended Shiloh or any other church since graduating from high school, but had for some time enjoyed the meeting-room
Masses that the hospital chaplain, Father Frank Tuchols, held for the staff.
No doubt Claire was part of the draw, but Dave says he was searching for
. . . well, he didn't know what, but the peaceful atmosphere in the room,
the rhythm of the liturgy, and the whole idea of a dozen or more co-workers
seated in a semicircle to share prayer and bread and wine gave him a warm
feeling. Except, Dave wasn't sure if he was allowed to receive communion
with his colleagues, so he stayed back, and no one ever invited him into the
inner circle.

By the time both Dave and Claire had left Children's—Claire for a
traveling job selling laboratory equipment, Dave (by then in graduate
school studying economics) to join Key Bank as a commercial loans officer—the couple had begun attending Sunday Mass together at St. Andrew's, the big, modern, sophisticated parish on Sheridan Drive. But Dave
didn't like it much. In the absence of an effective p.a. system, he couldn't
make out what was going on most of the time. The faithful struck him as
automatons, mumbling rote responses to mumbling priests—all the words
drowned out, more often than not, by the organ—and somehow knowing,
with no apparent script, when to stand and when to kneel. "What if the
priest played a practical joke and mumbled total nonsense?" he mused to
Claire one day. "Would you all still kneel, stand, and sit in the right
places?" The experience made him feel alienated from Claire, who, like all
the others, was totally at home with both words and movements and, like
all the others, clambered over his knees to leave him sitting awkward and
alone at communion time.

On Christmas Day in 1988, they decided to try St. Paul's, just down Delaware Avenue from St. Andrew's, for the family Mass at 10 A.M. Somehow, the older church's subtle balance between informality and reverence seemed a bit more comfortable to Dave, and he claims never to have felt out of place there, despite the intricacies of Catholic ritual and the parish's almost exclusively white complexion. Certainly, the p.a. system worked better. Dave even attended an "Inquiry" session of the Rite of Christian Initiation for Adults, usually known simply as RCIA—or, sometimes, by the ancient name of "the catechumenate."

But at home, Claire was by now feeling under increasing pressure to choose between Dave and her family. When her mother underwent surgery for uterine cancer, followed by radiation treatment, Claire couldn't resist the feeling that if she left Dave, her mom would somehow be OK. In February 1991, Claire moved out, taking Chanel, one of their two shih tzus, with her. Within months, Claire's mom was in remission.

Dave descended into bitter rage. He spent a lot of his time staring at the television set, stopped going to Mass, and started smoking again, a pack a day. It was at that time that he named the feeling he had toward Claire: hate. He hit bottom on a night he would later describe to Judy Nice's RCIA group as "the worst night of my life." Coming home from a tough day at the bank, he dragged himself into the apartment and decided on a dinner of popcorn. He plugged in the electric popper, and all the lights went out. So he called a neighbor to help him fix the fuse, and was cautioned against overloading the circuit again. So he put out every light in the place and plugged in the popper again, but standing there in darkness listening to kernels pop made him more depressed. So he turned the popper off and transferred the kernels to a saucepan on the gas stove, but the lid didn't fit snugly, and popped corn went flying around the kitchen and making little fires on the stovetop while Dave tried to kick his dog Charlie away from the hot corn on the floor. He took the saucepan off the heat and dug in, but the first mouthful produced an unpopped kernel that broke a tooth. Then Dave went straight to bed in his suit pants and shirt, pulled the blanket over his head, curled into a fetal position, and moped himself to sleep. The next day, he woke up with a decision to get his spiritual life together and became a regular presence at the St. Paul's "Inquiry" sessions; soon, he had graduated to the catechumenate proper, and was preparing for confirmation.

Claire, meanwhile, had watched her mom recover and, just before Halloween 1991, made up her mind that she was not, after all, going to let her parents defeat her love for Dave. She decided to call Dave and to say, before he hung up, at least this: "I want to talk to you today; I don't want to wait to see you in heaven."

But all she got out, in a voice that trembled over the line, was his name, and hers. "Dave? This is Claire."

Until that moment, Dave had known exactly what he would say if she ever called: "I hate your selfish guts!" Then he would hang up. But there was something in the shakiness of her voice that made his plan impossible. The phone call lasted about an hour; when it ended, they had agreed to meet for lunch the next day. A few days later, Dave applied to the Tribunal of the diocese of Buffalo for an annulment of his first marriage, and later that month, when Claire's dad showed up at Claire's house in Williamsville to help with some household project, Dave's dog Charlie was in the yard, so he left. From then on, when Claire's father called Claire, he would ask, "Is Charlie there?" It was as close as he could come to acknowledging Dave's reappearance in his daughter's life.

Dave was confirmed and received into communion at the Easter Vigil in 1992. By then, the involvement with RCIA had become a vital source of strength for both him and Claire. Judy Nice and her team of parishioners who helped guide Inquirers and candidates—Ruthie Hemerlein, Jamie Shaner, and Ken Monaco among them—seemed like family. Or, rather, better than family: here, Dave and Claire felt accepted and supported unconditionally.

It seemed automatic that they would continue to be part of the group after Dave's entry into the church. By Christmas, the annulment had come through and the wedding planning begun. When they took Claire's parents out to dinner to tell them these tidings, the response was explosive, and the months that followed saw the full spectrum of conflict from screaming matches to silent rage. Claire was informed that her parents had consulted various priests and received advice ranging from prayer to sending the couple away to live in a commune. There were no more dinner invitations for Dave. "The only people who live with black people are tramps and whores," Claire's mom said at one point, in the way of suggesting her daughter might need professional help.

Dave, hearing this, attempted to put it into perspective. "She doesn't mean it," he told Claire. "She's just trying anything she can to bring you to your senses." He himself had almost no direct contact with Claire's parents other than one frosty encounter with his future mother-in-law in Claire's driveway. Claire's distressed parents rarely telephoned when Dave was likely to be home, and if he answered, the conversation was short. "They don't know me," Dave complained to Claire when he was tired of being understanding. "If they would just take the time to talk to me and my family. My father is rich beyond compare—not in money but in ethics. Three of my brothers have Ph.D.s, three of my sisters have their master's. They don't know anything about me. All they know is that I'm Dave Taylor and I work at Key Bank."

When summer arrived and it became clear that the wedding would proceed, Claire's mom sniffed, "OK, be like E———," naming an aunt who had married a Jew. "Your grandfather will turn in his grave." And when Claire's parents declined to attend the nuptials, Claire's brothers, unlike her sisters, decided they would spend the wedding day with their parents, to keep them company.

At the Saturn Club, the wedding crowd cloistered itself in a shady courtyard where everyone settled into yellow folding chairs at tables clothed in white with sprays of lilies and baby's breath. Before the day was done, Dave's father would be persuaded to take a turn at the keyboard. Dave and Claire, touring the tables, approached Ruthie Hemerlein, seventy next month, sitting under a beech tree, her hands lightly clasped on the tabletop, a pressure bandage emerging from the short right sleeve of her dress. "My favorite person!" roared Dave, bending to embrace her. Ruthie it was who had given Dave his first Rosary. Every morning he touches the crucifix and then crosses himself, and he prays a decade or two whenever he's in an airplane. It was a beautiful service, Ruthie told Dave, and as for the shortage of chairs in the sanctuary, she figured Dave needed as much time on his knees as he could get. At this, Dave rocked back on his heels. "And rightfully so!" he shouted. "And rightfully so!" As his neigh crashed across the courtyard, people turned to one another and smiled. "That's Dave." Claire's arm, locked around his waist, led him on to the next group.

Talk at Ruthie's table, which was occupied entirely by RCIA team members, turned to mixed marriages. It was an easy jump from mixed races to mixed religions. Coty-Ann Henk, six years younger than Ruthie and a lot more spry, recalled having been forbidden to attend her brother-in-law's marriage in a Presbyterian church. "It was against church law," she told the others. "By attending, you would be condoning it."

"Nope, was *never* against church law," Ruthie said. "My cousin married in a Protestant church and we were all there—my dad even read a lesson. Trouble was, back then, all you knew about church law was what the priests chose to tell you." Ruthie, who is as devoted a Catholic as you will ever meet, who considers the Holy Mother a personal friend with whom she chats, woman to woman, almost every day, has known many priests in her day. There are many she admires (including Father Paul), but she is capable of harsh words (usually delivered with an ironic lilt and no bitterness) about those who spend their lives fund-raising, power-mongering, and law-keeping. Which was part of the reason she never bothered to apply for an annulment after divorcing her husband thirteen years ago. "God and I both know what kind of crummy marriage I had," she told Coty and the others. "Why would I need a bunch of men to sign a paper that says so?"

Across the table, Judy Nice said nothing as she listened to Ruthie. A tight nervous smile played on Judy's lips, and she held her hands clasped in her lap, which was her usual pose lately when sensitive matters were under discussion. Divorce was, to her, one such matter.

This past winter, it had fallen to Judy, as the parish's Director of Adult Sacraments, to tell a woman who had married a divorcé she should stop presenting herself at the communion rail until her husband's long-stalled annulment came through—if it ever did. Ever since, Judy had found herself increasingly uncomfortable with her teaching role in a church which was, she felt, often hard-hearted, legalistic, and discriminatory, especially in its dealings with women. More and more often, when talk at RCIA sessions turned from matters of faith and love to matters of doctrine and conscience, Judy was hearing herself steering the conversation clear of controversy. She didn't like it but saw, for the moment, no feasible alternative.

Like Judy, Marianne Parry said little during the discussion on divorce, merely nodding and smiling, her mouth puckering slightly under a thick mop of Beatle-style black hair. But then, Marianne, an intensive-care nurse at Buffalo General, is on the shy side. A faithful part of Dave and Claire's RCIA family, Marianne had done something new this summer: she had begun sponsoring a baptism candidate (catechumen) through the initiation rite.

The late-June sun had poured warmly through St. Paul's deep blue stained glass onto Marianne and her catechumen, tiny Janet Ehrensberger. As she faced Janet in the midst of the ten o'clock congregation, Marianne's right hand shook slightly tracing the sign of the cross first on Janet's ears (while a team member intoned, . . . *that you may hear the voice of God*), then on Janet's eyes (. . . *that you may see the glory of God*), and lips (. . . *that you may respond . . .*), and over her heart (. . . *that Christ may dwell there . . .*), her shoulders (*to bear the gentle yoke . . .*), hands (*that Christ may be known in the work that you do*), and feet (*to walk in the way of Christ*), by the end of which Janet's flushed cheeks had developed damp streaks.

"What do you ask of God's church?" Father Gary Bagley, a weekend assistant at St. Paul's, had demanded in turn of each of the four being welcomed into the catechumenate.

"Baptism," Janet had answered in her turn, her voice high but firm.

"What does faith offer to you?"

"A foundation," Janet had replied, a response that had come to her that very morning, when she woke up. By this, she meant that she needed something to base her life on, now that her husband was dead.

If you were looking for a single word to describe the life that Janet and Michael Ehrensberger had shared, the word would contain neither the harshest of consonants nor the most passionate of vowels. Its length would be polite: neither so short as to be curt nor so long as to be importunate. It should be a soft pastel word, to match the candy-land blue siding on their house on Englewood Avenue in leafy North Buffalo. A pleasing, unmenacing word, like the ceramic dolls that Janet used to mold and paint while Michael watched TV in the quiet evenings that made up their weeks and years. A word such as: "contentment."

They met at a common relative's funeral in 1978, when Janet was twenty-four. Mike was an easygoing, soft-spoken guy with soft, curly black hair and dark Germanic features; Janet was small, blond, and shy. He drove a forklift truck; she was taking a paralegal program. Before they married, they ascertained that neither was interested in having children, and al-

though Janet went through broody periods afterward, Michael didn't want
to know. He was distantly Catholic; she, distantly Protestant. They married
in the Kenmore Municipal Hall in 1980. He went to the Legion hall Friday
nights; she stayed home; Saturdays, they'd take in a movie, except in the
summer, when they moved to a park in Akron, N.Y., where they owned a
trailer next to that owned by Michael's folks.

They were, in their quiet way, happy. And then, in March 1992, Mike
fell down an elevator shaft at work and died.

Mike was buried from St. Paul's, where he had been baptized, and Janet
was invited to join the bereavement group run by Sister Mary Jude Rindfuss
of the Sisters of St. Mary of Namur (S.S.M.N.), the parish's Director of
Pastoral Care. It helped, at first, to hear other people talking about their
losses, but the other widows were mainly older and their husbands had
mainly died of natural causes—quite unlike Mike, who had gone to work
one morning and never returned. Janet had no wish to rehash her feelings
forever—she just wanted to figure out how to live without Mike, a puzzle for
which neither the group nor any of her friends or relatives had any clues.
People said, "Well, death is a part of life." Janet thought: "No shit."

Lonely and confused, Janet started spending a lot of time with the
woman who shared her loss most nearly, Michael's mother, and accompany-
ing her to Mass. She surprised herself by feeling wholly comfortable among
these Catholics. No fire or brimstone, no politics, not much noise. She
noticed that the people she met at St. Paul's were able to joke about religion, and to swear and stuff, like regular people. For the first time in her life,
she started toying with the idea of actually joining a church. One Thursday
night, for want of something better to do, she wandered into an RCIA
Inquiry session in the parish center. She thought it might help to fill the
gaping hole at the center of her life. She also was finding herself longing for
her own death; and if she was going to die, she might as well get baptized
first. By the summer of '93, she had decided nothing would ever fill the gap
Michael had left. She was also thinking less frequently about her own death.
But somehow, when Thursday nights came along, she still found herself
driving over to St. Paul's for Inquiry, where the topics ranged as widely as
anyone wanted them to—from the origins of evil and death to the existence
of angels and the sexual identity of God. And when three other newcomers
were ready to join the catechumenate, which met for study Sunday morn-

ings in the rectory, Janet resolved to go along for the ride. This group's sights were set on being received into the church at the following Easter Vigil, but, as Judy Nice kept saying, being in the group was a process, an exploration—not a commitment.

Besides, with Michael's parents heading off to the trailer park in Akron, it was going to be a long summer.

Summer: The smell of charcoal and newly mowed lawns. Flags hung over Kenmore's porches, ladders were propped against its walls, and gardeners were bent over flower beds. A time for boating on the Niagara and picnics in Delaware Park and excursions to Artpark, Chautauqua, the Shaw Festival over in Ontario. On Long Island, the currently vacationing but always Most Reverend Edward D. Head, D.D., Bishop of Buffalo, burned his hands in a spill of cooking fat and was rushed to the hospital. In Wichita, Kansas, a shooting attack on abortionist Dr. George Tiller came, as a Buffalo *News* editorial pointed out, "only days after an Alabama priest stirred controversy by . . . advocating the murder of physicians who perform legal abortions, calling such murders 'justifiable homicide.' " (Shortly afterward, the priest was suspended from parish duties by the Archbishop of Mobile.) The *News*'s religion reporter, on a slow day, surveyed an unspecified number of parishes in the Buffalo diocese and reported that in the absence of a clear policy, most priests did not permit girls to serve at the altar—and those who did permit them were unwilling to have their names printed in the paper. "For me, it's a nonissue," explained one such anonymous priest (who was, as it happened, Monsignor Paul Whitney, pastor of St. Paul's), "but I don't want to call attention to it. I'd get a ton of mail that I'd have to answer."

Summer: A time for nonnews and abstract reflections. "Have we lost our Catholic identity?" pondered an unsigned parish notes column in the St. Paul's weekly bulletin. "Not at all," it answered itself. "We are a eucharistic people and a service people. This is our heritage as Catholics. . . . Professor James Coleman of the University of Chicago asked why the dropout rate in Catholic high schools was so low. The answer, he discovered, was something called Social Capital—a reservoir of interest, love, care that surrounded the students. . . ."

Dick Shaner savors summer with the appetite of any devoted golfer, but somewhere in these past five summers there has been an acrid hint of irretrievable loss.

Before the sun began its westward fall on Saturday, July 9, 1988, Dick and Jamie were the kind of perfect young couple who had the kind of seemingly flawless life that often becomes the stuff of other people's jokes. Dick: articulate, dapper, tall and blandly handsome, upwardly mobile in public relations. Jamie: bookkeeper for real estate lawyer, liquid brown eyes, soft brown hair, usually trim and leggy but lately big with their second child due any day. House: comfortable, two-story, on a placid suburban street. Best friends: each other. Worst habits: none to speak of. Satisfaction-with-life quotient: moderate to high. Afternoon activity in the day's plan: a waterfront stroll with three-year-old Scott and his grandparents: Jamie's parents had driven up from Arizona for the impending birth, and Dick's parents were now on the road from their home in Olean, New York, seventy-five miles to the south. Neatly written note on the front door:

Dear Grandpa and Grandma Shaner,
    We've taken a drive to Sisters' Hospital—all of us. The doctor just wants to check on my progress. Someone will be back shortly with Scott and a progress report. Either all of us (if I'm not in labor) or someone will see you soon. Keep your fingers crossed!
                                                                    Jamie.

In the delivery room, Dr. Powalski waited with an easy smile, put the fetal monitor on Jamie, and listened, and listened. Gradually Dick noticed tension in the room. The doctor took up an ultrasound probe and moved it over Jamie's tummy while everyone watched the screen. There: the baby lay peacefully under Jamie's rib cage. He moved the probe to another angle. There: lying still, very still, not kicking, not twitching. Not moving *at all*. Another angle: not so much as a quiver inside the womb. No one spoke, until Dick's voice came from somewhere and said, "There's no heartbeat, is there?" And it was Dick who walked into the waiting room, where four grandparents (Dick's folks having arrived as the main party pulled out of the driveway) looked up at him, ready to be happy. He held out his arms and huddled everyone in as a quarterback might, everyone except Scott, who had hung back when he saw Dick's face. When Grandma Shaner broke away from the huddle, turned around, and threw her purse skittering across the floor, Scott came over and said, "What's happening?" All Dick could think of was to say, "There's no baby."

Early on Sunday morning, Jamie delivered a dead son. Dick, at her side, gazed at the boy's hands, curled as if in sleep. Jamie thought, "He's beautiful." A nurse baptized him in the name of the Father, Son, and Holy Spirit, naming him Cory Charles Shaner, although Dick's first impulse had been to keep this name, so carefully chosen, for another son, another time.

They asked to see a priest. They didn't know why exactly: despite Dick's being a lector at St. Paul's, they were strictly Sunday Catholics— more a matter of habit than of religious conviction. The hospital chaplain came and was, Jamie said later, "an asshole." He stood at the foot of her bed with his arms crossed and said, "Pretty tough luck, huh?" He didn't touch her, and didn't say a prayer, just stood there with the assembled family until, after a few awkward moments, Jamie asked him to leave. Dick called Father Paul, whom they then hardly knew, and when he arrived, it was as if he had brought along a roomful of oxygen. He held Jamie's hand and said in his virile drawl, "Heaven has a new little angel today," which was, somehow, exactly right.

Of the burial in Mount Olivet Cemetery the following Thursday, Jamie would recall little except for an image of herself sitting on a lawn chair near a young tree at the top of a rise; Dick would remember watching the funeral director carrying a tiny coffin to the grave on the palms of his hands. That was five summers ago—years which had seen Jamie pass through the depths of a crippling grief-driven depression and emerge with a faith that had grown into what sometimes seemed to Dick something like mysticism. Dick and Jamie together had progressed from the margins of church activity to the active core—Dick serving four years on the Parish Council, including two as president, Jamie leading the weekly RCIA Inquiry sessions. Both emerged as critics of Catholic legalism and a parish sensibility that too often seemed cold and unwelcoming. Quiet-spoken and popular among parishioners whom they knew personally, they would, in the coming months, surprise themselves and others by drawing more than one line in the sand.

Now, on another brilliant Saturday like that unforgettable one five Julys ago, Dick and Jamie and Scott and two-year-old Tyler made up a pot of flowers and took it up to the cemetery. When they reached the Garden of

Angels, a place where tiny stone markers flank a heart-shaped shrubbery, Scott insisted on singing a melancholy rendition of "Happy birthday, dear Cory."

"Who's Cory?" asked Tyler, not for the first time.

"He's our brother!" Scott explained patiently.

"Where's Cory?"

"Up in heaven with God."

Tyler stretched his head back so that he was looking straight up at the sky and said, "Hi, Cory. Happy birthday." Then he strolled over to the center of the heart of shrubs, where a stone angel stood with a stone child, waist-high to the angel, gazing up at her. Tyler walked up to the figures, and stood there for a minute staring into the child's granite face. "Hi, Cory," he said again.

For nearly a week that August, the footage from Denver filled the world's TV screens: tanned, straight-haired American boys and girls (between 170,000 and 375,000 of them, depending on who was counting) in T-shirts and shorts, joking or necking or solemnly singing, eating Big Macs and playing guitars in a clean-cut drug-free "Catholic Woodstock" (as *Time* called it), shouting by their sheer presence: *Don't count this church out.*

Kenmore's Michelle Pangborn was there in Colorado with them—the Catholic youth of America, the World Youth Day delegates from around the world, the bishops and cardinals, and Pope John Paul II himself. Of the seventeen summers that have so far left their taste on those in Michelle Pangborn's future, the summer of '93 was, she says, the most momentous.

Certainly, it was the thirstiest.

Thirteen miles, they had said. It felt a lot longer than that. Sure, you can walk thirteen miles easy, when you're seventeen and it's Saturday afternoon and the sun is glinting off snow on the mountaintops and they call it a "pilgrimage." A thirteen-mile walk behind a twelve-foot-high wooden cross, to camp out under the stars in Cherry Creek State Park and awaken for Mass with the Pope and a quarter or half million people. Hey, no problem. Except for the air, or lack of it. OK, they hadn't exactly said there *would* be air to breathe, but that surely was *understood,* the way Michelle saw it. But there was no air up there in the Rockies. "Big farce," she muttered to her roommate Amy, "no air, that makes me mad." Carrying a thirty-pound backpack of overnight stuff, she could have used some air. Some water too, come to think of it—*now there's an idea*. It was, after all, 98 degrees in the shade *(shade! ha!)*.

Michelle stopped, put her pack down, put her hand to her face, and looked at her fingers. Instead of being smudged with sweat, they were caked with dry salt. Suddenly, she realized her mouth was bone-dry too. She sat down on the road, and was dimly aware of someone running to find her some water. When it came, it was *(gross!)* carbonated, one of those ubiquitous bottles supplied to World Youth Day by the Coors company. The way Michelle figured it, Coors probably donated it on condition no *real* water would be available. She drank it down, burped, got to her feet, plodded onward. This was still a city street, they hadn't reached the park itself, and when the Denver householders realized how dehydrated the pilgrims were getting, they put their hoses out on the road for general use. Too exhausted to talk to her fellow marchers, Michelle spent the last eight miles thinking about the Israelites following Moses through the desert. Well, at least there was *air* in Sinai.

Savvy, independent, chubby, her sardonic smile and blue eyes cached among freckles, dimples, and bangs, Michelle is proud to define herself as "a nerd." For her, the word means you're smart, you work hard, you *care more about what you do than what you wear*.

OK, *some* nerds are like, incredibly antisocial. OK, there's a little Nerd Pride thing going in Michelle's crowd. After the summer, Michelle would enter her senior year at Kenmore West High with the expectation that she would, once again, finish first in her class. After that? Maybe chemical engineering at MIT, or history at Harvard—she'd probably get in but she'd need a full scholarship. Her dad is a biophysicist for a medical research institute (and a trustee at St. Paul's), her mom works for the parish, running the confirmation program for teens who don't go to Catholic schools, which is the bulk of them. Michelle herself, like her two older sisters—one studying organic chemistry at Caltech, the other research engineering at Cornell—went to St. Paul's School until the eighth grade and then switched to the public system because of the reputation for inferior academics at the local girls' and coed Catholic high schools.

Boyfriend? Dating? Michelle grimaces—you know, there are *some* teenage girls who have better things to do than moon over football players. OK, she goes out with guys, but usually in a group. Religion? OK, maybe she's slightly unusual: she never misses Mass on a Sunday or holy day, and taught a fourth-grade religion class in the past year. Her $675 air-hotel fare to Denver was paid by a special collection at St. Paul's, Michelle being the only young parishioner who had wanted to come. But to tell the truth, most of her church activity had been squeezed out during her junior year, with her being editor of the yearbook, plus on the environmental club, mock trial team, model United Nations, math team, welcome crew, students council, nerd stuff like that.

Michelle's group arrived at Cherry Creek Park at about 5 P.M.; the walk had taken seven hours. Far away from the huge, curving white-and-gold stage, the Buffalo crowd found some lawn on which to roll out sleeping bags, then got in line at one of the tents run by McDonald's, official caterer to World Youth Day. Michelle chose granola bars, dry cereal, and a Coke—all week long, the "hot" fare had been lukewarm and greasy-gray. She spent the following few hours taking care of Amy, who had heatstroke and was waiting for a ride to the hospital. At 11:30 P.M., the ambulance came for Amy and Michelle got into her sleeping bag. She put her hands under her head and stared at the stars, feeling as happy as she had ever been.

OK, the logistics sucked. The media made a big deal of that, by the way. Reuters said 7,000 people at Cherry Creek were treated for heatstroke, dehydration, hypothermia (overnight), and various minor maladies; the Associated Press put the casualties at 14,000; the Washington Post said 20,000; Newsweek said 63,000. During the Mass on Sunday, firefighters sprayed parts of the crowd with hoses but, a paramedic told the press, many pilgrims chose not to drink water because the lines to the bathrooms were half a mile long. The nation was further informed that a sixty-one-year-old man (or was he sixty?) had died of a heart attack during the pilgrims' walk (or was it later, during an evening prayer vigil at the park?) and that local health officials and Sheriff Pat Sullivan had denounced the scarcity of water fountains, the inaccessibility of medical tents, and the ubiquity of McDonald's-supplied burgers and sodas. McDonald's, in rebuttal, pointed out that fruit and green salads (and bagels) had been sold under the golden arches too.

Yet of all stories that the media told to mark World Youth Day, few had much to do with the bliss that Michelle and her fellow pilgrims found under the Colorado sky. When Michelle was flying to Denver, the airport news-stands were offering a Washington *Post* that wondered: "Is Sexual Dysfunc-tion Killing the Catholic Church?" and a *Newsweek* whose cover offered (all for one low price):

SEX
and the
CHURCH

Abortion, Birth Control and the Pope

· · · · · · · ·

Priests and Child Abuse

· · · · · · · ·

Celibacy Isn't the Problem

BY FATHER ANDREW GREELEY

All this, plus *(hey!)* a poll in which 503 adults who identified themselves as Roman Catholics (and may or may not have been practicing their faith) cast their collective verdict on the church's "positions" on human sexuality (43 percent said "about right"), and AIDS (34 percent). On birth control, most said "too conservative"; a majority also wanted women ordained as priests. On abortion, 43 percent approved of the church's position, while 62 percent said they, personally, did not know any Catholic woman who had had the procedure.

It was abortion that provided the media with a hard political angle on the Denver events. On being met by President Clinton at Denver's Staple-ton Airport Thursday evening, the seventy-three-year-old Pope, citing a "serious moral crisis" in developed countries, called for young people to be allowed to "mature as free and intelligent human beings, endowed with a robust sense of responsibility to the common good, capable of working with others to create a community and a nation with a strong moral fiber." Then, quoting from a speech he had given on his 1987 visit, he said this: "Amer-ica, you are beautiful and blessed in so many ways. If you want equal justice for all, and true freedom and lasting peace, then, America, defend life!" After the two leaders emerged from a private conversation about the carnage in Bosnia, reporters asked the pro-choice President what he thought of John Paul's airport remarks. Clinton gave a thumbs-up and said, "It was a great speech."

Asked the same question, White House press secretary Dee Dee Myers said the Pope had "tried to make his point without being confrontational," and added: "That's what we expected." But it was not, for some reason, what the press expected. Every use of the word "life" during the Pope's visit made news, as did every time he shortened a prepared address and, in the process, seemed to adjust a nuance of his abortion stance. For five days, it seemed not to occur to a single editor in the United States that it is not exactly big news for a Pope to oppose abortion.

If abortion was a major issue at the Denver festivities, Michelle Pangborn was unaware of it. Nonissue, more like. As she watched the airport scene on the scoreboard at Mile High Stadium, she found it refreshing, as the Pope cried out the word "life," to be surrounded by kids who were, she presumed, mostly pro-life like her. It was nice to be in the majority for a change. But conflict is so essential an ingredient in news that the reporters at Denver focused their energies on searching for it. And found it, of course, but mainly in the fringe events: the airplane trailing a "STOP THE POPE- ULATION EXPLOSION" streamer, the fundamentalists handing out anti-Catholic literature, the women's rights coalition that posted, on the door of the Cathedral of the Immaculate Conception, a notice accusing the church of sexism, homophobia, and abuse of power.

For Michelle Pangborn, who happens to think the Vatican's teaching against birth control is "impractical and unsafe in the real world" and believes that women should be ordained (but has no interest in being a priest herself), the protesters were a mild annoyance. The reporters were far more in evidence, mingling with the crowds, tape recorders in hand, seeking reaction to the Pope's having "lashed out" (as one reporter put it) not only at abortion but at alcohol and drug abuse, pornography, sexual "disorder," violence, and destruction of the environment. Big discovery: not everyone agreed with the boss on everything! *See, here's someone from Utah who is pro- choice!* And if the Salt Lake City pilgrim added that, for her, "the nice thing about being a Catholic is that you still can be a good Catholic, but not have to agree with everything the Pope says," this was a convenient bridge to the next discovery: that the Pope didn't like being disagreed with. There was no place in the church for "polarization and destructive criticism," John Paul II warned in one Denver address.

But the real story of Denver was almost entirely missed, even though it was under the frenzied reporters' very noses. They were looking for content—a message—and there was none to be found, or at least nothing new. An exasperated Gary MacEoin, writing for the *National Catholic Reporter*, noted that when the Pope arrived at Mile High Stadium, half of his speech, or more, consisted of merely listing the countries and U.S. regions represented there, so that each contingent could yell and stamp their feet. Other than this, John Paul had said "little of use to them. . . . 'You are the future,' the Pope told them. . . . There seems little point in gathering them from the four corners of the earth simply to tell them what they already know."

And yet, what was there to say? For everyone, from the Pope down, it wasn't anything that anyone said but the experience itself that was everything. The most manifest thing about Denver, and probably the most important, was also the most frivolous: it was fun!

Fun, from beginning to end. Checking out the Pope junk: the two-and-a-half-foot-tall Styrofoam white miters; the $18 Miracle Mug that showed the Denver skyline until you added hot water to reveal John Paul's face and outstretched arms; 300 other church-sanctioned souvenirs including fanny packs, commemorative plates, and the Popescope, for seeing above the crowd. Watching the pink sun gilding the state capitol while a bell choir played during the opening Mass at the civic center Wednesday night. ("That was a nice Mass, if you didn't pass out in the heat," said Michelle.) Dropping into a church to check out what the "Perpetual Adoration of the Blessed Sacrament" means. Watching two brothers and a sister from Boston replicating the Sistine Chapel ceiling on a dirty city sidewalk. Exchanging addresses with a guy from Pennsylvania in the hotel lobby, who was here with a marching band to play for the Broncos game on Monday night (the conversation begun for no better reason than Michelle's wearing a T-shirt bearing the name of an obscure band called They Might Be Giants, and he was a fan too).

On the flight home to Buffalo, the scenes that Michelle played over most often in her mind were not the freshest ones, from Cherry Creek, but those from the papal welcome on Thursday night. Ninety thousand rain-drenched youngsters waving white handkerchiefs and stamping their feet until Mile High shook, their excitement so infectious that a hundred bishops were caught up in an impromptu "wave" while the scoreboard flashed Coors Lite and Marlboro ads along with "Welcome" in dozens of languages. Saying the Our Father in hundreds of different languages simultaneously. Tens of thousands of hands joining for the singing of the week's theme song—*We are one body, one body in Christ*—with tears filling everyone's eyes, including the Pope's. For Michelle, it was fun just *seeing* the Pope sitting there in the stadium, a rainbow behind him, as he thanked a whole bunch of people: " 'I dunk this person, I dunk that person,' he dunked us all," she remembered later. "He just kinda sat on his chair with his head resting on his hands, sort of slumped over, and he looked sort of cute. It seemed weird that we were so excited to see this cute little man, he seemed so human sitting there."

The result: thousands of Michelles, leaders of the next generation of Catholics, carried away an intensely optimistic memory of the church, to cherish for their adulthoods.

Six months after Michelle came home from Denver, someone asked her what impact the events there had had on her. She wrinkled her nose, drew her feet up under her, thought about it for a moment, and then said this: "I think I'm not as pessimistic about the church as I was when I left. That doesn't necessarily mean I go along with the church in everything. I'm a very liberal person—not on abortion, but more on political lines, and environmental things: animal rights, pacifism, things like that. Things that the church really ignores. But most of the people who are active in those things are pretty strongly anti-Catholic. So for me, before Denver, it was like, the church will always be an important part of my life, but I will never get a whole lot out of it. But now, after Denver, OK, I have never had such incredibly wonderful emotions as I had there, just being there. And I'm really happy and proud that I found this in the church—*that the happiest I've ever been was in the church.*"

When the reporters at Denver breathlessly repeated all the disagreements that exist among loyal Catholics (young and old), they were within a hairbreadth of discovering what the Pope really means to the church. True, he often presents himself as a stern teacher, as did most of his predecessors. True, even while playing up his "cute" side, loving and "dunking" the kids in the Rockies, he was getting ready to launch upon the world an encyclical letter that would sound the charge against liberalism and excessive compassion in moral theology. That letter would even have some small impact on an ordinary parish like St. Paul's in the months ahead, marking a boundary between the liberals and the orthodox, as John Paul well intended it should.

All true, but at bottom, what the Pope means to the church is something other than a disciplinarian or ruler. The Pope is *Il Papa*—a "dad" to all Catholics. "John Paul Two, we love you," the kids at Denver chanted at every opportunity, by which they did not mean they agreed with him, or even that they especially cared what he thought—about theology or morals or anything else. And when the Pope moved to the edge of the stage at Cherry Creek and called, "John Paul Two, he loves *you*," he placed no conditions on this message either. *Il Papa* loves his children, and they love him, period. Who has never disagreed with their dad? Do you even have to *like* the guy—let alone agree with what he thinks or does? The thing about parents is not what they say, but that they are there. The thing about parents is that, by their being there, a family exists.

Late on the August afternoon of the Taylor wedding, as Dave and Claire set off for Nantucket and the honeymoon, the breeze off Lake Erie turned cool. Crowds gathered at Pilot Field, home of the AAA Buffalo Bisons, for a celebration of the tenth anniversary of the filming, right here in this city, of *The Natural*. Fans would arrive for the evening's Bisons game dressed in '30s garb, and the festivities would include a re-creation of Robert Redford's home run, the one watched in triumph by a standing Glenn Close, all in white.

Summer was almost over now, its warm frivolity a thing to be grasped and held against the approaching year.

Fall into Winter

Communion

September: Half a million dollars should not have been a huge amount of money for St. Paul's to raise. Given 5,555 adult members, the centennial restoration campaign target amounted to about $90 per member, or two and a half measly bucks per month over the three years ending with the parish's 1997 centenary. Not that it would be simple. As Monsignor Paul Whitney stepped up to the lectern soon after 10 A.M. on the twenty-fourth Sunday in Ordinary Time, he was aware of a certain stiff attentiveness in the air. Always was, always had been, when the pastor of St. Paul's talked about money.

Usually, the homily was delivered by whichever priest was presiding, but today the parish's sixty-year-old pastor would speak at each of the five Masses. Usually, Whitney switched on his roaming microphone and strolled up and down the center aisle to chat about love and life and death. Today, he remained at the lectern to refer to a script written by a downtown fundraising consultant. The campaign pamphlet was ready for mailing to member households; its green headings and gray-screened charts listed the needed capital repairs: $10,000 to replace the steeple roof, $10,000 to upgrade the parking lot, $15,000 to buy a new elevator for the school. . . . Today was for recruiting canvassers; next month, the volunteers would visit every parishioner (or every parishioner willing to open the door) to solicit a three-year pledge.

It should not be a tall order—but Whitney knew he could forget the number 5,555. Many of those nominal members were seldom seen in church and contributed scarcely a penny to it. . . . except on occasions such as a baby's baptism or a spouse's burial. The suggested monthly gifts in the campaign pamphlet didn't even mention the possibility of a $2.50 monthly pledge, the theoretical average. Rather, "patrons" were solicited to contribute at least $37 a month, the range of amounts rising to $1,250 for the status of "benefactor."

Ah, the good old days. Monsignor Timothy J. Ring, legendary pastor of St. Paul's from 1942 to 1975, builder of this church *and* the rectory *and* much of the school, terror of a generation of Kenmore altar boys, a man who ran this place with an iron hand, a part-time secretary, a hellfire homiletic predilection, and little evidence of tender loving care, scared up enough money to erect these impressive stone walls without a penny of debt. But Paul Whitney is no Timothy Ring.

No child is terrified of the current pastor; no adults either. At five feet seven, with his slight paunch, muscular arms, and weathered bespectacled face under salt-and-pepper hair, Father Paul (as everyone calls him, since he won't tolerate the honorific "Monsignor") is a cross between Gary Cooper and everyone's favorite uncle. It's easy to tell when he's angry—his sentences get shorter, his face reddens, and his eyes narrow—but few have heard his deep voice raised. When he came to St. Paul's in 1982, he earned a reputation as a vigorous manager of school and parish even while maintaining an outspoken presence on diocesan committees. But his energy waned at the turn of the decade, along with his health. Beset by arthritis and internal bleeding because of stomach and colon problems, Father Paul cut back on committee work and stopped writing regular notes for the weekly church bulletin. But he never refused to visit a sick, troubled, or bereaved parishioner, to hold a hand or offer a shoulder to cry on.

The differences between Father Paul and his celebrated predecessor go beyond personal style. By all accounts, Monsignor Ring was—like most pastors of his day—a priest with a clear vision of the church's authority. In this view, good Catholics obeyed their priests, good priests obeyed their bishops, and good bishops obeyed their Pope. Always. By contrast, Father

Paul takes pride in thinking for himself and makes no secret of his independent thoughts. He invites Protestants to receive communion at mixed weddings; he welcomes altar girls, and has done so since long before the practice won diocesan approval. When asked his opinion on artificial birth control, he says calmly, "I have no problem with it."

Many parishioners enjoy describing the scene in church one Holy Thursday a few years ago when Bishop Head was reported by the Buffalo *News* to have banned women from being included among the twelve "disciples" whose feet are washed by a priest during Mass in commemoration of Christ's Last Supper. That night, Father Paul stood in the sanctuary redfaced and declared to his congregation, "I know there is no proscription anywhere in church law against women's participation in this ceremony, but lest I give you scandal, there will be no foot washing at all here tonight." A year later and ever since, despite rumblings from parish traditionalists, St. Paul's (and many other churches in the diocese) quietly reverted to coed foot washings.

No one in Kenmore, therefore, would make the mistake of thinking that when the pastor of St. Paul's speaks, he speaks for Rome. If this diminishes his authority, he can live with that. But it doesn't help him exhort his people to action—including the writing of checks.

Everywhere, the days are gone when a priest said, "Give!" and every true Catholic gave. Father Andrew Greeley (wearing the hat of respected sociologist rather than pulp novelist) has reported that the average U.S. Catholic's contribution to the church halved itself, proportionate to income, between 1963 and 1984. Catholics have been donating slightly more to charity in the past few years, but the $1.40 that the average Catholic household donates from every $100 of income still lags behind the national average by half a dollar. As for specifically religious contributions, Catholic households managed an average of $308 in 1989, compared with Protestants' $653 and Jews' $498.

With an annual budget hovering around a million dollars, St. Paul's was far from poor, but neither was it one of the wealthier parishes in Greater Buffalo. The bulk of parish sum income went to running St. Paul's School, a K–8 operation with a good reputation that had been run by nuns from the turn of the century until the mid-'80s, when the need to pay an increasing number of lay teachers had forced the parish to start charging tuition—but at rates that had no chance of making the school self-sufficient. According to the parish's recent census of occupations, the three biggest employment groups (after "housewives" and "retired") were unskilled factory workers, secretaries, and retail store personnel; the median annual income of Kenmore's 7,101 households (just under half of them Catholic) was just under $31,000. For the average family, a "patron"-size monthly contribution would consume something like 1.5 percent of before-tax income. With just 1,750 people receiving envelopes for regular contributions to St. Paul's, the five hundred grand that Whitney was looking for in the next three years would amount to around thirty extra cents for every dollar currently hitting the collection plate.

The pastor's challenge was not small, and by the time he stepped up to the rubber to make his pitch, the kvetchers had been taking practice swings for a few weeks. Why was the church always asking for money? What would it be used for? More dumb innovations in the sanctuary, like when the tabernacle was moved last spring to a side altar from its traditionally central place? Or when the altar rail was dismantled two years ago and the marble used to construct that new lectern and that silly little stand—the ambo, or whatever they call it—for the lectionary? And now, hadn't there been talk of moving the baptismal font from its private room into the main part of the church? Maybe all this was just a disguised way of getting money for the bishop to pay settlements to the victims of sexual abuse by priests! How could anyone be trusted with cash anymore, especially since the diocesan comptroller had pleaded guilty, just two years before, to embezzling $1.4 million in Chancery funds?

Both Whitney and Parish Council president, Dave Baxter, would spend much time in the following days and weeks patiently fielding pop flies. Not one cent of campaign money would be spent, they promised, on interior renovation; not one cent would leave the parish. And if these promises did not entirely satisfy the dugout grumblers, enough team players took the field to provide a full complement of canvassers. Only time would tell what would happen when they started knocking on Kenmore's doors.

After delivering his spiel for the fourth time that day, a weary Whitney turned the ten o'clock Mass over to the bullpen priest, Gary Bagley, the diocesan youth minister and St. Paul's "weekend vicar." Headed for the umbilical corridor to the rectory and a cup of coffee he should not drink, the pastor attempted to slip unnoticed through the sacristy. Unfortunately, this was the rare day when Pat Blum, one of the parish's three part-time religious education coordinators, was having trouble keeping the attention of the four dozen kids, aged three through eleven, squatting on the sacristy's big Oriental rug for the Children's Liturgy of the Word.

Pat's problem today was the thorny content of the lectionary's Gospel reading, in which Jesus instructed his apostles to be ready to forgive those who trespassed against them—not just seven times, as Simon Peter had suggested, but "seventy times seven." So, as the pastor moved through the room, Pat called for help: "Oh, Father Paul, some of the kids are kinda wondering about this forgiveness thing."

The pastor sighed very quietly and allowed as how forgiving was not always a breeze. He asked if any of the kids had seen the TV reports that week of the trial of two men charged with beating up a truck driver during the Los Angeles riots of 1992. A few of the older ones' hands went up. "And did you see that truck driver, Reginald Denny, embracing the mothers of the two accused?" Some heads shook, others nodded solemnly, others did both in turn. "If it's possible for him to forgive, then it's possible for us too."

A recently published book might have provided the pastor with an even more dramatic—and specifically Catholic—reference. The book, called *Dead Man Walking,* was the memoir of Helen Prejean, a Sister of St. Joseph working as a spiritual adviser to Death Row prisoners in Angola, Louisiana—and a minister to the bereaved and enraged families of the condemned prisoners' victims. In the book's final passage, Prejean recalled a predawn prayer vigil with Lloyd LeBlanc, the father of a boy who had been murdered by the first man she saw executed. The nun and the bereaved father prayed together before the Blessed Sacrament in a rural chapel:

> Lloyd and I kneel on the prie-dieu. He takes his rosary out of his pocket [and] we "tell" the beads. . . . We pray the sorrowful mysteries. Jesus agonizing before he is led to execution. Jesus afraid. Jesus sweating blood. Were there beads of sweat on [Lloyd's son] David's brow when he realized the mortal danger? Was it when the kidnappers turned the car down a road that he knew ended in a cane field? Was it when he was told to lie face down on the ground? . . .

Lloyd LeBlanc has told me that he would have been content with imprisonment for Patrick Sonnier. He went to the execution, he says, not for revenge, but hoping for an apology. Patrick Sonnier had not disappointed him. Before sitting in the electric chair he had said, "Mr. LeBlanc, I want to ask your forgiveness for what me and Eddie done," and Lloyd LeBlanc had nodded his head, signaling a forgiveness he had already given. He says that when he arrived with sheriff's deputies there in the cane field to identify his son, he had knelt by his boy—"laying down there with his two little eyes sticking out like bullets"—and prayed the Our Father. And when he came to the words: "Forgive us our trespasses as we forgive those who trespass against us," he had not halted or equivocated, and he said, "Whoever did this, I forgive them."

But he acknowledges that it's a struggle to overcome the feelings of bitterness and revenge that well up, especially as he remembers David's birthday year by year and loses him all over again: David at twenty, David at twenty-five, David getting married, David standing at the back door with his little ones clustered around his knees, grown-up David, a man like himself, whom he will never know. Forgiveness is never going to be easy. Each day it must be prayed for and struggled for and won.

"For-give. Us. Our. Tres-passes. As. We. For-give. Those . . ." Bernice had slowed right down—one syllable, one breath—but it was no good: Jo, who had fallen behind from the first line, was gurgling meaninglessly, and struggling against the gurgle, and losing the struggle for very effort. *She's getting worse,* Bernice acknowledged to herself as she realized that Jo was near to choking over mere words. Usually, that came later, when Jo tried to swallow the host—an inch in diameter, a thumbnail thick, and Jo battled every time to force her throat muscles to drag it down. Now, Bernice accelerated the Lord's Prayer a notch, figured it was kinder to get it over with. ". . . Who trespass against us. And lead us not into temptation, but deliver us . . ."

Josephine Kamuda was in her early forties, Bernice thought, and still beautiful, in a way; her mouth and eyes could still produce a hint of a wry smile through blotchy cheeks, and she insisted that her nurse brush her stringy, formerly blond hair and paint her long fingernails every day. She was a devoted wife; she was mother to a thirteen-year-old boy; she had advanced multiple sclerosis. Every second Monday, when Bernice brought communion to the little house on Nassau, she would stop at the side door, hand half raised to knock, and take a deep breath, wondering what small deterioration Jo would display today, which fragile muscle command Jo would have lost. At first, Bernice had often found Jo sitting at the dining-room table finishing a breakfast of pancakes and blueberries, holding the spoon herself. But nowadays, Jo was propped strengthlessly against a complicated pile of pillows. Bernice hadn't seen Jo take solid food, apart from the holy wafer, for months.

Bernice had to rely on force of habit to conduct a conversation with Jo—it was often hard to make out exactly what she was saying, but she tended to say much the same things each month.

"How's. Your. Hus-band?" she would moan.

"He's fine, dear, he was reading the newspaper when I left."

"Do. You. Drive. Him. Nuts? I. Drive. My. Hus-band. Nuts."

"Oh, I'm sure you don't, dear. Is he working? I heard he was laid off."

Jo thought about that, then repeated: "I. Drive. Him. Nuts." Bernice wasn't sure, but she didn't think there was anything wrong with Jo's comprehension—just a bit of memory loss, and a physical limit to the number of remarks she could manage to spit out. But now she added one Bernice hadn't heard before: "He'll. Miss. Me."

Bernice, not sure she had heard right: "He'll miss you? Where you off to?"

"Not go-ing any-where," Jo managed, and left it at that. Bernice pulled a dining chair close to Jo's sofa, laid her pyx on the coffee table with its sacred cargo, and dug into her purse for the little blue "Communion of the Sick" book that Sister Mary Jude had given Bernice and the couple of dozen other Special Ministers of Holy Communion.

"You've got mi-ll-ions in there," Jo sputtered at the purse, as she usually did at this point.

"Sure," Bernice said with a gay laugh. "But behave yourself now, Josephine, because we're gonna pray."

Jo started singing, ponderously, almost tunelessly, just five syllables, but one at a time: *Ain't misbehavin'*. Bernice laughed and applauded. Then she looked determinedly down at her book. "Ready to pray now? In the name of the Father and of the Son, and of the Holy Spirit, Amen." Jo produced a single finger and somehow crossed herself, just reaching her forehead, chest, and shoulder blades.

Bernice chose a reading from the Epistle to the Romans, and when she read, *Nothing can stop Jesus from loving us, forgiving us, and embracing us joyfully forever,* Jo interjected, "Thank you."

Bernice looked up, smiled, and went on to read an explanatory note from the book: "Sometimes it seems that God is so far away and even unconcerned. Jesus felt that way on the cross but he still trusted his father. Jesus told his father that he felt abandoned but then he prayed, 'Father, I put my life in your hands.' And so . . . we can pray, 'Father, I put my life in your hands.' "

"I do," said Jo. Bernice looked up and smiled again, and then looked down fast. At times like this, her own faith felt puny next to Jo's. But after the Our Father had descended into a mess, Jo seemed close to despairing tears.

"I'm sor-ry."

"Don't be," Bernice said softly.

"I drive you nuts," Jo said.

"No, you don't," Bernice said, and placed a single sacred wafer on Jo's tongue. (*This is the Lamb of God who takes away the sins of the world . . .*) Immediately, she picked up a glass of water, watching Jo intently, praying silently that this time Jo wouldn't choke.

She didn't.

Afterward, after inquiring fruitlessly how Jo's son was doing in school, after reporting once more that her own husband, Art, was just fine and not yet driven nuts, after applauding Jo's reprise of *Ain't misbehavin'* and her rendition of *Let me entertain you* and (Bernice having announced she would have to take off soon) *Hit the road, Jack*, after announcing that she really did have to move along now and hearing Jo say suddenly (shockingly clear and quick), "Don't go," after staying a little longer for more singing and family news, after listening to Jo's increasingly weary efforts at vocalization decline into gibberish, after getting up at last and being sent off with *I'm savin' all my love for you*, after the nurse closed the house door behind her, Bernice leaned against the doorpost for a moment, and finally released her breath in a loud "Phew." She knew so little about this disease. Was Jo saying goodbye, as she seemed to be? Was she dying now? Bernice hoped not, but, she murmured, as she reached into her purse for the car key, "If she's gotta go, I hope she goes quick."

At sixty-seven, Bernice Graff, a small woman with a warm unflappability, was no stranger to death. It had been sixteen years since she joined the crew of Special Ministers and began bringing the sacrament to housebound St. Paul's parishioners, all of whom had been seriously ill. Last week alone, her list had gone down by two. She attended all the funerals and kept the memorial prayer cards in the little notebook where she recorded her visits.

Often as not, the cards offered the Prayer of St. Francis—*Grant that I may not so much seek to be consoled as to console*—which held a special meaning for her. As she would put it, "We've got a Franciscan up in heaven," meaning her son Paul, who died while in the novitiate at age nineteen. That was December 1980, and for many years afterward, Bernice couldn't pray that prayer without crying.

Paul's picture stands beside that of his brother Bob on the living-room mantel of Bernice and Art Graff's house on Parkwood. Every flat surface, except for floor and kitchen table, seems occupied by framed photographs. Bernice enjoys taking a visitor on a tour of the pictures—Ray, wife, and four children a couple of miles north of here in Tonawanda; Barbara with her husband and three daughters across the river in Ontario; Russell and Steve, with their wives and children, in California. And here's Carolyn and her husband in International Falls, Minnesota—the faces of Carolyn's nine kids sprawl over the entire length of the dining table, and there's another on the way. Altogether, nineteen grandchildren's faces jostle for table and shelf space with the Graffs' three living sons and two daughters. But Paul and Bob—unmarried, childless, dead—have that quiet piece of mantel all to themselves.

If the visitor asks how her sons died, Bernice lifts her shoulders and slowly drops them, then describes the auto accident when Paul was in high school—how Paul nearly bled to death and lost his spleen, and how, from then on, his life had been on the line every day. Unable to fight infection, he could die if he merely caught cold. And that's what had happened, on a trip to New York City in 1980. Paul died of pneumonia in his Massachusetts monastery on December 15 that year.

"And this young man"—Bernice touches the frame of the picture of Bob—"he died of AIDS, in New York City, on Christmas Eve 1987." She says it tenderly, but that's all she says, and gazes at the picture for just a moment before turning away—"Here, take a look at this"—and strides clear across the dining area to examine a huge family shot taken at Russell's wedding in 1985, leaning forward to point out an emptiness between two shoulders. Bernice thinks of this as "Paul's space." She can almost see him standing there, his lean handsome face and blond hair, ageless at nineteen. "He was there, no question."

Bernice and Art met just after World War II at the Dellwood dance hall. He was a twenty-nine-year-old ex-GI; she was nineteen, transformed by war into a factory draftsman. In accordance with Art's wishes, Bernice quit her job when their first child arrived; Art took care of radio and TV transmitters for WHLD Buffalo and was an engineer in the control room of WBEN-TV when he retired in 1977. The seven kids all went from St. Paul's School to Cardinal O'Hara High and, the '60s notwithstanding, attended Mass at least on Sundays and holy days.

Bernice herself has never known a time when she didn't attend Mass regularly. When she was a child, the house rule was that if you claimed to be too sick to go to Mass, you had to spend the entire Sunday in bed. In the early '50s, when Bernice had three kids, young mothers in the parish, who often felt isolated and cabin-crazy, were invited to join a daytime discussion group program under the odd name of Bishop's Committee. She went along with a neighbor and became head of one of the groups, which met in members' homes to discuss kid stuff and the odd bit of husband stuff. Later, she joined the Mothers' Club at St. Paul's School and, later still, Sodality. Art, in turn, became a member of the Knights of Columbus and attended a few Holy Name Society men's breakfasts. He rallied to Monsignor Ring's call to contribute sweat to building a big stone church to replace the wooden building which had become so small for the growing Kenmore that two Masses were often said simultaneously, on the main floor and in the basement. But Art was never what you'd call a joiner.

By 1993, with Paul dead thirteen years and Bob six years, Bernice's church busyness included fund-raising, catering, and sacristy duties with the Sodality as well as distributing the Eucharist both at Mass and in the homes of shut-ins like Jo Kamuda, and reaching out to the widows of men she had cared for—inviting them out to lunch, just to chat, or whatever. She tried to keep it light. . . . *Grant that I may not so much seek to be consoled as to console* . . . For Bernice, ministering to others was one way to avoid thinking too much about her own loss.

Mementos of faith, hope, and love pressed into the little notebook in Bernice's purse:

The memorial card from Paul's funeral, bearing a prayer of consecration to Mary (. . . *when I am called from this life, may I be found worthy to embrace you at the gate of heaven* . . .).

Bob's high school graduation picture (the suit, tie, vest, and shirt all made, at his request, by his mom).

A paragraph clipped from one of Father Paul's church bulletin notes (. . . *Mary is the mother who holds her dead son, looks into his face and cries the tears of all mothers and fathers of history, all those stunned by tragedy who see the ashes of their dreams slip through their fingers* . . .).

A dozen or so memorial cards (for dead communicants and dead priests).

Miscellaneous prayer cards (Prayer of Reparation, Prayer to the Sacred Heart, Prayer for a Family, Prayer for Missionaries), including a well-worn *Memorare* card (*Remember, O most holy Virgin, that never was it known that anyone who fled to your protection, implored your help, or sought your intercession was left unaided. Inspired by this confidence we fly unto you, O Virgin of Virgins, our mother* . . .).

Bernice says the *Memorare* every time she prays the Rosary, which is every day. For her, each Hail Mary is an intensely personal act—a salutation from one bereaved mother to another. "I never could have pulled through everything," Bernice says, "without her pulling me through."

Hard as it has been for Bernice Graff to "get over" her two boys' deaths (as if a parent can actually cross so high a mountain), she is certain that death was not the final word on Paul and Bob, any more than it was for Jesus, or Mary, or any of the saints. This is the life-preserving nub of Bernice's faith. When she unites herself with Christ in the Eucharist each morning, she achieves communion with every other member of his mystical body—living or dead. So Paul and Bob are still with her. She can talk to them, and feel their presence with her, anytime. And since they are closer to God than she, they can help out by interceding for her.

"Paul and Bob, you listen to me," Bernice would say often that autumn, shaking her finger at both of them. "You better make sure your sister has a perfectly healthy little baby"—referring to Carolyn, forty-five, in her fourteenth pregnancy with four miscarriages behind her. "Work on it, you boys." Or, the previous Christmas: "Now, you two, we want to have a nice day tomorrow"—referring to the planned family gathering at Barbara's house in Niagara Falls. "Not too much snow, boys. See what you can do." And when the snow came pouring down anyway, Bernice wagged her finger again and shook her head: "You guys weren't listening to me. I'm still your mom, you know!"

D̲o you mean to tell me that if Jesus Christ were here today he would refuse to have supper with me because my husband does not have a piece of paper?"

Father Paul meant to tell the outraged Rosemarie Konsek McKenna nothing of the kind—only that the church's rule on this matter was firmer than either he or she liked. Bill McKenna, whom Rose had married at the town of Tonawanda courthouse on the Memorial Day weekend of 1991, had been married before. They had chosen not to wait for Bill's previous marriage to be annulled by the church. Ergo, the earlier vows were still binding. QED: Rose and Bill were adulterers. To present oneself at the altar while in a state of so grave (or mortal) a sin amounted to an act of defiance, thus compounding the sin.

Rose knew all this—had known it when she and Bill had decided to go ahead with the civil wedding. She had required no persuasion to suspend herself from communion. It just turned out that breaking the habit had been harder than she had expected. A *lot* harder. So here she was, three weeks after the wedding, reading the riot act to her parish priest: "Is this the same Jesus Christ who welcomed Mary Magdalene as a friend? This Mary Magdalene, who, I understand, was a prostitute? And don't we *all* say every time we go to Mass, 'Lord, I am not worthy to receive you . . .'?"

Rose was probably born stubborn. Stubborn as her waitress mother, Maureen, who was raised in an area of Belfast where to be Catholic was a statement of obduracy. Stubborn as her father, Josef, who, in the summer of '58, on the evening of a day spent lying on a Canadian beach, finally got a response to the classified ad the heavily pregnant Maureen had placed for him ("Young Polish immigrant willing to work") and reported at Eduardo's bar in Buffalo to carry beer kegs up the basement stairs despite his third-degree sunburn.

By the time Rose was born that October, the first of three girls, Joe was part of the establishment at Eduardo's, where he would rise to become pizza baker and then assistant manager. His wages combined with Maureen's waitressing earnings to send their three daughters to Catholic high schools; Maureen's mom took care of the girls after school, taught them to say the Rosary by age six—and then made sure they did. Unlike Maureen, Joe was not big on churchgoing but generally agreed to accompany his wife and kids to Mass at Holy Name on Bailey Avenue, at least until the girls were grown.

The family story goes that when his third child was born, he was sleeping off his night shift. When woken up by his mother-in-law, he asked, "Boy or girl?" Told it was the latter—again—he turned over and went back to sleep. So Rose became Joe's tomboy. He taught her to paint and do household repairs, but he had no favorites. On the day Rose accidentally broke a window during one of the frequent fights between her and her sister Michele, each girl denied responsibility, so Joe took his belt to both of them. That way, he could be sure the guilty party got punished.

At nineteen, Rose was waitressing at Eduardo's. She had quit nursing school after listening to a dead firefighter's eight-year-old son's shouts of "Why *my* dad? Why?" echo through an emergency ward. On the Friday of the following Fourth of July weekend, the restaurant was extra-packed with a busload of Canadians and Rose felt her left leg dragging as she rushed from table to kitchen to bar. The family doctor put her in Millard Fillmore Hospital for observation, diagnosed neuritis, and prescribed an IV medication that seemed to do the trick. Rose went back to waitressing by night while working at a supermarket by day and figuring out what she wanted to do with her life. The occasional numbness in her limbs seemed nothing to worry about.

At twenty-one, her life changed course.

It was September, and she had returned to UB to start a B.Sc. in accounting. One morning, her left eye seemed to be peering through a fog; a day later, she couldn't see through it at all. After ten days in Millard Fillmore, her vision had returned, and the results from a new round of tests had come in.

"When will your parents be in again?" asked the doctor at the foot of Rose's hospital bed.

"Anything you have to say about my health," said Rose, her temper rising, "you say it to me."

The doctor looked at her. "You have multiple sclerosis," he said.

After he left, Rose stood at the window for most of the night, smoking two packs of cigarettes while she stared at the city lights. She didn't know much about MS, but remembered seeing a fund-raising billboard on the Kensington Expressway—a picture of a wheelchair with two crutches crossed over it, and the caption: "MS, destroyer of young lives."

She spent much of the night staring out the window, but by dawn she was talking back to the billboard in her mind. "I don't care," she said. "It's not going to destroy *my* young life." Rose returned to school, and to Eduardo's nights, and worked on the campus newspaper. She lived with her parents, went to Mass with her mom every Sunday and holy day, and walked or rode her bike everywhere. She loved to ride that bike, but by the time she graduated in 1984, her balance was going, and when she walked into job interviews (too proud to use a cane), she was aware of having a slightly drunken gait.

This may have been one reason it took nine months to land her first job, at Buffalo City Hall as a typist for what is now called the Mayor's Advocacy Office for Persons with Disabilities (Rosemarie McKenna, Executive Director).

In 1989, as a volunteer for the Multiple Sclerosis Society, Rose chaired a panel of people with MS mainly for the benefit of others who had been recently diagnosed. "Life doesn't stop just because you have MS," she said in her introductory remarks. One of the panelists was an extremely nervous man with broad shoulders and thin reddish hair who was there only because he couldn't say no to the society which had helped him buy his first wheelchair. Bill McKenna was bowled over by the calm woman steering the discussion, with her fiery optimism and her blue-green eyes that burned below a single wild curl of black hair. After the meeting, Rose walked him back to his car, and they exchanged phone numbers.

Rose found the stranger interesting—part shy boyish smile, part quick sardonic wit. She waited three days for him to call, and when he didn't, she called him. "This is Rose Konsek. How are you?" Bill took a couple of gulps, said fine, and they talked for a while. He asked her if she liked movies; had she seen *Driving Miss Daisy?* No, she hadn't.

They talked all the way through the movie, discovering that they both loved Bogart movies, *Jeopardy!*, and Trivial Pursuit. Later, they learned that they both hated going to bars, that he was a conservative Republican and she a liberal Democrat, that he enjoyed John le Carré and she had a weakness for Danielle Steel. And that was how the good Catholic girl fell in love with a married man.

Bill was in the process of finalizing his divorce from his separated wife, the mother of his two sons. Three months later, when he asked Rose to marry him, she said yes, but in the morning called him, in tears, to say no. When he asked again six months later, Rose pointed out that he had not yet done anything about getting an annulment, and he said OK, he would give it a try. But Bill's sister had secured an annulment 10 years previously, and the process sounded to him like something out of the Inquisition. Bill, who had considered his involvement with canon law over on the day he was confirmed, did nothing.

On the last night of 1990, Bill asked a third time, and Rose said yes, but she really did want him to get the annulment. Yet, mere weeks before the planned civil wedding, Rose and Bill were out looking at apartments and Rose, staring through the windshield at one building, found that at this moment her potential future home looked to her like a mausoleum. She turned to her fiancé, and sobbed: "Bill, please, *please*, go for the annulment. This is important to me." Bill realized that the marriage could end right here, before it started, and promised that this time he really would.

And maybe he would have, all on his own, sooner or later. But then Rose saw an ad in the Buffalo *News* under the heading "Take Another Look." It was an invitation from St. Paul's Church, Kenmore, for alienated

Catholics—including those who were divorced—to come and explore the prospects of reconciliation to the church. She dragged Bill along. They met a number of other couples in more or less the same boat, who were given the opportunity, for three or four Sunday nights, to vent their rage at the pastor of St. Paul's and, through him, at the entire holy Catholic Church. Rose and Bill started attending Mass at St. Paul's together—the ten o'clock Sunday Mass, the one with the folk-style ensemble and the equally folksy homilies by Father Gary.

Bill had told Father Paul that he was reluctant to go through the annulment process unless he could be sure it would end well, and the pastor had suggested a compromise. If Bill would write an account of his first marriage, Father Paul would ask a buddy of his at the Tribunal to take a look to see if he foresaw any difficulties.

Days before the courthouse wedding, Bill wheeled himself to his favorite spot in the living room of his apartment, armed with a tape recorder and a list of headings that Father Paul had supplied. *Family background*, the list began. Bill pressed the record button and spoke:

> *The dominant one was and is my mother. She is the one who always tried to make sure the household was a happy one. She would work eight hours a day teaching, come home, fix dinner for the family, and prepare for the following day at work. My mother was the one and is the one I always wanted to speak to when I have a serious situation to confront. Her answer was always responsible, thoughtful, and sincere. My father always struck me as the older brother I never had. As a parent he was selfish, terrible-tempered, and more concerned with appearances. . . .*

Working his way down the list of headings was, at first, fairly smooth sailing. *Relationship with siblings*: endless competition with his younger brother, the superior athlete; not much to speak of with his sister. *School and social life*: did well enough academically, could have tried harder; friendships during liberal arts studies at Canisius College mostly with people who shared interest in theater arts. *Medical history*: nothing unusual until diagnosed with MS about eight years ago. *Sex*: none before meeting Ruth, his first wife. *Personality traits*: tendency to feel inferior, a dummy to his father and an athletic klutz to his brother; quick-tempered, sarcastic tendency; not nervous, moody, selfish, ungrateful, unpredictable, or dishonest. *Wife's interests: horseback riding, peer acceptance . . .*

> *. . . I knew Ruth through a friend in college. I thought she was kind of an offbeat person and somehow we got together . . . on St. Patrick's Day 1972 at a bar. From that time, I saw her just about every evening. I cannot tell you what the initial source of my attraction to her was, but I will tell you that the continuing source of the relationship was nothing more than physical. . . . We always looked for any and all opportunities to engage in carnal pleasures. I would stay over at her parents' house every weekend when I was going to school in Virginia. And just about any Saturday night, after her parents had gone to bed, we would engage in sexual relations in her parents' dining room. . . .*

The next heading—*Doubts, hesitations, or pressure before the marriage—* brought back a memory that Bill had buried. For some reason, it made his voice shake as he went on recording:

> *. . . I can remember telling Ruth by a long-distance telephone call that I didn't want to remain at Emory and Henry College after spring break of 1973. After much crying on her part, and the ever-ready threat to return the engagement ring, I acquiesced. . . .*

Bill pressed the stop button, buried his face in his hands, and sobbed for a while as the memories of that spring came flooding back. He had wanted to stay in Buffalo rather than return to Abingdon, Virginia, where he had followed Ruth after her dad had been transferred by Westinghouse. At twenty, he had wanted with all his heart to go on being young and free; yet he wanted to remain Ruth's lover. He was persuaded to return to Virginia, and they advanced the nuptial date by a few months to be married by a hippie priest on farmland on July 6, 1973.

When Tim was born the following March, Bill was finishing his teaching degree at Buffalo State College and working the four-to-midnight shift at Columbus McKinnon, assembling chain slings. Soon after his second son, Sean, turned two, Bill quit teaching to work at the Erie County legislature as a committee clerk for the Republican majority. For fifteen years, his marriage slowly deteriorated; the couple argued over money, choice of friends, and Bill's not spending enough time at home. In 1983, playing tennis with a buddy, Bill clean-missed an easy overhead smash; soon afterward, he noticed his foot dropping out of control as he walked. When the diagnosis came in—MS—Bill fell into a two-year depression. He worked on a public golf course for a while, cutting the greens, before landing his present position as an interviewer for Erie County's Department of Social Services. By then, his marriage was over.

On the eve of his second nuptials, Bill handed the tape of his testimony to Rose as a wedding gift. The bride wore a cream taffeta dress and brocade jacket with pillbox hat and short veil; Rose's boss, Mayor Jimmy Griffin, joined the crowd of two hundred at the reception. The first time someone tinkled a glass, the happy couple offered the customary kiss; the second time, Rose fished a red squirt gun from her purse and promised to drench the next offender. Rose's visiting cousin from Ireland caught the bouquet, after which Bill lifted himself from his wheelchair to a restaurant chair and his bride spread-eagled herself on his lap while he groped under her dress for the garter. Bill's son Tim caught the toss, and the Irish cousin didn't know enough local custom to hit Tim's hand away as he worked the garter up her leg, over her knee, and onward, up her thigh. The crowd roared.

When Rose's mom complained about the civil wedding, they explained that the annulment was just a matter of time. "But which anniversary will you celebrate?" Maureen Konsek persisted. "This one or the *real* one?" And when Rose tried to stay away from communion, a huge hole opened up in her happiness—she felt as if she were being punished for falling in love. It was the first time she had ever thought ill of her church. Her husband called Father Paul: "It's killing her," he said.

"Tell her to come see me," the pastor replied.

Rose arrived at the rectory ready to offer a piece of her mind, and did so, complete with the references to Jesus Christ and Mary Magdalene. But she had no idea what to expect from Father Paul. Other priests, whether from the old school or from the wave of young conservatives now graduating from many seminaries, might have quoted the Gospels right back at her: "Any man who divorces his wife and marries another woman," said Jesus according to St. Luke, "is guilty of adultery." Instead, Father Paul heard her out and then said, quite calmly, "Rosemarie, you must follow your own conscience."

She needed to hear nothing more: next Sunday, Rose McKenna once more held her hands out to receive the body of her Lord and was reunited with the communion of saints.

Meanwhile, she had transcribed Bill's tape. Father Paul sent it downtown with a note to Father Sal Manganello, a former parochial vicar of his and now a canon lawyer at the Tribunal, who in turn sent Bill a handwritten note:

William, can you please clarify the following:

1. On page 3 you talk about a relationship with another woman (before the first marriage). Can you explain why this relationship ended and what attracted you to the woman whom you married?

2. You didn't talk about any formal engagement. Was there one? If so, please elaborate.

3. You mentioned that the date of the marriage was changed. Please explain why.

4. Ruth threatened to return the engagement ring. Would you please explain the circumstances involved in this? Did she have doubts, or did you?

No idle curiosity was involved in composing these questions. Manganello, playing the canonical role of "auditor," had the task of deciding if there were any likely grounds for annulment. He was mining some rich territory opened up by what Bill considered minor details.

There is no such thing as a Catholic divorce. Since canon law considers the sacrament of marriage irreversible in its very essence, an annulment is a declaration that the marriage bond never existed. This means, in the words of the guidelines issued by the Buffalo Tribunal, that "one or both parties may have entered the marriage with goodwill, but lacked the openness, honesty, or emotional stability or capacity to establish a community of life and love with another person."

So broad an interpretation of the law would not win approval in some corridors of the Vatican, but the liberal canon lawyers who now run many

American diocesan Tribunals make their stand on a crucial change in the 1983 revision of the Code of Canon Law. Under the old code, annulments were granted only upon evidence of fraud or other technical grounds, or if the marriage had not been consummated, or if the possibility of having children had been excluded—since the "procreation and education of children" was then considered essential to the purpose of the sacrament. But the new code enlarged the definition of marriage with references to partnership and relationship, and also contemplated annulments based on psychological factors that constituted "grave lack of discretion or judgment."

Now, as explained by Sister Sandra Makowski, S.S.M.N., a lawyer at the Tribunal (and former Director of Adult Formation at St. Paul's), most annulment investigations center on "the commitment that the couple made when they said, 'I do.' The question is: 'Was this commitment based on a free, mature, and reflective consent by both parties?' So we have to prove that their consent was flawed when they got married."

One frequent example of "flawed" commitment: a marriage entered into because the bride was pregnant and the couple thought of marriage as the solution to their problem. Or the Tribunal lawyers might discover a history of abuse in one or both families. Bill McKenna's auditor had clearly found, in the written testimony, reasons to wonder about other frequent scenarios: a rebound relationship from Bill's previous romance, or possibly inappropriate reasons for attraction. Pressed to describe relationships and attractions, petitioners sometimes confess flawed motives: "He reminded me of my dad," or "She was just like my former girlfriend," or "He owned his own car."

The same goes for the question about what Makowski calls "timeline issues" (was the wedding rushed? was the commitment "thought through"?) and the auditor's particular interest in doubts that surfaced before the wedding day. Simple questions can bring much bigger issues to the surface: Makowski remembers one wedding date that was changed because the bride had two black eyes. That annulment was no problem.

But to Bill, Manganello's questions seemed pernickety at best and dumb at worst. The replies were contained in one single-spaced page. The previous relationship "was never anything more than a very good friendship, a status that continues to this very day." (So much for a rebound scenario.) His attraction to Ruth was chiefly physical (nothing wrong there either).

Yes, there was a formal engagement—Bill had bought Ruth an engagement ring in the fall of 1972, and they had a small party for family and friends. (Strike three, but canon law provides no limit on pitches taken.)

Bill's answer to the question about the altered marriage date was:

> *The reason was that Ruth's father had left the household to take up with another woman. . . . It was our reasoning that since I had left school and was working for Household Finance Corp. full-time with the attendant benefits, I could at least care for Ruth insofar as hospitalization was concerned.*

And right there, Bill may unwittingly have scored a base hit against "mature and reflective consent." (He will never know, because the Tribunal is not required to give reasons for its decisions.) In any case, by October he had been invited to make a formal application for annulment. And so, finally, he drove down to the Chancery on Main Street, took the brass-doored elevator to the mezzanine balcony with its marble floor and saints' statues and polished brass railings, and wheeled himself over to the door that said "Tribunal." He announced himself to the woman typing behind a glass partition, got a friendly smile and an invitation to sit in what looked like a doctor's waiting room. In an inner office, he talked, for less time than he had expected, to a priest in a black suit.

Unknowingly, Bill had already crossed the only real hurdle in the annulment process. At the Buffalo Tribunal, between eight and ten new cases receive an auditor's attention each week (which is about half the number of phone calls the office gets to inquire about the annulment process). Of the sixty to seventy cases that any auditor handles at a time, about a quarter will be found to lack apparent grounds. But of the remaining cases, the ones accepted for formal consideration (at a prescribed fee of $350), 99 percent, according to Sandra Makowski, achieve (usually within somewhat less than a year) what she calls "an affirmative result."

Along the way, the minutiae of adversarial legal procedure are observed. The Tribunal assigns one of its officials to serve as advocate to the petitioner, another as advocate to the respondent, and a third as "defender of the bond." (The latter's duty, according to Makowski, is "not to play a prosecutorial role but to see to it that the rules are followed.") Another staffer acts as judge. (If it's the turn of Makowski to act as judge, the law requires that two other judges be appointed to the case, because she, alone among the lawyers, is not a priest. But in practice, the other judges merely co-sign the documents pro forma, leaving the decision to her.) There are no actual hearings—the various officials do most of their communicating by paperwork.

It takes time. Corroborating testimony must be obtained from witnesses who knew the partners before and during the marriage, and the former spouse—if she or he can be found—must be given an opportunity to testify. And if an annulment is granted, the decision must be confirmed by another court—a statewide interdiocesan court or, in some larger dioceses, including Buffalo, a second court of the same tribunal.

The two courts hardly ever disagree, but if they do, the case is kicked all the way upstairs, to Rome. And that's usually bad news for the petitioner, because Rome strongly disapproves of the high success rate of American annulment requests. Of the 54,137 Catholic annulments granted worldwide in 1991, 75 percent were awarded by U.S. dioceses; the United States grants 44 times the number for Italy, which has a roughly equivalent Catholic population. Sandra Makowski acknowledges that once a case is in process, the Tribunal officers in effect "look for a way to grant it." A former Judicial Vicar used to say of the Tribunal he headed that it represented "a ministry of justice, not compassion," but today's watchword for both advocates and judges in Buffalo is "equity," a word which they interpret as meaning "justice lined with charity." The cover of the Tribunal's guidelines brochure now shows the Prodigal Son returning, with the caption "RICH IN COMPASSION." The introductory text quotes both the ideal of law ("What God has joined, let no one separate"—Matthew 19:6) and the promise of grace ("Be compassionate, as your father has compassion"—Luke 6:36).

Bill McKenna received his judgment of mercy by letter in December 1992. The marriage of Bill and Ruth McKenna had never happened. That night, Bill and Rose went out for an Italian dinner, came home to consummate their indisputably nonadulterous love, and began preparations for the renewal of their vows at St. Paul's on the following Memorial Day—thus settling the "which anniversary?" concerns of Rose's mother.

And now, on a Saturday evening in September, the waiting and raging behind them, Bill and Rose could settle into their tiny TV den to watch once more the video of their long-awaited nuptial Mass. Bill wheeling himself down the aisle with Rose walking beside him on a tripod cane. Vows, rings, a huge smoochy kiss. Bride and groom sipping from Father Paul Whitney's heavy personal chalice (the one inlaid with the diamond from his mother's engagement band) while the folk ensemble sang Rose's favorite hymn: *I, the Lord of sea and sky, I have heard my people cry: / all who dwell in dark and sin, my hand will save* . . .

Hanging on the living-room wall, near the picture of Our Lady of Czestochowa that Rose's dad brought back from Poland last summer (which, if you look at it from the right, shows Our Lady of Perpetual Help and, from the left, St. Joseph and Child), was a gift from Paul Whitney. The framed certificate, signed by a Roman cardinal, bore a familiar kindly likeness and the words:

His Holiness

John Paul II

lovingly imparts his

Apostolic Blessing

on

William J. McKenna

and

Rosemarie A. Konsek

on the occasion of

their marriage

May 29, 1993

Yet, blessings notwithstanding, His Holiness's troops in Rome were, that September, stepping up their public attacks on the American annulment machine. Archbishop Vincenzo Fagiolo, a senior canon lawyer at the Vatican, had strongly condemned the U.S. annulment rate as causing "grave scandal" by undermining the irreversibility of the sacrament.

As if to prove Fagiolo's point, the recent engagement of Representative Joseph Kennedy II to a member of his staff had produced a *Time* magazine story entitled "Till Annulment Do Us Part." The story noted that the divorced congressman was confidently awaiting an annulment, and quoted an unnamed prelate who demanded: "Is it possible that there are that many Americans—and it's only Americans—suffering from grave psychic deficiencies?" Theologian Jon Nilson of Chicago's Loyola University responded: "We are perhaps a little more psychologically sophisticated than certain parts of the world. . . . It is the American church trying to be both realistic and compassionate."

September: The Buffalo Philharmonic, teetering on the brink of bankruptcy, had announced that its season was in jeopardy. Bills quarterback Jim Kelly had opened his huge, gleaming bar and restaurant at Main Place. The U.S. Senate had confirmed President Clinton's nomination of the fervently pro-choice Joycelyn Elders as Surgeon General despite vigorous protests from the National Conference of Catholic Bishops and other religious leaders.

September: From Ruth Hemerlein's eleventh-floor window, Kenmore and the neighboring Town of Tonawanda were a rich green carpet that stretched north toward I-190 and the river. It was this view that had sold Ruthie on her apartment building, which she described bluntly as an "old folks' home." Unfortunately, the window was above her line of sight as she sat in her gray velvet armchair every morning, back straight, Rockports crossed, right arm wrapped in its pressure bandage, Rosary beads clicking over her slight paunch, Miraculous Medal hung, as ever, around her neck. She got the medal as a wedding present in 1949, and was wearing it the day she divorced her husband, a gambler and philanderer, two decades ago. She wore it too on the day, shortly afterward, when she told her then parish priest, "Monsignor, I know you don't approve but I had to do it for my own sake and my children's sake, and so will you pray with me now that God will show me the way to go?" Whereupon the priest had said, "What makes you think God wants to help you, when you've turned your back on him?" Whereupon Ruthie had begun vainly seeking a spiritual home in various Protestant churches, without quitting her habit of beginning each day by saying good morning to the Lord's dear mother. This habit Ruthie had learned from her stepmother, who (well understanding the little girl's fear of abandonment, given the death of her natural mother in bearing a thirteenth child less than a year after Ruthie's own birth) had promised that the Holy Mother would never leave her side.

"I was scared to death of God," Ruthie recalls in a slight Irish drawl that emerges from a definitely Irish overbite and dark blue Irish eyes, "but I *loved* the Blessed Mother." Once, she had overheard a Protestant neighbor remonstrating with Ruthie's stepmother about the latter's appeals to Mary as mediatrix. The Irish Catholic woman had replied mildly, "Now tell me: if my son had a business and he was hiring help, and your son was out of work, would you hesitate to come and ask me to ask *my* son to help *your* son? Sure, it's just the same with Mary and *her* son."

September: time to get things going again. On the last weekend of the month, Church Bulletins of Buffalo, Inc., had to haul out their smallest type to accommodate the notices sent over from St. Paul's. The choir needed new singers; the pastoral care ministry needed more visitors to attend the sick and housebound; the world's hungry needed sponsored walkers in the annual Crop Walk; the Kenmore Mercy Hospital needed volunteers for the pregnancy hot line; the Appreciation Campaign for Catholic Education needed money. Sodality's monthly meetings were up and running, as were Holy Name communion breakfasts and Father Dick's Thursday scripture group. Coming up: the Youth Ministry rummage sale, the Home School Association craft sale, the Red Cross bloodmobile visit, the Kenmore Mercy Guild fashion show, the First Saturday pilgrimage to Our Lady of Fatima Shrine in Youngstown, New York, the Cardinal O'Hara High School open house, and Bishop Head's "Religious Educators of the Year" awards, where Jamie and Dick Shaner would be among those honored. As well, the bulletin contained appeals from the Respect Life Committee—

Make a statement! Take a stand! Show you respect Life! Sunday, October 3rd, on Niagara Falls Boulevard, Christians will be standing together to show they support the unborn child's right to life. There is no Buffalo Bills game this day!. . . .

—and from the Restoration Fund Campaign:

Although we are asking for your sacrifice, we are reminded that sacrifice leads to good things, and most importantly we need to remember that the Lord is never outdone in generosity.

Finally, on a white insert sheet, under the heading "Answer the Call," this appeal:

The St. Paul's "OCIA (Order of Christian Initiation of Adults)" is in *critical* need of parish sponsors for our Inquirers and Catechumens—these are the people who are interested in or preparing to enter the church, as well as those adults who will be receiving the sacraments of communion or confirmation. . . . A parish sponsor is someone who is . . . *ready* to become more involved in their parish community. . . . *willing* to be a friend and fellow journeyer for the candidate. . . . *able* to share their faith with others. . . . *interested* in deepening their faith relationship with God.

Before the ten o'clock Mass, a small altercation took place in the rectory. Father Don, the junior parochial vicar, priest in charge of liturgy, and resident stickler for detail, had noticed a stray character in the white insert sheet. "OCIA?" he said, addressing the catechumenate director, Judy Nice. "*Order?* Didn't you know the diocese had decided to stick with *Rite?*"

"Well," said Judy, "the national forum—the North American Forum—decided to make the switch—"

"But we're part of the *Buffalo* diocese, and the *diocesan* Liturgical Commission said—"

"Look," Jamie Shaner cut in. Mass was about to start, and she and another team member were supposed to be giving a short presentation on the OCIA, or RCIA, or whatever, in the effort to get sponsors for this year's record crop of candidates. Judy had already suggested she avoid the controversy by calling it neither O nor R but simply "the catechumenate," not that Jamie particularly cared one way or another. Jamie said, "Judy already told me to say—"

"I don't care what you say," Don said, turning on his heel. "Just don't call it the OCIA."

Afterward, Father Don would recall this whole conversation as being a lighthearted one in which he had expressed mild amusement at the bureau-crats downtown and offered an equally mild suggestion that the confusion of a name change be avoided for now. Jamie, meanwhile, would never be entirely sure why she didn't just wink at Judy and forget the whole thing. But the incident irked her.

And then, during Mass, Father Gary happened to say something in his wide-ranging homily about how "it doesn't matter what we call ourselves, whether we're Christians or Jews or whatever we are, what matters is what we do with that." So, when Jamie stepped up to the lectern to deliver her prepared talk, she ad-libbed a preface, describing the pre-Mass conversation about what to call the catechumenate, and quoting Father Don's parting comment. "And it just seems to fit here," Jamie said, "to say that, as Father Gary said, it really doesn't matter what we call ourselves. What matters is what we're doing, and that's what I'm here to tell you about. . . ."

It would be some months before Jamie found out just how much her blithe remarks bothered Father Don.

A mid the frenzy of that last weekend of the year's busiest month, few parishioners noticed a small story that appeared on page 3 of the Buffalo *News*:

NEW ENCYCLICAL BY POPE RENEWS CONSERVATIVE VIEW

LONDON (AP) — Pope John Paul II, in an encyclical to be published next month, reasserts his opposition to abortion, di-vorce, contraception, homosexuality, and premarital sex, the *Times* newspaper re-ported Thursday.

The Pope has been widely expected to use the document to reaffirm his conserva-tive views on Catholic morality.

The *Times* said it obtained a copy of the encyclical and noted that some parts, including that on papal infallibility, have been toned down, but that the Pope calls contraception "intrinsically evil."

The Vatican is expected to release the document Oct. 5.

Truth

October: After the Offertory at the ten o'clock Mass any Sunday that fall, if you were to follow the adult candidates for baptism and confirmation through the sacristy, along the umbilical corridor that joins St. Paul's Church to its rectory, up a half-dozen stairs and through double doors into the priests' dining room, you might find a spare seat at the big table, and if not, someone would fetch one for you. You would certainly find a smiling welcome, a hot drink, a doughnut, and some cheerful chatter about God, the universe, and everything.

"What kinds of evil are there in the world?" asked Judy one such day.

"War, numero uno," said Dennis Hurley, the team's newest member— and one of the two or three most talkative. A parishioner of St. Paul's for most of his thirty-seven years, Dennis had only this past Easter come up to Judy at a coffee hour and asked if he could help out with the initiation process.

"Hatred," said Dave Taylor, the newlywed, who was another of the talkative ones. "Stereotypes. You can find evil everywhere, even in the most beautiful home." His wife, Claire, kept her eyes on the table and no one mentioned the empty front pews at her August wedding. "It's confusing," Dave finished.

"Sometimes," said Judy, "I think confusion is evil in itself. But what's our response to evil, as Christians?"

"Patience, I guess," said Dave. "But sometimes, I run out of patience. Sometimes, my impulse is to get it out, right away."

"But there was evil from the beginning of time," said a confirmation candidate who, engaged to be married to a Catholic at St. Paul's the following year, had the looks of an unspoiled country girl with her tousled blond hair and pleasant smile. "I don't think anyone can do anything about it."

"So why does God allow it?" asked Judy.

"That's my question."

"Well, we don't give answers here," said Judy. "It's OK to raise questions, but I warned you, we don't have all the answers."

"Well," persisted Dennis, "I've heard people say that God allows evil in order to give people a free choice."

"But not all evil is so personal, Dennis. There are children starving in Africa. . . ."

"Right," said the country girl. "That's the kind of thing that bothers me."

"Well, that's true, but even there, other people are making choices."

"Like fat Americans eating well?"

"Right," said Dennis.

"But I still don't think we have answers to all these questions." This was one of Judy's two most apparent preoccupations in these sessions—to encourage her candidates to voice questions without expecting hard dogmatic responses. The other was to draw them out of themselves, to encourage them to explore the meaning of faith in the context of their feelings and experiences. For Judy, this table was not so much a place for teaching—"catechism"—as it was a place for "searching and sharing."

One morning, after everyone had added their Styrofoam cups to the litter of doughnuts, napkins, Bibles, and missalettes that surrounded a stubby lit candle, Judy began the session by asking one of the candidates to read that day's Gospel to the group. She had chosen her victim with forethought. An athletic twenty-two-year-old auto mechanic, Tony was at the very opposite end of the spectrum from Dennis and Dave: he seldom said a word. Today, Judy had decided to do some gentle pushing.

Tony, who was marrying shortly and wanted to be confirmed so that his children would belong to a proper Catholic family, grimaced at Judy's request but bravely limped through a few lines of Matthew.

" 'When Jesus came to the neighborhood of, ah—' "

"Caesarea Philippi," proposed Judy.

" '—he asked his disciples this question: "Who do people say the Son of Man is? . . . And you, who do you say that I am?" "You are the Messiah," Simon Peter answered, "the Son of the living God!" Jesus replied, "Blest are you, Simon, son of John. No man has revealed this to you, but my heavenly Father—" ' "

Tony stopped, and went back to drop in the period with a bump. " ' "—but my heavenly Father. I, for my part, declare to you: You are 'Rock,' and on this rock I will build my church, and the jaws of death shall not prevail against it. I will entrust to you the keys of the kingdom of heaven. Whatever you declare bound on earth shall be bound in heaven. Whatever you declare loosed—" ' or is that 'lost'?"

"No, 'loosed' is right."

" ' "—loosed on earth shall be loosed in heaven." Then he strictly ordered his disciples not to tell anyone that he was the Messiah.' "

"Thanks, Tony." Judy's voice, usually gentle, was even a shade softer when she spoke to Tony. He was so shy; she couldn't help thinking of him as hugely fragile, even though she had not yet managed to get him to say enough about himself to learn much about him. "Those aren't words we use every day, Tony, so they don't exactly flow off of our lips."

"Well, I'm not that great of a reader anyways."

"Well. So. Some background on this Gospel. It's been two and a half years since Peter first said yes to Christ, and now the big question is asked—what does he make of him? And when he answers, 'You are the Messiah, the Christ,' it's his profession of faith. Then Jesus says words that are very famous for us Catholics. In Greek, the text reads: 'Thou art *Petros*, and on this *Petra*, I will build my church.' See, it's a kind of double meaning. 'Peter' means 'Rock.' "

"Yes," said Tony, surprisingly. "That's Latin. *Petra* means stone."

"You took Latin, Tony?"

"No, but a lot of Italian words, and Spanish too, are derived . . ."

Across the table, Dennis was nodding and murmuring, "That's right."

"So, Tony," Judy said softly, "you could be quite a scripture scholar!" But when she looked directly at Tony as she asked her usual question of the table at large—"What struck you in this reading?"—Tony merely thrust his chin almost into the neck of his T-shirt and looked silently across at Dennis.

For once, Dennis hung back and returned Tony's stare.

"The two of you," said Judy after a moment of this, smiling her always hesitant smile while shaking her head, "you're so—"

"He knows," said Tony, frowning and pointing to Dennis. "He's just waiting for me to say something."

Dennis bobbed his head. "Oh, I don't want to hog it."

"No," insisted Tony, "he knows. He has a comment but he's waiting for me to say one."

"No, no," said Dennis.

Still, Judy waited for Tony, but he had clammed up. So Judy sighed quietly and looked at Dennis. "You're on."

"OK. People that I talk to—people from other churches—that is, Protestants—they'll argue with you about this one."

"Mm-huh."

"About the rock. They'll say that Jesus was talking about himself: 'and on *this* rock I will build my church.' "

"Really?"

"Yeah. I don't want to get that technical about it, but that's what I was told. But when they say that, they're starting to split hairs, getting away from what the meaning is."

"Which is?"

"Well, what I like is what you said there, about the faith."

And then Tony surprised Judy again. "The way I take it," he said, "is that Jesus is the rock, but he has to build. One rock doesn't make . . . doesn't make a building. He's the rock, but he has to gather more people . . ." Tony trailed off with a shrug.

Judy was leaning forward, as close to Tony as she could get from her place, her broad shoulders almost touching the dark wood, her big breasts pressed into it. "The builder in you is speaking, Tony, you have that first-hand experience."

Silence, and then Tony did, indeed, speak again. "Because Jesus him-self couldn't touch everyone." Judy was nodding vigorously, her shoulders pointed straight at him like spurs. "So that's why he sent Peter—"

"Not that he didn't—" Dennis broke in. Judy's shoulders slumped. "—want to, Tony, but he wanted the disciples to go out and do it, he wanted that faith to build that church, person to person, so that people would get involved with each other, because if he went around to convert everybody, there'd be no need for everyone to—"

"Mm-huh," said Judy flatly, her blue eyes fixed unblinkingly on Tony.

"—to, ah, commune, more or—" Dennis continued.

"Mm-*huh*," said Judy, a bit louder, still watching Tony.

"—less."

Dennis stopped, but the moment had passed. Eighteen long seconds went by, Judy pressing into her side of the table, eyes fixed on Tony. He said nothing.

Finally, Judy straightened up, adjusted a strand of her short light brown hair, and handed out some half-letter-sized sheets. "Why don't we take a few minutes to jot down some answers to these questions. 'Cause I feel like we're still all up in our heads, and we've got to get down out of our heads."

What have you learned about Jesus in the past several weeks?

List some of the names you know Jesus by.

Jesus asked the disciples, "Who do people say that the Son of Man is?" He then asked Peter, "Who do you say that I am?" Who is Jesus to you? Why?

How do you live your life so that people will know Jesus through you?

For ten minutes, the room was quiet. Tony scratched sporadically, intently, holding his pencil in a tight claw of forefinger and thumb, left hand crooked into a rest for the tip of his nose. Judy wrote slowly too, her smile fixed in place at the edges of her mouth. Now and again, she looked up to say, "Take your time," or "Remember, your answers are private; you'll only be sharing what's comfortable to you." Dennis, meanwhile, worked his way easily to the last question, which he attacked with the air of a high school sophomore in a year-end exam. He wrote, in block capitals that could be read by someone sitting six feet away:

I PRAY TO BE AS HONEST AND

He paused, thought, scratched out "as," then resumed:

NOT

He paused again, drew a careful line through the last word—

~~NOT~~

—and pondered. Then, as if inspired:

HUMBLE, NOT HURTING OTHERS IN ANY WAY.

Dennis sat back and read it over carefully. Then he leaned forward again, scratched out the period, and added:

BY MY ACTIONS.

Months later, team members and candidates would think back over these congenial fall sessions and wonder if they had missed any clues to what was going on in Judy's head, or in Dennis's. Only a few—Jamie Shaner above all—had heard from Judy's own lips of the war being waged inside her. A few had noted the way her nervous smile seemed especially fixed on the ends of her thin pale lips when certain subjects came up, such as the all-male priesthood or the authority of the Pope. But then, that was Judy: self-effacing, yielding—shy, basically. As for Dennis, he was sitting on a big surprise: easygoing Dennis, expansive and bighearted, betrayed no hint of even the most loyal brand of opposition.

Judy's crisis had begun the previous spring, when she was forced into the role of ecclesiastical bad guy. As she explained the circumstances half a year later, Judy's voice was at its shakiest, and she picked at the base of her left thumbnail so intensely that before she was done talking it had gushed blood and she had to race from her sunroom to the kitchen for a Band-Aid.

Jeffrey Tredo worked as a custodian for a book distribution company. Never baptized, he had been married and divorced before siring two children with his present wife, Jennifer, a Catholic. For several years, Jeff and Jennifer had attended churches of various stripes, and Jeff had begun worrying relentlessly about the prospect of spending eternity in hell. Soon after they settled at St. Paul's, in the spring of 1992, Jennifer (who tended to do the talking) called Judy Nice to introduce herself. She said she and Jeff had decided it was time for Jeff and the children to be baptized.

The children were no problem—Pat Blum, as coordinator of liturgical matters for kids, would prepare them for baptism with no particular difficulty. Jeff, however, was a special case. Because he had remarried without an annulment, he could not be baptized. But because he was unbaptized and his "ex" not a Catholic, canon law made annulment especially complicated. Catch-22.

Nevertheless, Jeff had applied for an annulment and started attending catechumenate sessions during Lent 1992; after his fellow catechumens "graduated" that Easter, he and his team sponsor, Ken Monaco, had often sat alone with Judy at the dining-room table. Despite constant queries from both Judy and Ken, the Tredo case dragged on for more than a year, and by the following Lent, it had become clear that when Jeff's children were baptized on Holy Saturday 1993, Jeff would be in the congregation with Jennifer, still waiting his turn but less patiently than before.

"Jeff is a simple man," Judy recalled, clawing at her thumb. "He really didn't understand a lot of the concepts or process. To him, it was like getting another divorce, and in his words, he had already been put through the wringer once, by the legal system, and now he was being put through it again, by the church's system."

Sometime that Lent, Father Paul had strolled over from the rectory to Judy's office in the parish center to talk about Jeff's wife, Jennifer.

The problem: Jennifer had for some time been coming to Mass and receiving the sacrament. If she were to do so on Holy Saturday, with her newly baptized children, it might get noticed. People might talk. Judy would have to take Jennifer aside, explain the situation.

Obediently, Judy sat down with Jeff and Jennifer and laid it out. Their marriage was not valid; the family had a high profile in the parish just then, what with Jeff's difficulties downtown and the two kids getting ready for baptism. It, well, it really would be best if . . .

Jennifer was, as she put it simply sometime later, "hurt." Judy herself was devastated.

"I looked at this woman, I felt her pain," Judy said, picking more furiously at her thumb. "The way she saw it, she had been an unwed mother who had been living in sin, and by marrying Jeff, she had undone the wrong and put herself right with God. She had felt worthless before and now she felt valid. How could I make the judgment that she was now for some reason unworthy to receive? It was like saying, 'Jesus isn't with you.' Afterward, I shut the door of my office and cried, and cried, and cried.

"That night, I swore that I would never again do someone else's dirty work for them. That's when I realized the big tension in my situation, the tension between being part of the official Catholic Church and being true to me. It isn't a conflict often but when it is, it's always when faced by an individual person.

"And at the same time, I realized that the same thing would have been true for Father Paul if he had spoken to her himself. Even talking to me about it, it wasn't because he himself was worried about Jennifer—*he* was doing someone else's dirty work. This case had become too visible, so some of his freedom to do his own thing quietly had been taken away," Judy said, moments before her blood started flowing.

"And even so, I think in the beginning of his time as a pastor here, he might have been more willing to rock the boat. But Father Paul had been through some difficult years—priests resigning all around him all the time, and him having been sick—in some ways, he wasn't any longer the pastor who had hired me. When I started working here, it was a close team of priests, two young priests who looked up to him, but when they moved on, the priests who came in—after the first one, who was great—were mostly men who had personal crises and all kinds of stories. And I think Father Paul really had to confront a priesthood that was disintegrating, and it really had to be disheartening. I mean, set aside the priesthood, imagine living in any home where people are always colliding, one member always in tension with others or in some personal crisis. . . . I just think he got worn out.

"I really like Father Paul. I respect him. And I hate to see where he is now compared to where he might have been some years ago. But also, I'm still mad at myself for not challenging him about Jennifer. But at the same time, I didn't want to hurt him, to make more waves in his life. And Easter seemed to be a down time for him, and . . ."

Judy looked down at the red mess on her hands—"Oh God, yuk, sorry!"—and dashed into the kitchen.

Jennifer Tredo quickly accepted the situation—rules are rules—and never fully understood why Judy was so upset. The annulment case dragged on; Jeff stopped coming to the dining-room sessions, and when the Tredos came to Mass they no longer sat with the catechumens in the front pews. But Judy found herself brooding over the Jennifer affair and her own growing ambivalence about being an official of the Catholic Church.

In the summer, Judy, feeling herself to be in "a crisis of faith," increasingly unable to pray or feel God's presence, took herself to a retreat. The three-day event was conducted by one of her heroes, James R. Dolan, S.J., a nationally admired spiritual director and author on meditative prayer.

"Let go of all the *shoulds* and the *oughts,*" Dolan told the retreatants at the St. Columban Center on the south shore of Lake Erie, an hour's drive away from Kenmore and all its freight. Judy felt as though Dolan were talking directly to her. "You put a lot of burdens on yourself," he said, "because of trying to think what someone else is thinking, or to be what someone else is putting on you to be." He also said this: "A mystic is a person who stays in the present moment." And this: "How powerful is a sacred idea." And: "To be upset is a choice: the pain happens, it's not a choice. But to be upset is a choice."

Dolan pressed a button and male voices, a cappella but for the beat of a drum, filled the room with words that would echo through Judy's head, somehow sustaining her, for months ahead:

> Is your God so small that an unkind word
>   can destroy your faith?
>   Is your God so small?
> Is your God so small that you cannot rest
>   'til your wrong's made right?
>   Is your God so small?
> . . . Is your God so small that his only Son
>   hanging on the cross
>   for the love of all
>   couldn't reach your heart
>   couldn't change your life? . . .
> Is your God so small that you're not quite sure
>   that he's God at all . . . ?

Judy came back from the retreat feeling, for now, as if her questions had been answered. Above all the legalisms, all the personal failings, all the cruelties that people could inflict, there was God. And as for the church's rules and dogmas, well, they were smaller than God. "If I believe something is true, then it is true," she told herself, "or at least, it's true for me. It has the validity of being something I experience. Something from God." No longer would she allow herself to worry unduly over whether or not her truth was "validated by the structures of the church." This was her promise to herself.

And what difference would this promise make? "The difference," Judy said in her sunroom that fall after fixing her thumb, "is that when I looked into Jennifer's eyes and said what I had to say to her, and went off and cried, it was partly because I felt so mixed up—because I felt I had done it wrong, by allowing her to see I didn't believe in what the church was saying. And now, I wouldn't be so confused. I wouldn't own it, the church's teaching, as being true. Because for me, it *isn't* true. It's just all those men. . . . Pardon? Oh. (Phew.) Yes, OK, including the Pope. (Phew.) I mean, oh God, he's probably a very good man, he's just—they're just putting God in a box.

They're saying, 'God is saying this.' But God is bigger than all of that, and all of us."

From the Buffalo *News*, Wednesday, October 6:

ENCYCLICAL IS REMINDER OF MORAL TRUTHS, AREA CATHOLICS TOLD

By Dave Condren
News Religion Reporter
The encyclical released Tuesday by Pope John Paul II was written to remind Catholics that good moral decisions must be based on "the law of God and the teachings of our church," Bishop Edward D. Head said Tuesday.

"We just cannot do what we want to do," said Bishop Head, explaining the thrust of the document. "Our freedom to make good moral decisions must be rooted in the truth."

Bishop Head, leader of the 780,000 Catholics in the diocese of Buffalo, said the Pope had written the encyclical "because he is very concerned about certain attacks [by theologians] that have been made against the moral norms that the church has used for centuries."

Those moral norms, the document maintains, "are not dependent upon the historical moment."

In the encyclical, *Veritatis Splendor*, Latin for *The Splendor of Truth*, the Pope characterized such attacks on the traditional morality of the Catholic Church as "systematic questioning" and called on bishops to crack down on that dissent. . . .

Quoting from the Second Vatican Council, the encyclical said the list of acts the church considers to be "intrinsically evil" includes homicide, genocide, abortion, euthanasia, suicide, physical and mental torture, slavery, prostitution, and degrading conditions of work that treat laborers as mere instruments of profit. . . .

The Splendor of Truth was much trumpeted in the media both before and after its official release. TV newscasts compared it briskly to *Of Human Life (Humanae Vitae)*, Paul VI's 1968 encyclical on birth control. The New York *Times* declared: "Papal Encyclical Says Church Must Enforce Basic Morality." *Time* explained: "A Refinement of Evil: In perhaps the most important document of his papacy, John Paul II frames the boundaries of what's right—and includes contraception among the wrong." While the Reuters newswire pitted orthodox exegesis . . .

Cardinal Joseph Ratzinger, head of the Vatican's doctrinal office, said the encyclical wanted to show that "faith includes morals, not just general ideals. . . . A purely individualistic notion of freedom, which would become mistaken for arbitrariness, can only be destructive; it would finally pit all against all," Ratzinger said.

against dissident outrage . . .

A liberal U.S. group, Catholics for a Free Choice, has criticized the encyclical's stands as harsh and uncompromising. "This document is an assault on the dignity and goodness of every Catholic who in conscience disagrees with any of the moral positions taken by the church," the Washington-based group said.

Associated Press writer David Briggs plumbed the depths of iniquity:

> . . . The idea of mortal sins—individual acts that could mean the difference between heaven and hell—largely died out in the period following the Second Vatican Council in the 1960s. . . . Now, in a new encyclical condemning moral relativism in the church and society, Pope John Paul II wants to reaffirm the church's teaching that damnation is possible for a particularly ill-chosen act. . . .

Given all the publicity, Judy Nice felt obliged to secure a copy of the Pope's 180-page letter. She scanned a few dozen pages, felt swamped by its dense style and unyielding tone, and put it aside for a better day that never came. It was Ken Monaco, an investigator for the U.S. Labor Department and John Paul's main man in the St. Paul's catechumenate, who dove into it with pen in hand. Ken ground bold black arrows into the margins of sections 29 and 30, with their affirmation of the duty of the magisterium (the teaching office of the Pope and his bishops) to identify moral truth:

> . . . Certainly the church's magisterium does not intend to impose upon the faithful any particular theological system, still less a philosophical one. Nevertheless, in order to "reverently preserve and faithfully expound the Word of God," the magisterium has the duty to state that some trends of theological thinking and certain philosophical affirmations are incompatible with revealed truth.
> . . . The magisterium continues to carry out its task of discernment, accepting and living out the admonition addressed by the apostle Paul to Timothy: "I charge you . . . convince, rebuke, and exhort, be unfailing in patience and in teaching. For the time will come when the people will not endure sound teaching. . . ."

(As he read this passage out loud at his kitchen table one Saturday morning while his schoolteacher wife Karen flipped her famous apple pancakes, Ken savored this phrase and took up his pen again to underline it. " 'Sound teaching,' " Ken repeated aloud. " *'Sound teaching'!* Powerful words. Powerful words.")

". . . but having itching ears they will accumulate for themselves teachers to suit their own likings and will turn away from listening to the truth and wander into myths. . . ."

Even before receiving the text, Ken had eagerly followed the publicity surrounding *Veritatis Splendor*, and had suggested to Judy that the candidates be instructed on the encyclical's message. He was scheduled to lead a mid-October Sunday dining-table session: why not do it then?

According to Ken, Judy was horrified at this suggestion. "She told me, 'You can't do that.' She said, 'Telling people what to do and what's a sin is just *not what this process is for*.' " Judy denies using these words. In any case, Ken, who felt that teaching people about sin was, in part, precisely what the catechumenate was for, nevertheless let the matter drop, for now. When he led the scheduled session, he confined himself to an aside.

His opening came when the group was chewing over a hazy question he had posed: "How do people today respond to God's call?" Someone had referred to the many extremist cults present in America today, and someone else had said, "Cults attract people who want someone to tell them all the answers."

This led Coty-Ann Henk to say, "Don't you think that's what's happening in the Catholic Church right now? We are getting away from saying, 'This is the way things always were and this is what you have to do.' And conservative people are going bonkers: they want everything in that nice little neat package that was always there, but now we're being told, 'It's your free will, it's your conscience, it's your relationship with God.' And I think that's why so many Catholics have left and are looking for something that has that order and that structure that we used to have, because they need to be told. They don't want to find their own way."

Around the table, Dennis and Tony and Dave and Claire and Janet were all nodding together as if some puppet master in the ceiling had succumbed to a coughing spell.

But Ken frowned. "Then again," he said, "I disagree with the idea that, you know, it's your free will and your conscience and wherever your conscience leads you, with God and so forth. You've got one extreme—you had the Pharisees back in Jesus' time, who had some six hundred and twenty laws, and over three hundred of them were prohibitions. But on the other hand, I think what's happening today in the church is that people are expounding on free will and on conscience so much that it comes down to 'Well, if it's good for me, I'll do it.' "

"Mm-HMM-huh," said Coty-Ann.

"Well," said Ken, "I think what the church, in terms of the direction it's going in now, with the new catechism coming out, with the latest encyclical and so forth, it's saying that, for our faithful, we need to educate our conscience, as to what is right and what is wrong.

"The point is," said Ken, now well launched into a speech that had him bouncing up and down in his chair as he wagged a pencil between forefinger and thumb, "so many people are looking at things with so many gray areas, and are not listening to where the Holy Spirit is directing us. Look at what Paul says, in the second reading today, to the Thessalonians. The proofs of faith—love, and hope, and so on—are very evident. *Very evident.* And I think in today's church that we really need to *educate* our consciences, to rely on what has been tradition, to rely on scriptures, in terms of leading faithful lives.

"And there Paul is thanking the church—*thanking* the church—and yet here we are, how many times are we *criticizing* the church today? How many times do we, quote, *reluctantly support* today's Roman Catholic Church? And how many times are we just *tolerating* what's there today?"

It was the kind and style of speech people expected of Ken—his enthusiasm building, his warm voice rising and falling, the words tumbling out, the key phrases repeated, the rhetorical questions. Around the table, as Ken talked on, there were nods and inscrutable stares.

"And I think the Holy Father, in terms of appealing to the youth in Denver, had a very powerful prophetic message—his message was extremely simple—and among the most often heard words in his message were 'What is the truth?' *What is the truth?'*"

Ken paused and lowered his voice for the answer. "Follow Christ, follow the Gospels and so forth." He paused again, and looked around the table deliberately.

"It's not easy to be Catholic," he finished.

There was a tightness in the room's air now, as if people were suddenly finding it a little harder to breathe. When this happened, it was always good to have Dave Taylor around.

Dave said, slowly, "I think . . . I think that it's all . . . It's all part of being part of the community." What he meant by "it," Dave did not explain, but he drawled on, having somewhere found, or somehow built, a bridge into more familiar and more consensual territory. "That's part of the answer: being community-minded. It's, like, getting out into the community, seeing where the needs are, where the hurts are. For some people that's an easy thing to do, and for others it's not, and that's OK. Because the community is so big that there's enough room for everyone to make a significant difference no matter how lightly they may think that they are walking. Not having read that en . . . What was it?"

"Encyclical."

"Well, it's hard to grasp that, what you said, because immediately I think of, there's so many complicated issues in any community. I remember watching 60 Minutes or one of these programs, where they went and interviewed some of these gang members in Los Angeles, and so on, and asked them, 'Why did you become a member of a gang, raping, robbing, stealing, et cetera?' And one kid said—and this stopped me dead in my tracks—he said, 'Well, I have parents who don't care about me. My mother is never home; my father, I have no idea who he is. My mom and my dad would not give their life for me. But my gang would. They stand up for me. They would give their life for me.'

"And I remember that when I was a kid, one thing that I knew, living in some pretty rough neighborhoods, my father was willing to lay his life on the line, and at one point he did exactly that. So I grew up knowing that I had a family, and knowing my father would give his life for me. And for this kid on TV, the gang was this kid's family.

"And to me, I don't know, I haven't read that en . . . That letter. But it's just, you know, there are just so many sensitive issues that have a variety of answers coming from all different directions." Around the table, people were nodding again, as blank-eyed as before, but they were breathing easier. If Dave's reasoning was at times confusing, talk of community was assuredly more comfortable than talk of absolute truth.

"But I agree," Dave continued. "I agree, those basic rules, those basic philosophies, are something we need to have. I just feel, staying with the basics and being a part of the community and going in there and, at least, putting your life on the line, which is not an easy thing to do—but, believing in God, as you said before, I mean, it's paradoxical, because it's tough, but as long as you focus, God on your side, it's easy."

When Dave trailed off, there was silence. Ken frowned for a moment, but said nothing, and the discussion was over.

Judy was grateful to Dave for kicking the ball out of bounds, but she wondered how long the truce between her and Ken Monaco would last.

The funny thing was, they really liked each other. Ken was a decent, compassionate man; Judy found his jokes funny, his enthusiasm infectious, his confidence enviable. And, just as much, Ken liked and admired Judy's tender warmth, her way of drawing strangers out of their shells, her willingness to provide a sympathetic ear to anyone in trouble.

All the same, a tension was mounting. It concerned the very purpose of the catechumenate, and the questions of authority and moral absolutes. Although the matter of the encyclical rested, for now, John Paul's words would yet thunder through the zone of free expression that Judy Nice had helped create at St. Paul's.

From *The Splendor of Truth*, Introduction, sections 2 and 4:

No one can escape from the fundamental questions: What must I do? How do I distinguish good from evil? The answer is only possible thanks to the splendor of the truth which shines forth deep within the human spirit. . . . The church remains deeply conscious of her "duty in every age of examining the signs of the times and interpreting them in the light of the Gospel . . ." (Second Vatican Council.) . . . Today, however, it seems necessary to reflect on the whole of the church's moral teaching, with the precise goal of recalling certain fundamental truths of Catholic doctrine, which, in the present circumstances, risk being distorted or denied. . . .

Ken and Judy might be light years apart on the issue of religious authority, but they were raised in strikingly similar worlds. Both were born of working-class immigrant stock; both attended parochial Catholic schools; both were inculcated with conservative family values. But whereas for Ken this background meant solid roots and a sense of the inherent worth of tradition, Judy's relationship with her faith has always been a tad more complex.

Ken was one of four children. His Polish-American mother had an administrative post with the U.S. Department of Justice and his Italian-American father, like his father before him, worked in the Bethlehem Steel plant at Lackawanna, just south of Buffalo. One of Ken's most vivid speeches begins with grandfather Monaco, who could speak no English when he arrived in western New York, who worked sixteen-hour days on the coke ovens and came home from work with his face filthy, whose eleven kids slept three or four to a bed.

"Tough times? Absolutely, absolutely," says Ken, continuing his speech and remembering to note that his own father was shaken out of bed whenever an altar boy failed to show up at the church across the street. "And with all these children, how did they make it? Their family life was centered on the church, *centered* on the church. There was a profound belief in God; there was a profound belief that if you did good things, good things would come to you. And with all these children you wonder, where's the individual attention? Where's all this 'quality time' that parents should spend with their kids? But all the children turned out great, because of the roots that these children were given, the foundation that these children were given when they were really young."

Ken's memories of St. Barbara's parish school carry a palpable sense of belonging—living in the shadow of Our Lady of Victory Basilica, the whole family attended Mass every Sunday, and Novenas every May and October. Today, Ken speaks with reverence of the nuns and priests of his childhood, and if he even once questioned the faith of his parents and grandparents and great-grandparents, Ken has forgotten when that might have been. Ken says he wanted to be a priest from eighth grade, but in the end "felt called to be married and have a family." At Canisius College, where he started an accountancy program before switching to education, Ken met Karen, who was studying to be a teacher across the road at Medaille. They married in 1980, while he was working as a federal education program specialist in Washington, D.C. Karen taught at a D.C. parish school for a year and a half. By the time their son Chris was two, the Monacos were back in Erie

County; Ken now roams upstate New York in search of embezzlements by labor unions. They make their home in a split-level house in the Town of Tonawanda with a golden retriever named Molson and a statue of Our Lady of Fatima in the backyard.

By contrast, Judy's childhood romance with the Catholic Church was stormy. Her father, a Pennsylvanian millwright, was brought up in the Brethren, and married his wife, Pam, an Italian-American from Buffalo's West Side, in the rectory of her parish. Judy's mom saw to it that Judy went to St. John the Baptist School and Cardinal O'Hara High, and that she never saw any of the movies blacklisted in *The Catholic Union and Echo*. Judy always felt there was something wrong about her dad not being allowed to receive communion with the rest of the family, and bitterly resented being told at school—first by schoolmates, then, in class, by a nun—that her father would not go to heaven unless someone first converted him to the true faith.

"Do you really believe that?" her mom said quietly when Judy came home with this dire warning. No, Judy decided, she did not. Didn't her dad kneel in prayer every night of his life? Wasn't it he who had taught her to say the Our Father with the fancy ending—"For Thine is the kingdom . . ."—that no one at school knew? No, she didn't "really believe that," and ever since, she has been filtering Catholic authority figures' words through her own common sense.

And yet, little Judy wore her St. Anne medal to ward off evil, and loved listening to the nuns tell the lives of the saints—Therese, the little flower of Lisieux; Francis and his animals; Martin de Porres.

Wholly unlike Ken, who questioned nothing, Judy grew up trying to sort it all out. What, if anything, did the sermons about Communist plots, and the nuns' warnings of sin lurking under short skirts, and the priests' tantrums in dark confessional boxes, have to do with the justice and peace preached by the Franciscans at O'Hara, with the visits of "God's Peace Corps" to the inner city, with the Peter, Paul, and Mary songs at Mass, and with the renovation of the church by Pope John's great Council. (Unknown to Judy, the Council had declared all baptized Christians to be "incorporated into Christ," thus resolving any doubt over her father's admission into heaven.)

By the time she was a senior, Judy had decided that the times were a'changin', and you no longer had to be religious to be good. She would keep going to Mass until graduation; after that, whether Mom liked it or not, came freedom time.

From *The Splendor of Truth,* Chapter Two, sections 32 and 34:

> Certain currents of modern thought have gone so far as to exalt freedom to such an extent that . . . individual conscience is accorded the status of a supreme tribunal of moral judgment which hands down categorical and infallible decisions about good and evil.
>
> . . . If we wish to undertake a critical discernment of these tendencies—a discernment capable of acknowledging what is legitimate, useful, and of value in them, while at the same time pointing out their ambiguities, dangers, and errors—we must examine them in the light of the fundamental dependence of freedom upon truth, a dependence which has found its clearest expression in the words of Christ: "You will know the truth, and the truth will set you free."

On Sunday, October 17, the same day the encyclical had been mentioned at the rectory dining table, it was mentioned, briefly, over a splendid dinner at Marotto's restaurant by Monsignor Paul Whitney and a crowd of old buddies, all priests. Only one of those present, a philosophy teacher at Christ the King Seminary, claimed to have read the product of the Pope's years of labor (written, it was said, in Polish in longhand). "It's really heavy going," the professor said. "I doubt that ten priests in the diocese will ever read the whole thing." The conversation moved on. Paul Whitney himself would not be sweating his way through the dense theological text anytime soon. The way he saw it, his time would be more efficiently spent reading a few of the inevitable commentaries in the independent Catholic journal *Commonweal,* or the Jesuit review *America,* or the *National Catholic Reporter.* He certainly was not planning to be preaching about it.

No imaginable papal encyclical would have much impression on Paul Whitney after the one that had, in his words, "slam-dunked" him twenty-five years ago. *Of Human Life* had marked an epoch in the development of Whitney's mind, in much the same way it had for the collective mind of the Catholic Church in the United States. When the dust had settled over Paul VI's directive on birth control, the American church had been forever altered. If the majority of Catholics could not abide the Pope's thinking on contraception, neither could they contemplate leaving the church (although thousands did leave during the years that followed). Most Catholics simply stayed put, and followed their own consciences.

In this small way, an epochal change began. If Catholics could follow their consciences at home in bed—if they could think that the Pope, speaking officially and almost to the limit of his authority, might be wrong—then they could also think for themselves concerning other matters. And so, they did, and have been doing, ever since.

Humanae Vitae's arrival in the summer of 1968 coincided with Paul Whitney's appointment to the diocesan major seminary of St. John Vianney. Three weeks and a day after the encyclical exploded on the Catholic world, Whitney was summoned, together with the entire faculty he was about to join, to see Bishop James A. McNulty for a "clarification" of the duties and responsibilities of seminary professors.

The show trial that ensued in the Chancery chapel was occasioned by a much-publicized national statement of theologians. Drafted by Father Charles Curran, then a professor of moral theology at Catholic University, the "statement of dissent" had encouraged couples to decide about contraception "according to their conscience." More than six hundred priests and Catholic theologians signed the statement, including the Buffalo seminary's moral theologian, Father Tom Daley.

In the national capital, Patrick Cardinal O'Boyle, Archbishop of Washington, had immediately moved to assert authority over Catholic University—an authority which the following years would prove to be tenuous, at best. In the Buffalo diocese, Bishop McNulty was similarly moved to demonstrate who was boss when half the faculty of Christ the King signed a letter in support of Daley's renegade position. The bishop fired Daley from the seminary and sent him to be pastor of Paul Whitney's home parish of St. Mary's in Batavia, New York. Next: the show trial.

The thirty-six-year-old Whitney, not yet having been officially appointed at the seminary, had not been invited to sign the statement, but was nevertheless in the Chancery chapel that day as his livid bishop addressed each professor in turn.

"Father, if a young lady came into the confessional to confess to you that she was practicing birth control, how would you advise her?"

"Well, Bishop, it depends on the circumstances . . ."

It did not seem to young Whitney that the prelate was paying much attention to the answers—he merely waited until each man had finished, and then moved on.

"Father Faiola, what do you think of the Holy Father?"

At this, Whitney could hear the swish of hands gesticulating in the row behind him, but, at first, no words. "Bishop, what do you mean by that question? It's obvious. The Holy Father is our major superior, he's the vicar of Christ on earth. . . ."

Everyone but the young Whitney was asked a question, and answered it in some fashion, and then, according to Whitney's recollection, the bishop said something to the effect of "OK, I've heard everything that you have all said, and is there anything else that anyone wants to add?"

No one spoke.

"Well, then, I would like to make it clear that the following men's services to the seminary have now ceased."

Bishop McNulty then listed the names of six among those present, and that was that. The purge executed, McNulty admonished those remaining to attend to their duties, and left the room. Whitney sat there stunned. To his ears, there had been nothing about the cautious answers of these six to distinguish them from their peers. For the first time, Paul Whitney had seen, as he said later, "the naked power of the church on display."

And yet, these events were about more than ecclesiastical politics. Paul Whitney had been watching the birth control doctrine torment faithful and even not so faithful Catholics ever since he started hearing confessions. He would never forget his first crisis in the confessional. Only recently ordained, he had heard the flutter of a woman's clothing on the other side of the screen, then sobbing, and then a stammered confession to contraceptive transgression.

The young priest recognized the voice, a pretty young woman with a handsome husband who, Whitney figured, just couldn't keep his hands off her, "safe" or "unsafe." Later, he couldn't remember how he had responded to the penitent that day—just that he had tried to engage the woman in a discussion of her sin, that she had fallen into uncontrollable tears, and that she had walked out of the confessional before receiving absolution.

Whitney never heard her anguished voice in a confessional again, and years later learned that she had died of cancer. What stayed with him was the moment he heard the other door slam and was left sitting alone in the gloom.

It set him thinking—mainly, at first, about matters of pastoral style. The next time someone entered the confessional in a clearly emotional state, he decided, he would address the feelings, rather than the imputed sin. "She was a fine person," he says, "a good person, and when she needed me, I didn't do anything to help her.

"I didn't diagnose the condition of the penitent soon enough: when someone comes in and is sobbing out a confession, saying she feels unworthy and that God condemns her, well, there was a whole bag there that I didn't sort out very well. The way we had been trained, many times we were sitting there isolating these moral problems or sexual problems and not dealing with the person, where he or she was at. But if you don't deal with the person, where they're coming from and what their definition of God is, you might as well save your breath.

"In later days, I would say to people like that, 'Maybe this is something we can sit down and talk about somewhere, face to face in a private room.' That's what I still do in that situation. Occasionally someone takes me up on it, comes to see me in the rectory afterward. And sometimes, at the end, it's 'Father, would you give me absolution?' And I say, 'Sure.' Because often-times, it isn't just the one problem, the moral problem, but there are lots of other things they need to talk about. Often, it has to do with how they perceive God, what their experience of authority is in their life—their relationship with their parents, their husbands, their wives. So, do they see God as a loving father who cares for them, or do they see him as a menacing God lurking behind a tree and ready to write down every little peccadillo? Back in the old church, that old definition was the dominant one, and that's why a lot of people came to confession. It was fear—fear that God was madder than hell at them and would get back at them."

It did not occur to Whitney, in those early days, that a papal encyclical might be wrong—about contraception or anything else. Growing up in Batavia during the Depression, the son of an auto salesman (later a factory worker) who didn't hesitate to use the razor strap, eating dinner every night at a table where "children were seen and not heard," he had developed into a conscientious and well-mannered adolescent, the head altar boy at St. Mary's, a diligent though not brilliant student at the minor seminary (high school for potential priests) in Buffalo. His grandmother, the housekeeper at St. Joseph's rectory across town, told him, "I want you to say three Hail Marys a day to ask Our Lady not that you will become a priest, but that you'll be a good one." He took this to be a comment on some of the priests who had passed through St. Joseph's over the years.

His memories of minor seminary are of "joyful boyhood years" spent busing it to Buffalo every Sunday night, sleeping in a bunk bed in a room with thirty other boys, playing baseball or touch football in the good months and basketball or handball in the winter, returning to a classroom filled with the odor of young male sweat and the cacophony of eight hours of Latin each week, eating donated unripe apples and sauerkraut and sandwiches of dry cheese on dry bread, drinking powdered milk.

Always at pains to please others, especially those in authority, young Paul was prefect of the first-year class and later prefect of the boarding school. He sometimes served as a Latin tutor in his senior year, and was one of the favored few boys invited to drink tea with the rector in his room and to run the rector's personal errands. At twenty, he moved on to St. Bernard's major seminary in Rochester (now the Rochester Colgate ecumenical divinity school) for the mandatory two years of philosophy and four of theology, mostly taught and examined in Latin. In sermons to this day, he sometimes catches himself swaying to the old fundamental dogma texts—*Tu es Petrus et super hanc petram* . . . Even after the modifications of Vatican II, he likes to think of himself as a priest who knows how to say Mass with reverence and precision, maintaining the proper "custody of the eyes" (although nowadays, that includes making eye contact with the congregation) and moving about the sanctuary with the proper balance between decorum and ease, so that attention remains focused on the sacramental drama rather than the person of the priest.

Ordained in Buffalo Cathedral at twenty-six on a snowy day in March 1958, he used ordination gifts to make the down payment on a new silver-blue Chevrolet. He was a junior priest at Blessed Sacrament Parish in Delavan, New York, when he had the traumatic confessional encounter over birth control. But it was a couple of years later, while teaching Latin and social studies back at the minor seminary of his "joyful boyhood," that he started questioning the contraception doctrine itself.

By then he had become part of a group of noisy golf-addicted priests who have, ever since those delirious Conciliar days of Catholic revival, fed each other's most critical and independent streaks on weekly days off and annual links-bound holidays. He had also begun helping out with pre-Cana (marriage preparation) conferences and volunteered one Friday evening a month at the diocesan family life clinic, where Catholic couples came for help in practicing natural birth control, then known as the "rhythm method." At the clinic, a priest worked alongside a Catholic gynecologist, the priest covering theological aspects while the doctor took care of technique.

From doctors and clients at the clinic, and from the married pre-Cana team members, he learned some hard realities about the world inhabited by real live married couples—matters not covered in the moral theology textbooks he had read at St. Bernard's. "They would say to me, 'It's just too hard, Father. We've got six kids, we love each other, her periods are not always on time.' They would ask good intelligent questions about the church's teaching, which I took back to dinner with my fellow professors who were more theologically adept than myself, asking them, 'When is the church going to do something about this?' "

Meanwhile, he helped out in parishes on weekends. At Easter and Christmas the lines outside the confessionals were long, and the tales of connubial disorder dreary: "I used a condom six times." . . . "I'm on the pill again." . . . "We had intercourse and he withdrew." Although the church counted such acts as mortal sins, Whitney, like most other priests, treated them as routine—much like the venial lists: "I lied seventeen times." . . . "I yelled at my kids." . . . "I haven't been saying my prayers before and after meals."

What could you do? Merely murmur comfortingly, "I know it's difficult." Or: "Ask God for help and strength to see your way through this problem, so you and your husband can live up to the ideals you have for yourselves." Or: "I understand the tremendous tension you're under, but don't let it impair the love you have for your wife."

And, most important: "I absolve you from all your sins, in the name of the Father, the Son, and the Holy Spirit." Unlike some priests, Whitney never denied absolution, not even to the most obdurate sinner. "As far as I was concerned," he says, "we weren't there to patrol the gates of heaven, but to forgive, and to give consolation."

Then came the invitation to move up to the major seminary as spiritual director, and then came *Humanae Vitae*, and then Paul Whitney was off to St. Paul's University in Ottawa to get his master's in theology and immerse himself in the exhilarating papers of the Second Vatican Council. Not only did he return to Buffalo "refreshed" by a year sitting at the feet of liberal Catholic theologians, but he now possessed "a stronger theological analysis of the teaching authority of the Holy See. I now realized that in certain areas the Pope does not speak with infallibility, and that this [contraception] was one of those areas.

"Theologically, I felt very comfortable with the idea that if couples left themselves open to the possibility of having children sometime in the life of the marriage, then they were fulfilling what Vatican II taught, with that dual concept that Vatican II came up with, that sex was meant just as much for building the love of husband and wife as it was for the procreation of children.

"So if couples are strapped financially, or whatever, and they're going to put off having children for a few years, or they've already had all the children they can take care of, I have no problem with that. It's their decision, and none of my business. I can no more tell you how to deal with your conscience than you can tell me how to deal with mine.

"Now, if Bishop Head were sitting here and heard me say that, he would probably have to say I was an unfaithful priest. But then, he's no theologian. He's from Long Island, that long line of New York Catholic conservatives. But then again, he's a very pastoral man, and if he were sitting here in this room and totally private, and heard me say it, maybe he could hack it—*personally*, privately. But he could never say it publicly, or teach it."

From *The Splendor of Truth*, Chapter Three, sections 113 and 116:

While exchanges and conflicts of opinion may constitute normal expressions of public life in a representative democracy, moral teaching certainly cannot depend upon respect for a process. . . . Opposition to the teaching of the church's pastors cannot be seen as a legitimate expression either of Christian freedom or of the diversity of the Spirit's gifts. When this happens, the church's pastors have a duty to act in conformity with their apostolic mission, insisting that the right of the faithful to receive Catholic doctrine in its purity and integrity must always be respected. . . .

A particular responsibility is incumbent upon bishops. . . . It falls to them, in communion with the Holy See, both to grant the title "Catholic" to church-related schools, universities, health-care facilities, and counseling services, and, in cases of serious failure to live up to that title, to take it away.

October: The carpet beneath Ruthie Hemerlein's window became a tapestry of amber, ruby, and rust, and Ruthie began wondering whether she would see another Erie County fall. Since her son Roger was moving his family from nearby Pendleton to Atlanta to work with a pest control firm, Ruthie, with both her sons now out of state, was contemplating a move to be closer to one of them. She had lived in western New York for all but a handful of her seventy years, educated in parish schools around the region as the family followed her father, a railroad conductor, through his various postings.

"I'm gonna tell ya," she chortles (for she chortles often and pleasantly), "I got more religion on my own than I ever got in those schools. We had the catechism each day in grammar school—*Who made the world? God made the world*. I don't remember a lot of the stuff from higher grades, like the seven capital sins and all, but I know they stressed a lot of church law—what you must do, what you can't do, and of course they had us all terrified of our chastity. I didn't really know what in the Sam Hill chastity was, but I knew damn well that I'd better have it. They made you feel like you really weren't very good, but if you worked real hard on it, maybe you could squeak by. And that stuff's not religion, not like the religion you get now, the New Testament, which is basically Love God with your whole mind and soul, et cetera, and love your neighbor as yourself. I don't ever remember that idea being put across to me."

Not, that is, until many years later, when a priest attached to a renewal center "looked me in the eye and said, 'Don't you know that God loves you?' It sounds silly, but I had never heard that. Everything I had ever been taught was: Fear the Lord."

October: On Respect Life Sunday, members of the Buffalo diocese bundled into winter coats to form a twenty-four-mile human chain from Lake Erie to Niagara Falls in support of the unborn. That same day in nearby Rochester, New York, Bishop Matthew H. Clark, one of the nation's most liberal prelates, summoned 1,300 delegates to a downtown hotel for a synod—still an unusual event in Catholic dioceses. The delegates chose "lifelong religious education" as their diocese's top priority, and asked their bishop to press Rome to ordain both women and married men. In California, Governor Pete Wilson signed into law a gender-free rape law and a spousal rape law, developments that *The Wanderer*, an ultraconservative Catholic weekly, reported under the headline "The Insanity Goes On." The paper cited views that the spousal rape bill was "the first step on the feminist agenda in the process of doing away with marriage."

At St. Paul's, the St. Vincent de Paul Society urged parishioners to new heights of generosity in donating food for the poor because "our pantry is bare." A half dozen people and their pets braved pouring rain in the rectory parking lot to attend the annual blessing of animals. The Sodality held its annual Living Rosary in the school gym: sixty women, one for each bead on the Rosary, sat in darkness holding candles which they lit one at a time as the murmur moved around a great circle: "Hail Mary, full of grace, the Lord is with you . . ."

As October, the Month of the Holy Rosary, drew to an end, most of the parish's 3,000 households had been visited by canvassers for the restoration drive, which the pastor had formally committed "to the protection of Our Blessed Mother and her title, Queen of the Most Holy Rosary." In a bulletin note, Whitney asked for special prayers to the Holy Mother for "her blessing on our Drive. . . . Offer your Rosary for this intention or pray the *Memorare* to ask Mary's help."

Sure enough, when the volunteers arrived at the Wednesday-evening report-back sessions, they brought good news of widows' mites and more bountiful promises averaging over $250 a year. The total of three-year pledges slightly exceeded the drive's $500,000 target.

True, some canvassers also told of doors being slammed in their faces. One Wednesday evening, a worried volunteer took the pastor aside.

"Father, do you know Mrs. C.?"

"Oh, sure," Father Paul said. "Did she tell you about O'Hara?"

"You know!" About eight years ago, Mrs. C. had called the pastor in distress, alleging that her son had been sexually fondled by a Franciscan teacher at O'Hara High. Not fully believing it—this being a while before such charges became commonplace—Whitney had hedged. He had said, "This is a very serious charge, and you'd better be prepared to substantiate it. If it's that serious to you, my suggestion to you would be to go downtown to the Chancery and make a complaint. You can't ask me to go and invade the Franciscan order's territory; I have no jurisdiction there." As far as he knew, no official action had ever been taken in the matter, but the Franciscans had later quit O'Hara abruptly after a salary dispute with the diocese.

"Oh yeah," Father Paul told the canvasser, noncommittal. "She's still pounding that drum?"

"Uh-huh. They don't want to give anything. They say the parish didn't support them, nor the diocese either."

"OK, I understand," the pastor said, and patted the canvasser on the shoulder before walking away. Whatever the truth of the matter, it was water under the bridge. His only real worry, as the drive drew to a close, was that regular collection-plate giving seemed to be taking a bit of a dive. Were parishioners already taking back from their envelopes some of what they had pledged to the capital drive? It would bear watching.

On Halloween a snowstorm blanketed the city but failed to deter a sellout crowd from cheering the Bills to a decisive victory over the Redskins.

That afternoon, to provoke the catechumenate into a full exploration of the humanity of Jesus, Judy Nice photocopied a set of statements for discussion, including:

TRUE/FALSE: Jesus was as much a human being as you are.

TRUE/FALSE: Jesus knew all things since he was a child.

TRUE/FALSE: Jesus grew as a human being through the affection of his parents and friends.

TRUE/FALSE: Jesus made a free decision to die on the cross for us.

TRUE/FALSE: Jesus had sexuality.

As a Roman bureaucrat once asked a Jewish preacher, what is truth? Judy's dispute with Ken—a dispute that hinged on the church's authority to proclaim truth in all John Paul's "splendor"—now simmered quietly. But both knew that, sooner or later, they would have to confront the issue. More than either Ken or Judy cared to acknowledge, the running debate between them was part of a war being waged across North America, and beyond. Its outcome would be pivotal for the shape of Catholicism to come.

The war of the Catholic laity gets its urgency from the decline of the clergy, a decline already catastrophic enough to force a massive renovation of the idea of Catholic leadership. In the late '60s, more than 900 men were ordained in the United States each year; in the early '90s, the number was under 300. And even these numbers speak too softly. There were fourteen men in the graduating class of Father Dick Sowinski, one of St. Paul's two parochial vicars. Of these fourteen, ten were still active as priests in 1993. Of the ten, only one was in charge of a parish. The other nine had "no sense of great urgency" about becoming pastors, according to the understatement-inclined and administration-allergic Father Dick (one of the nine).

Nor were there religious sisters around to pick up the slack—in 1992, the median age of the 99,337 U.S. nuns was reported at sixty-five, which was twenty years older than in 1968, when there had been 176,341 sisters. The diminishing number of nuns has been matched by a marked change in their national profile. Unlike the shrouded loyalists of old, modern nuns, in their business suits or denim jeans, tend to be highly educated (eight out of ten have master's degrees) specialists such as statisticians, professors, and doctors; many are outspoken dissenters from Rome's teaching on issues such as women's ordination and even abortion.

The near-disappearance of nuns has had a two-edged impact on parishes like St. Paul's, where the only nun in sight is Sister Mary Jude Rindfuss, S.S.M.N., who coordinates the team of lay pastoral visitors. On the one hand, it has forced laypeople into leadership roles: St. Paul's School has an all-lay staff, as does the religious education program for public-school children. But at the same time, a cadre of powerful female role models has disappeared—women who played pivotal roles forming the identity of every previous generation of Catholics.

It now seems inevitable that, fairly soon, the running of most parishes will be entirely in the hands of lay staff, with the few remaining priests relegated to the role of itinerant Mass providers. That's already true in places with sparser Catholic populations than the state of New York, and no one seriously disputes that the trend will spread.

Which leaves a big question to be resolved: what kind of leaders will these lay ministers be? In their attitudes and culture, will they be as diverse as the present crop of clergy, or will their ranks slowly become restricted to the orthodox? In the wake of *Humanae Vitae,* liberal priests had gained from Paul VI's legions the tacit acknowledgment of their right to question the magisterium. In the wake of *Veritatis Splendor,* the fates not of liberal clergy but of lay questioners—people like Judy Nice and her counterparts in Catholic parishes, schools, and hospitals—would be at stake.

But the lay rebels of the '90s are at a threefold disadvantage as compared with the ordained rebels of '68.

First, they don't have the tenure of ordination. Nothing short of a high-profile Curran-style confrontation with his bishop—and possibly not even that—could threaten Paul Whitney's job security or his retirement plan. Lay staff like Judy Nice are usually appointed from year to year, and thus cannot help but fear for their jobs when they make waves.

Second, all priests, but few laity, stand behind the intellectual levee of a seminary education. After six years in minor seminary, six more in theological school, and a postgraduate year studying the documents of Vatican II, Paul Whitney had returned to Buffalo in '69 armed with a quiet confidence in his ability to argue against—or simply ignore—*Humanae Vitae* and, if he chose, any future orthodox outbursts from the magisterium. Judy Nice's part-time religion courses at Canisius College were little match for Ken Monaco's Rome-approved treatises.

To all of which, add loneliness. Priests have each other—classmates going back decades and, sometimes, soul mates within the rectory. Nuns too have their communities. Judy's husband, Rick, is a sweet and gentle man who, that year, had spent many hours hearing her out and comforting her with his caresses. But Rick's kindness did not translate into a grasp of theological nuance or church politics.

So Judy dreaded the next sounding of the trumpet and was glad to focus, for now, on other business: she would shortly welcome a new crop of candidates into the catechumenate, making a record six in the group being prepared for next Easter. Ken Monaco, she knew, likewise had other things on his mind. He and his wife, Karen, unable to conceive a sibling for their son Christopher, had had the dispiriting news that one of two orphans in India whom they were hoping to adopt, an eight-year-old boy, had been diagnosed as having chronic hepatitis B, and given only a slim chance of achieving adulthood. The Monacos remained optimistic that the adoption of a six-year-old girl would be approved by Christmas; they believed God's hand had guided this process, and planned to change their daughter's name from Manjula to Maria, in honor of the Holy Mother. ("Has infertility been a cross? Yes," declared Ken. "Have we rejected that cross? No, because it has deepened our faith. Deepened our faith!")

Weeks after the appearance of *Veritatis*, Judy brooded over the rifts among faithful Catholics, and friends. "Why does my truth feel and sound so different from Ken's? And what do I do about that? I used to try to accommodate everybody, but now I'm beginning to feel that I can't do that anymore. It feels dysfunctional to me. It feels like the kind of thing that goes on in a dysfunctional family. You keep secrets, you don't say what's on your mind."

She paused, and then asked again, "How does God speak such contrary truth to each of us?"

Choices

November: On the feast day of Christ the King, which, being the Sunday before Advent, was the last Sunday of the liturgical year, 140 second-graders, from both parish and public school, sat on the green tiled floor of the St. Paul's School gym and got ready to rehearse their first confessions.

Each child wore about the neck a large piece of kraft paper, its color (green, blue, red, or yellow) indicating the group to which she or he had been assigned for "Gathering Day" in preparation for First Reconciliation. On the colored paper was printed the child's name; the paper itself had been roughly cut into an animal's shape. "It's a kitty cat," said one girl. "Naw, it's a sheep," said the boy next to her. The chatter died as Pat Blum, herself little taller and no less thin than many of the children, turned on a lectern microphone with an electronic bang and donned half-moon glasses to read in her quiet but no-nonsense voice:

> *Oh be careful little eyes what you see,*
> *be careful little eyes what you see,*
> *for the Father up above is looking down in love,*
> *so be careful little eyes what you see.*

Oh be careful little ears what you hear,
be careful little ears what you hear,
for the Father up above is looking down in love:
be careful little ears what you hear.

Be careful little hands what you do . . .

When Mrs. Blum finished, she looked around at a room full of wide little eyes. "Our Father," she began, and little voices echoed shrill off the hall's walls. "In the name of the Father, and of the Son, and of the Holy Spirit. Amen," she concluded, and little hands fluttered like butterfly wings across 140 little chests, the solemnity of the day seemingly cemented.

One of the red sheep, Samuel Thomas Forlenza, known as Sammy to distinguish him from his dad, wiped first his forehead and then his right cheek with four flattened fingers while being herded out of the gym. He wiped again, in the way he always did when bewildered or excited or both, as the herd emerged into cold sunlight and turned left, past the rectory and toward the church. As he followed the adult leader in erratic loping steps, Sammy cradled his chin in a hand that had disappeared into the overlarge sleeve of his Buffalo Bills winter jacket (even though the cuff had been turned up at least six inches).

The leader, a big schoolteacher with a scratchy voice, stopped at the top of the steps to calm her already raucous sheep. "This is God's house," she called in her loudest outside voice. "If God were actually waiting for you in there, you wouldn't be talking and fooling around, would you? And he really is in there, you know, so you need to just sit down and think about what we're doing here today.

"And remember," she said, "this is just practice today. It's just pretend. You won't really be confessing your sins today. Today we're just pretending." Sammy wiped his face and suddenly bent over to tie the laces of his tiny black Nikes.

The sun brightened the deep blue south transept window above the red sheep as Father Don, wearing black short-sleeved clerical shirt, black trousers, and a diamond stud in one ear, launched the spiel he would shortly be repeating for the blue, green, and yellow sheep. "Last I heard, the Bills were losing three-nothing. But it's real early in the game, so I'm sure we're gonna win. OK, now can anyone tell me why we're here today?"

"To practice Reconciliation," said a girl in front of Sammy.

"To practice Reconciliation, exactly. Because the first time we do something, we're nervous. And we don't want you to be nervous, so we're going to practice. So don't be nervous. There's nothing to be nervous about."

Sammy wiped his face and hunched deeper into his big Bills jacket, pressing his shoulders into the back of a pew. Father Don ran carefully through the rite of confession and emphasized the importance of memorizing the Prayer of Sorrow, which Sammy's mom (who called the prayer by another name—actofcontrition, Sammy thought) had helped him learn, one line a night, in the preceding weeks.

"That's not so bad, is it?" concluded Father Don. "It's nothing to worry about at all!" Sammy wiped his face again. "And believe me, I've heard some adults say some pretty bad stuff, and I've never yelled at them, and I'm not going to yell at you either." Wipe, wipe. "There is nothing you can tell me that I haven't heard before. So," the priest said with friendly smile and raised voice, "DON'T GET NERVOUS." Wipe, wipe, wipe.

The seven-year-olds and eight-year-olds lined up in the center aisle and trotted, one by one, to meet Father Don to the right of the altar, or Mrs. Blum to the left, to just practice, just pretend, to confess their sins. Sammy waited until the big teacher asked for the last time, "Who hasn't been yet?" before joining the line. As he stood on the outside edges of his feet, the teacher stage-whispered: "And remember, it's a secret. You don't even have to tell your mom and dad what you confessed!"

"This is Sammy, Father."

"Well, hi, Sammy, how ya doin'? Nervous?"

Sammy nodded, climbed into a red vinyl chair facing Father Don, and crossed his legs. He was so small for the chair that his calves were almost horizontal, and as the priest leaned forward to engage him, the black-and-white Nike on Sammy's right foot waved in the air dangerously near Father Don's nose.

"How come?"

"I dunno," offered Sammy in a tiny voice.

"There's nothing to be nervous about, OK?"

Sammy nodded, and wiped his face.

"Don't worry about it. Promise not to worry?"

Nod. Wipe.

"OK. Remember how we begin?"

"Um-ah, bless me for my sins."

" 'Bless me, Father, for I have sinned'—OK, close enough. OK. Then you're gonna tell the priest your sins, but for now I want you to give me one sin, tell me one thing, one example of a sin."

"My little sister."

"What about your little sister? Is she the sin or do you do something to her?"

"Um-ah, I usually do something to her."

"Something nasty, huh?"

Quick nod. Wipe. Behind the small "penitent," the green herd was now tramping into the church.

"Then the priest is gonna talk to you about that, OK?"

Sammy nodded and smeared his hand over the top of his head.

"And then he's gonna ask you to do something to make up for your sins. Maybe, ah, do something nice or special for your sister."

Nod.

"And then he's gonna ask you to say your Prayer of Sorrow. Got that memorized?"

This time, Sammy's nod was a bit bigger. He wiped his cheek and then his brow, his big brown unsmiling eyes fixed on the priest's as he rattled off: "OhmyGodIamsorrythatIhavesinned, pleaseforgiveme. Iwannaloveyouandbegoodtoeveryone, helpmemakeupformysins, I'lltrytodobetterfromnowonamen."

"Wow, great job on that, Sammy, OK!"

Sammy did not crack a smile.

"Then he's gonna pray over you, and"—Sam shrank into the chair away from Father Don's big hand—"bless you; he'll give you a pin and send you back to your parents. How about a handshake?"

Sammy's fingertips disappeared into the priest's palm.

"Wasn't so bad, was it?"

Sammy didn't smile, didn't move except to tug at his fingers.

"You gonna be nervous? No, you're not, because you know what you're doin'. Just remember that: you do know what you're doin'."

Sammy retrieved his fingertips to wipe his left cheek as he slipped off the chair and scurried, just short of running, to join the red herd now assembling for their journey back into the cafeteria, where, to his apparent relief, Sammy found familiar territory in the form of activity books and crayons. Sammy *loved* activity books. He opened his book and explored it while a strange mom read a Bible story to the group.

". . . The people complained: 'Zacchaeus is a sinner.' But Zacchaeus said to the Lord, 'I will give half my money to the poor. If I have cheated anyone I will pay that person back four times more.' And Jesus said, 'Salvation has come to this house today. . . . The Son of Man came to find lost people and save them.' "

Sammy turned a page to begin finding "lost sheep" hidden in a field.

"Stinker. Stinker. Stinker," Sammy muttered as he pounced on each sheep and colored it blue. Finally, he counted the blue shapes and printed the result at the side of the page, "11 SHEEP," simultaneously stretching out his free hand to snare a passing sugar doughnut.

When the universal *Catechism of the Catholic Church*, available in French since 1992, finally appeared in its English translation, paragraphs 387 and 1440 of this encyclopedic recapitulation of church doctrine about everything, the most massive achievement of John Paul II's papacy, would state:

> . . . Without the knowledge Revelation gives of God we cannot recognize sin clearly and are tempted to explain it as merely a developmental flaw, a psychological weakness, a mistake, or the necessary consequence of an inadequate social structure, etc. Only in the knowledge of God's plan for man can we grasp that sin is an abuse of the freedom that God gives to created persons so that they are capable of loving him and loving one another.
>
> ¶ Sin is before all else an offense against God, a rupture of communion with him. At the same time it damages communion

with the church. For this reason conversion entails both God's forgiveness and reconciliation with the church, which are expressed liturgically by the sacrament of Penance and Reconciliation.

In fairness to Sammy, his little sister Allie was a formidable temptation to sin. Ailsa Marina Forlenza possessed a three-year-old's diabolical cornucopia of techniques for grabbing any straying adult attention. From the washroom, she might yell, for the edification of parents and guests, a descriptive name for her feces, the cries of "T. Rex!" or "Tiddlyosaurus!" echoing through the Forlenzas' 1927 granite former farmhouse. Wandering into the living room, she might announce, "I'm gonna clean my clock," and attack the grandfather clock, her father's pride and joy, with a sticky washcloth. "Please, Allie, I don't want you to do that," Sam Sr. would say. But when she turned her gap-toothed smile on him, he looked the other way.

Sammy, who favored more serious pursuits such as Lego, SuperMario, and dinosaur books, whose mother, Mary Ann, was frequently able to pin to the kitchen bulletin board admiring notes from teachers about good manners and intelligence, sometimes found the commotion attached to his sister a little too much. The resulting shoving was usually brief, loud, and within acceptable limits of violence. Strictly venial matter, but still, as Sammy's beloved Mrs. Rizzo would say, a Wrong Choice.

Annette Rizzo, that was, a full-lipped young mother and bank official with long red-painted nails and a taste for tight sweaters and jeans. Mrs. Rizzo was a volunteer teacher in the St. Paul's religious education program, known to many parishioners simply as "Religion." At St. Paul's, the second-grade Religion program for the fall semester consisted entirely of preparation for the rite variously known as the sacrament of Conversion, of Penance, of Confession, of Forgiveness, and of Reconciliation.

The word "sin," although it did crop up in the "actofcontrition" memorized nightly by Sammy and his mom, had seldom, if ever, been heard in Mrs. Rizzo's Saturday-morning class. The phrase that Mrs. Rizzo used, over and over again, was: "Wrong Choice."

"Did anyone here make a Right Choice this week?" Mrs. Rizzo asked near the beginning of one such class. Sammy, and most of the other children, nodded solemnly. "And did anyone make a Wro-o-o-ng Choice?" Mrs. Rizzo asked then, drawing out the W-word comically to dilute its threat. Sammy, and a few others, nodded again. "Are you sorry for the Wrong Choice? No, Alison? If it was a Wrong Choice, you would have hurt someone. Sure, you are sorry. What was the Wrong Choice that you made?"

"I, um. My brother and I were playing together, and, um. I pushed him."

"Oh!" said Mrs. Rizzo in mock horror. "Did you tell him you were sorry?"

Alison shook her head.

"Maybe you oughta go home and give him a big hug and tell him you're sorry for doing that. Was that a nice thing to do? Was that a Right Choice?"

Alison shrugged.

"Well, I don't think that was a Right Choice. Well, we have to think about that. OK, now, God has given us rules to follow, so that we can make the Right Choices, and we're gonna read about those rules today. Can everyone turn to page eighteen? Who would like to read first today?"

Sammy's hand shot up. This was not the cowed Sammy who would hide in his pew on "Gathering Day" a few weeks later. This was a quick, keen, bright-eyed, and occasionally smart-aleck Sammy, who read the required passage carefully and fluently.

"OK," said Mrs. Rizzo. "Let's go back and think about that. Jesus wants you to follow him. How can you follow him?"

"Um-ah, making Right Choices," said Sammy at once, his eyes meeting hers just long enough to check for approval, then moving on in endless activity—exchanging a wry secret glance with the girls on either side of him at the front table, scanning ahead in his workbook, and peering around the room. It could almost have been his public school homeroom, with its map and flag of the United States, illustrated cutout numbers and letters, READING IS FUN poster and dinosaur stickers, but for a small crucifix over the front green board and a statue of Mary high in a corner.

"That's right," said Mrs. Rizzo. " 'Cause he made good choices, and he wants you to do that too. But God loves us even when we do make Wrong Choices. He forgives us. And that's what Reconciliation is all about. At baptism, your parents, your family, your godparents, and all the people around you, they all promised to help you make Right Choices. They help you learn the rules God gave. Anyone heard of the Ten Commandments?"

Amy, a husky-voiced pensive girl with a ponytail, put her hand half up, then brought it down fast as she noticed the sea of shaking heads. Various kids then read one commandment each from the workbook, Mrs. Rizzo adding a word of explanation here and there:

" 'In vain' means 'in a bad way': we speak God's name only in love, OK? . . . 'Honor' means 'love' your father and mother: don't talk back to them. . . ."

There was an awkward moment at the Sixth Commandment, which happened to have been omitted from the edition that Mrs. Rizzo used.

"Do not 'mit adulty," read Carl.

"Oh, that one's not in mine," said Mrs. Rizzo. She took a breath. "OK. You have to . . . You have to take good care of yourself, OK? In other people . . . Um, I think we're gonna have to get back to that one, OK? How about number seven? Joe?"

"You shall not steal."

"OK, I think everyone knows what *that* is, huh?"

Catechism of the Catholic Church, paragraphs 1857–58, 1861–63, and 1458:

For a *sin* to be *mortal*, three conditions must together be met: "Mortal sin is sin whose object is grave matter and which is also committed with full knowledge and deliberate consent."

¶ *Grave matter* is specified by the Ten Commandments. . . . The gravity of sins is more or less great: murder is graver than theft. One must also take into account who is wronged: violence against parents is in itself graver than violence against a stranger.

¶ Mortal sin is a radical possibility of human freedom, as is love itself. It results in the loss of charity and the privation of sanctifying grace, that is, of the state of grace. If it is not redeemed by repentance and God's forgiveness, it causes exclusion from Christ's kingdom and the eternal death of hell, for our freedom has the power to make choices for ever, with no turning back. However, although we can judge that an act is in itself a grave offense, we must entrust judgment of persons to the grace and mercy of God.

¶ One commits *venial sin* when, in a less serious matter, he does not observe the standard prescribed by the moral law, or when he disobeys the moral law in a grave matter, but without full knowledge or without complete consent.

¶ . . . Deliberate and unrepented venial sin disposes us little by little to commit mortal sin. However, venial sin does not set us in direct opposition to the will and friendship of God. . . .

¶ Without being strictly necessary, confession of everyday faults (venial sins) is nevertheless strongly recommended by the church.

Wedding portraits of Sam and Mary Ann Forlenza show a sultry petite, impossibly thin redheaded bride and a handsome stubby-athletic groom with a dark brush cut and glowing dark eyes. Mary Ann Forlenza grew up among fellow Italian-Americans on the lower West Side of Buffalo; she attended grade school at Holy Angels and went on to Nardin Academy Catholic high school. At Buffalo State College, she studied journalism and public relations. She was taking orders in the duty-free store on the Peace Bridge when, in the summer of 1980, she was smitten with Sam, a UB junior paying for his science degree by schlepping merchandise onto the bridge.

The young couple had been married two years when Sammy was born in 1986. They had no technical difficulties conceiving their perfectly planned family, and no moral qualms about family planning either. "In these times, it's irresponsible," says Sam of those who spurn artificial contraception. "None of our friends have more than two kids. It's the norm, I guess." As for church-commended natural methods, Sam shrugs: "That's impractical." Mary Ann adds: "Besides that, I have endometriosis, so I have to be on the pill. I don't think the Pope could argue with that." None of the grandparents—Catholics all—argued either. The whole thing was a non-issue.

When the children arrived, Mary Ann quit work and she and Sam, who had formerly enjoyed long nights spent drinking with friends, became homebodies, absorbed with every development in Sammy's and Allie's lives. Sam Sr. would come home from work around five-thirty most days, and liked to play with the kids, take his turn at bath time, read bedtime stories. Afterward, he and Mary Ann were content to watch TV or battle their way through the high-tech maze of Sammy's SuperMario game.

They enrolled Sammy at St. Paul's School because there was no pre-K in the public schools and he seemed to crave the stimulation. But while Mary Ann had no complaint with Sammy's pre-K teacher, she was unimpressed by what she saw of the parochial school. Although it had a full curriculum, computer room, and Spanish classes, Mary Ann had the impression that the school was operating on a shoestring with religion and discipline its chief priorities. By contrast, Hoover public school was modern, brightly lit, and well equipped, and had a reputation for enlightened policies and academic excellence. It was also nearer to her home, and free.

If Mary Ann's attachment to church ends, more or less, with the weekly obligation, her husband Sam has almost no interest in religion at all. He too grew up in a Catholic household, and his parents took him to Mass most Sundays, but otherwise did not discuss religion; Sam and his older brother and sister attended public grade school. The two boys did go to Canisius for high school, but strictly because of the academics. Both took science degrees—big brother Ron went on to be a surgeon; Sam became an engineer for New York Telephone. Ron has been known to refer to himself as an agnostic, but Sam is not sure what he himself is. He does, however, consider the Catholic Church "overly focused on guilt and rules" and sometimes "ridiculous and punitive—on divorce, for instance."

Nevertheless, Mary Ann takes Sammy to Mass most Sundays, and she notices that when Sammy goes off with the other kids during the Liturgy of the Word for their own special service, he always comes back with a smile on his face. The only part of the exercise that she complains about is the Kiss of Peace. On one recent Sunday, the woman sitting next to her hacked away into her hand all through Mass and then offered the same hand for the exchange of peace. Mary Ann, who doesn't want anyone to think she has "a thing about cleanliness," nevertheless cites sanitariness for her refusal to take advantage of the post-Vatican II availability of the chalice, and admits,

"Sometimes I want to say to the priest, 'Look it's the flu season, couldn't you just this once say, "Why don't we just smile at each other for the Peace today"?' "

Some Sundays, Sam Sr. consents to go along, since only he can keep Allie quiet in church. He never receives communion. Sammy, however, was enrolled in Religion when he hit the first grade. Even Sam Sr. feels church instruction is important for a child—it provides, he says, a sense of belonging, helping to establish a child's roots in the community and in history. "It gives the child a sense of heritage," Sam says. "I want Sammy to hear the stories that his parents and grandparents heard as children, and part of that is the traditions of the church."

So there had never been any question that Sammy would, like his mother and father before him, begin preparing to make his confession. And when the notice had come of a meeting for parents of second-graders, Mary Ann had gone along to get the dates and logistics. She entered the St. Paul's School gym feeling both a little sad and a little happy that her son was suddenly grown up enough to have arrived at this milestone. She was soon bored, though, as she found herself sitting through a forty-five-minute background lecture by Father Don.

"The process of Reconciliation has changed over the years," said Father Don, who this time was wearing a gold earring. "When each church was a small community of a handful of people, everyone knew when someone sinned. What they considered sinful was not the petty trash, the venial garbage"—Father Don pronounced it garBARGE—"that is ninety-seven percent of what comes in the confessional today. There was public acknowledgment of the sin, and then the person was placed in the order of penitents, removed from communion for a time—in some cases, being made to wear sackcloth or ashes or other public symbols of penitence—and restored to communion just before Easter.

"Over time, the emphasis moved from social relationships to the vertical—the relationship with God. A heresy, or false teaching, crept in, called Jansenism. The Jansenists taught that everything to do with the flesh was evil; everything to do with sex was sinful. The effects of this heresy linger; there is still a sense in the church that earthly concerns are bad, and only heavenly concerns are good. The Irish were especially influenced by Jansenism, and it was Irish monks too who invented a dark corner to deal with those sins. Can anyone guess what that invention was?"

A woman's voice from the back of the room: "The confessional."

"Right, the confessional. A dark lonely box, where the only relationship that matters is me and God. No wonder people today hate going to confession. But luckily, in the last twenty to thirty years we've moved away from the Middle Ages and Jansenism. . . ."

Like her husband, Sam, Mary Ann Forlenza remembers nothing about the first time she made Reconciliation, then generally called Confession, but she does remember subsequent confessions as being terrifying encounters in a gloomy closet with a gruff disembodied male bark that became an angry howl over the smallest thing—a missed Sunday Mass, for instance. (If Mary Ann ever understood neglect of the Sunday obligation to be no small matter, but a mortal sin, she forgot this a long time ago.) It was an enduring puzzle to her that at parish picnics and the like, the priests were so friendly, remembering every family's every joy and trial, but turned so malevolent in the pulpit or confessional. "It turned you off," she says. "It wasn't about forgiveness, it was more like 'Don't do it again, ten Hail Marys and five Our Fathers.'"

Mary Ann was glad when Sammy came home from Reconciliation classes with what seemed a wholly different concept, one that placed not guilt but forgiveness—the possibility of a fresh start after every "Wrong Choice"—at the center of things. She approved of the values he was learning about in the class; the lessons seemed aimed at inculcating compassion, tolerance, and a positive attitude toward the world. And she was more than glad to discover that Sammy would make his first confession—and, if he chose, subsequent ones—not in a dark closet but sitting with a priest, face to face. She even enjoyed memorizing the revamped act of contrition (or, rather, Prayer of Sorrow) with her son. It certainly was a lot easier than the old one, which, she thinks, she can still remember: "'O my God, I am heartily sorry that I have offended thee. I detest all my sins because . . .' I can't remember the next part."

Sam Sr. offers: "Something about 'thy just punishment,' I think," but the rest, for both of them, is a blank.

"But the worst part was listing your sins," says Mary Ann. "If you didn't have any, or if you didn't think you had enough, you'd add: 'And I lied five times.' It was terrible to do that, I guess, but the more sins you had, the bigger a penance you'd get, and it seemed to make the priest happier to dole the penances out."

There was, of course, no possibility of *not* having sinned. Mary Ann had been taught that Adam and Eve had, in their Original Sin back in their garden, destroyed the possibility of a state of grace. So everyone had evil impulses as well as good ones, and all too often, evil won. Because of this Original Sin, God had been obliged to establish rules for his children's guidance: the rules, or commandments, were there to help you avoid sin. And when you broke the rules, he forgave you through the sacrament. Then you could start sinning all over again.

Sammy was receiving this identical teaching in Mrs. Rizzo's class, except that the language had changed to filter out the terror. For one thing, the phrase "Original Sin" went unspoken. Instead, one Saturday morning that November, Mrs. Rizzo passed out a song sheet and switched on her ghetto blaster to conjure up the sweet voices of children, singing at a merry clip:

> *Willa-Mena Amphisbena is a beast you know.*
> *Willa-Mena Amphisbena has two heads to show.*
>   *One is happy. One is sad. Willa's good. Mena's bad.*
>   *One is happy. One is sad. Willa's always's laughing.*
>   *Mena's always mad. . . .*
>
> *Willa-Mena Amphisbena is a scary sight.*
> *Willa-Mena, if you've seen her, you won't sleep tonight.*
>   *One is happy. One is sad. Willa's good. Mena's bad. . . .*

The beat slowed right down for the punch line, sung by just one voice:

> *You won't find an Amphisbena in your local zoo.*
> *Willa-Mena Amphisbena IS IN ME AND YOU!*

"Is that true?" asked Mrs. Rizzo. "Willa-Mena in me and you? Sometimes we're happy, and sometimes we're sad? Sometimes we're good, and sometimes we're bad? It's almost like we're two different people, like we have two heads!"

Lauren, a mischievous blond in a wheelchair, stretched her head way over the back of her chair so that she could see Mrs. Rizzo standing, as it were, upside down behind her. She displayed her widest smile and shouted, "Four!"

Mrs. Rizzo, who had no idea what Lauren meant, said, "OK, turn to the next page in your book—"

"Six!" yelled Lauren.

"—page twenty. Six what, Lauren?"

"Six heads!"

Mrs. Rizzo paused, looked back at the song sheet, and considered. "Oh, yeah. That's true too. A happy one, a sad one, a good one, a bad one, a laughing one, a mad one. OK, who needs a pencil?"

Contrary to the popular stereotype, it is forgiveness, rather than guilt, that lies at the heart of Catholic spirituality. Guilt is a fact of life—no more a religious invention than is sin; even the children of atheists are born with a conscience. The difference between religions lies not in the facts of sin and guilt, but in the remedies. All Christian children are taught that God stands ready to forgive every penitent sinner. And, yes, this message was obscured for many among the generations educated in the harsh era preceding Vatican II—obscured by a pedagogy based on fear. But even so, only the Catholic tradition has elevated forgiveness—the remedy for sin—to sacramental status. While Protestants hold that conversion and baptism wash every sin away, the fact of sin *among the reborn* is a problem for them, a paradox that requires major theological know-how to solve. For assurance of divine forgiveness, Protestants can only hope for a feeling, a subjective experience of absolution. It is Catholics—the supposedly guilt-ridden Catholics—who can walk away from the confessional tearing up lists of sins.

Mrs. Rizzo explained Reconciliation as making peace after doing something to hurt someone. "Sometimes you make the Wrong Choice," Mrs. Rizzo said. "This can make you very sad. You need the peace of Jesus." She wrote the word "Reconciliation" on the green board, as Sammy's mouth slowly opened into a huge silent yawn. "That word means forgiveness. Making Reconciliation means thinking very hard about if you've made any Wrong Choices, and if you're sorry, then you tell Father about the Wrong Choices you have made, and through him, you get the forgiveness of God."

To demonstrate forgiveness, the class made finger puppets and used them to act out "Wrong Choices" of their own invention. These sins mostly consisted of one puppet punching another's stomach. Each time around, the culprit said, "Sorry," the victim said, "That's OK," and the puppets lived peacefully ever after, or at least until the next assault.

Then, reconciled, everyone exchanged a greeting of peace. They did this in pairs, starting at the back of the room, but because there was an odd number of kids in the room, Sammy was left alone, and sat there for a moment looking forlorn, a long delicate forefinger poised on his upper lip. Mrs. Rizzo walked up to him, extended a hand, and said, "The peace of the Lord be with you, Sammy." She pinched his nose lightly between her forefinger and thumb.

Sammy smiled and murmured, "And also with you." He wiped the touch off his nose and returned his forefinger to its place on his lip.

C*atechism of the Catholic Church*, paragraphs 397, 399–401, and 405:

Man, tempted by the devil, let his trust in his Creator die in his heart and, abusing his freedom, *disobeyed* God's command. . . . ¶ Scripture portrays the tragic consequences of this first disobedience. Adam and Eve immediately lose the grace of original holiness. They become afraid of the God of whom they have conceived a distorted image—that of a God jealous of his prerogatives.

¶ The harmony in which they had found themselves, thanks to original justice, is now destroyed: the control of the soul's spiritual faculties over the body is shattered; the union of man and woman becomes subject to tensions, their relations henceforth marked by lust and domination. Harmony with creation is broken: visible creation has become alien and hostile to man. Because of man, creation is now subject "to its bondage to decay." . . . ¶ After that first sin, the world is virtually inundated by sin. . . .

¶ Although it is proper to each individual, original sin does not have the character of a personal fault in any of Adam's descendants. It is a deprivation of original holiness and justice, but human nature has not been totally corrupted: it is wounded in the natural powers proper to it; subject to ignorance, suffering, and the dominion of death; and inclined to sin—an inclination to evil that is called "concupiscence." Baptism, by imparting the life of Christ's grace, erases original sin and turns a man back toward God, but the consequences for nature, weakened and inclined to evil, persist in man and summon him to spiritual life.

November: Lighted candy canes, candles, and little trees appeared on the lampposts on Delaware Avenue, and the trees under Ruthie Hemerlein's window were a carpet no more. Instead, a shimmering veil of yellow and gray allowed Ruthie to peer down Kenmore's neat rows of multicolored roofs trimmed with always fresh paint. Nancy, Ruthie's New Jersey daughter-in-law, was expecting a baby at last, and Ruthie hoped for her first granddaughter, but did not mention this in her prayers to the Blessed Mother, concentrating instead on good health—for Nancy, then stricken with colitis, and for the baby she bore.

November: At St. Paul's as at most parishes, this was high season for activity, a time to implement the plans of September and October and to get ready for Christmas, winter, and spring. The Liturgy Committee put the final touches on preparations for Advent. The Senior Youth Group announced a doughnut sale after all Masses. The Sodality planned a demonstration of Oriental flower arranging. Adult Formation announced a "Faith Sharing" series and an Advent Evening of Reflection, and raised $500 with a line dance. The monthly catechumenate team meeting having been canceled because of all-around busyness, Ken Monaco had to wait for his chance to present John Paul's views on truth's splendor.

November: The month's news included much about bishops. From Chicago came a new allegation of sexual abuse, this time leveled at one of the most senior and universally respected of U.S. prelates. A former seminary student, Steven Cook, thirty-four, had filed a $10 million lawsuit accusing Joseph Cardinal Bernardin of Chicago of sexually abusing him as a teenager. In Washington, the U.S. bishops, gathered for their annual fall meeting, joined the Pope himself in expressing confidence in Bernardin's innocence. (A few months later, Cook would withdraw the allegation, which had been based on a "recovered memory.") At the same meeting, the bishops officially released a pastoral letter on marriage and the family. The Buffalo *News* had already given the draft front-page treatment:

CATHOLIC BISHOPS ENCOURAGE SPOUSAL EQUALITY DURING MARRIAGE

By David Briggs
Associated Press
Men, submit to your wives: share your tears—as well as the laundry and the bathtub scrubbing.

Women, be not afraid to get mad at your husband, or to tell him to spend equal time with the children.

In perhaps their most comprehensive attempt to address relations between the sexes, a committee of U.S. bishops is proposing a document on marriage that encourages Catholics to move beyond the sexual stereotypes they grew up with. . . .

The 5,000-word letter described the family as sacred, called for families to spend more time together, and urged couples to "move beyond gender stereotypes" toward a relationship of "mutuality." The bishops' conference also approved a statement on world peace, urging the United States to avoid both isolationism and "unwise" foreign interventions.

At St. Paul's, on the twenty-first day of that November, the feast day of Christ the King, Father Don, the junior parochial vicar, was steeling himself for a fateful meeting with the Most Reverend Edward Head, Bishop of Buffalo.

Father Don's homily at the ten o'clock Mass was a concise reflection on the Judgment Day parable of the sheep and the goats. He told of an old Irish monk who wrote in his journal: "I sought my soul, but my soul I could not see. I sought my God, but my God eluded me. I sought my brother and sister, and then I found all four. . . ." Father Don said the day's liturgy was a call "to contemplate Christ's kingship from the point of view of how he will judge us in the end." And, he said, "it becomes very clear that Jesus will judge us on how well we care for one another."

Judgment Day, Father Don said, was a call "to examine our lives, which means we have to be totally honest, and sometimes make very hard decisions about the direction our lives are going. And today we are given one way to lighten the load, a simpler way to find God.

"If you are having trouble loving God," Father Don said, "try loving people." It was as apt a way as any to begin saying goodbye to his life as a priest.

This life was, by Father Don's own account, one into which he had slid, rather than one self-consciously chosen. In high school, he had shone at history and English, failed ruinously at sports, and been overshadowed socially by his more gregarious, more attractive, and more athletic twin brother. He found his niche—or it was found for him—in his sophomore year, outside school hours. St. Barnabas Parish was having trouble securing a teacher for Don's younger sister's fourth-grade religion class, and Don, who then foresaw a teaching career for himself, volunteered. Soon he was attending the "home seminary," a group for high school students considering careers in the priesthood. Not one to spend hours in prayer (either then or later), he would never claim to have a deeply spiritual sense of vocation. It was more a case of having discovered a place where he seemed to belong.

And so, in the fall of 1979, he found himself a freshman at the seminary of Christ the King in the Buffalo suburb of East Aurora.

Whatever the status of its titular monarch, the campus seems, from Father Don's description, to have been ruled by youthful hormones. Like all Catholic seminaries, Christ the King required its students to avoid "particular friendships" with people of both sexes, and taught that even to touch or to be alone with another person unnecessarily was to invite temptation. But ideal was not reality. Off campus, men pursued women; on campus, they pursued each other; in neither case were heroic efforts made to keep the liaisons secret. Father Don says that he himself had felt attracted to men since high school but, as he puts it now, had done "nothing about it except masturbation." He says that at the seminary, straights ("jocks") and gays ("sisters") knew who each other were, or thought they knew, and an undercurrent of tension existed between the two. The latter group adopted openly effeminate ways and used feminine pronouns for each other, although some "sisters" played touch football and "some jocks were getting it, with other guys, every night."

It is inconceivable to Father Don that the faculty could not have known how much sex was taking place in the dorms. The seminarian concluded that his Franciscan teachers preferred *not* to know, troubling themselves only if someone openly had an "exclusive" friendship, which could too easily lead to "scandal." Only in such an instance were the men involved asked to leave, although usually on stated grounds that had nothing to do with sex. The latter subject was taboo, yet it seemed always to lurk just beneath the surface. When a visiting presider at the seminary Mass made the mistake of introducing the penitential rite with the words "And now, let us bow our heads to examine ourselves," half the congregation collapsed in stifled laughter.

Even in the lust-laden ether of Christ the King, Father Don says he himself didn't so much as maintain a "particular friendship"; rather, he hung out with a half dozen men almost all of whom happened, as he later realized, to be gay. (Among these, two men were regular lovers: they were both ordained and one is now dead, of AIDS). "I was very naive," Father Don says. "I was told afterward that there were a couple of guys who wanted me bad but I wasn't aware of it at all." He was still a virgin at the time of his ordination in 1983.

Father Don served three and a half years at his home parish of St. Barnabas before moving on to St. Rose of Lima in North Buffalo and then, in 1991, to St. Paul's. What he loved most about being a priest was the liturgy—the music, the sheer goose-bumps-grade beauty of sacramental ritual at its best. "The sanctuary became my theater," he says, "and I was pretty damn good at it." More than once in his early years, his habit of taking liberties with the details of the missal got him in trouble with pastors and people. "The Mass is less a matter of adhering to ritual than of maintaining a dialogue," he says, "with the priest as the mediator and the words as the medium. There I was, trying to make it a real experience of meeting God, and all they were worried about was whether I was leaving out one word, or that this time of being with God had to be less than an hour long."

If liturgy was both a joy and a strain, the daily grind of pastoral duties was a chore at best and an affliction at worst. Father Don hated rectory life—an intense existence of sharing a home with men with whom he often had little in common. A home? Well, an office with bedrooms attached; a meeting place for parish groups; a magnet for strangers in search of a helping hand or simply a handout.

Father Don says, "It was kind of hard at one o'clock in the morning when someone's pounding at the door because they've been out drinking and have had a fight with their spouse. Or in the middle of my dinner, when someone decides that a crisis that's been building three years or more has now reached breaking point.

"Our setup says to the people, 'The priest has no life; his life is yours.' If doctors can trust an answering service to screen calls and patch through emergencies after hours, why can't clergy? And how often does a true emergency arise anyway? Or maybe the parishioners are thinking, 'If you keep them busy twenty-four hours a day, it's less likely that they'll be whacking it off.' "

In the confessional, he was sometimes able to feel something approaching competence in his pastoral role. Though impatient with the many who seemed to approach Reconciliation purely out of a sense of religious obligation, he occasionally felt a powerful sense of the divine presence, and healing, in confessional encounters. "There were times when someone left and I was crying almost as much as they were," he recalls. But as a counselor back in the rectory office, he felt "grossly inadequate."

"Within a year and a half of ordination," Father Don says, "I had got tired of dealing day in and day out with other people's problems. From marriage counseling right on down. A lot of it had nothing to do with the religious side. I was, like, 'Your marriage is breaking up, so go see a marriage counselor! Not me. I've only had one course in counseling.' I felt like I was the dumping ground. They could all dump on me, but God forbid the priest dump on them. I was supposed to listen to everything they say and not make any judgments, just absolve them, in a sense, whereas if I were to say what was going on in *my* life and *my* turmoil, I'd have been kicked out or condemned."

The turmoil in Father Don's life had come to the fore a little over six years after his ordination, when he lost his virginity in an encounter with a fellow priest. Afterward, he was, by his own account, "a wreck." If his prior use of homoerotic magazines and videos had troubled him, it was a strictly private trouble. Now, he was obliged to face a reality about himself for which he was both unready and, by profession, unsuited. The young priest's spiritual director suggested a visit to the clergy counseling center, and it was in a fraught session with a nun there that Father Don first heard himself say the words "Yes, I am gay."

The counselor showed no sign of being shocked by this revelation, and probably was not. While no one can know how many priests are sexually active, let alone what their preferences are, a 1993 article in the Washington *Post* by high school teacher and former seminarian Patrick Welsh took some educated guesses about the number of clergy who are gay. Welsh quoted Catholic University sociologist Dean Hoge, who in turn cited estimates by priests polled by two national surveys: "In seminaries now," Hoge said, "the percentage is higher than in the active priesthood. In many dioceses, estimates are as high as 50 percent. It's too hot to handle as a scientifically researchable topic."

Also quoted was former Jesuit John McNeil, author of *The Church and the Homosexual,* who said gays had provided considerable talent to the church: "There is some truth to the fact that there was no place for gay men to go until recently. Either you got married or entered the clergy to have a cover for the fact that you were not heterosexual."

Inevitably, Father Don's years with the counselor opened up other, older personal turmoils. "Low self-esteem" was a topic that came up a lot, as was the emotional isolation the priest had always felt from his stoic, disapproving father, a postal worker. Another was the habit of taking responsibility for others' lives, probably the result of his dad's shift work and his older-brother status in relation to two sisters. There was also the pain of his father's massive paralyzing stroke, which not only cut off meaningful communication between father and son when the latter was twenty, and eliminated any chance of healing the rift between them, but changed the older man's prevailing mood from cold remoteness to violent rage.

But equally inevitably, the growing self-awareness led Father Don back, again and again, to the conflict between his chosen career and his longing for intimacy.

Ironically, Father Don's arrival at St. Paul's in 1992 marked the beginning of his most rewarding time as a priest and the beginning of the end of his priesthood. Paul Whitney fostered the curate's liturgical bent as had no previous boss, and Father Don quickly made a number of friends among the parishioners. But the rage inside him was building steam. By the end of his first year in Kenmore, Father Don had privately decided that his time as a priest was nearly up. "It was too lonely," he says. "I felt isolated. I had a lot of friends but I needed a particular friend and hadn't allowed myself to have one, because I was too afraid of scandal."

All the same, Father Don was slowly growing more active sexually. His second partner, like the first, was a priest—this time, there were a few encounters before the liaison ended. Another affair followed, with a layman. Meanwhile, Father Don had begun revealing his secret. He had come out to his mother in 1990 and by the summer of 1993 to his siblings—but not his father. In the parish, he no longer made any effort to conceal his slight effeminacy. The summer of '93 was when he had his ear pierced, but, in a peculiar compromise with the truth, it was the *left* ear, which is supposed to signal that the adorned man is straight, not gay.

"One lady in the 7 A.M. Sunday congregation took exception," Father Don recalls, "but no one else. Most of the kids thought it was cool." But several parishioners, unhip to the status signals of modern jewelry, would claim no surprise when, a year or two later, they learned that Father Don was gay.

In any case, by the beginning of fall, Father Don had already decided to quit, and when Advent loomed without "the right time" having arrived, he walked into Paul Whitney's front room and announced the truth about himself, a revelation that was greeted with the pastor's usual matter-of-fact grace. The hard part was calling Bishop Head's office for an appointment. But eventually he got up the courage.

On the Monday following the feast of Christ the King, Father Don would go downtown to ask, as is customary in such cases, for a leave of absence to consider his future. But he had little thought of returning. Just one more priest lost to the church, at a time when 10 percent of U.S. parishes had no resident pastor, when the number of seminarians nationwide had dwindled to 5,891 from 48,000 in 1965, when, of the Buffalo diocese's 388 priests, just fifteen were under thirty-four years old. Eleven of the diocese's priests had died the previous year, five while still on the job; to replace them, just one man had been ordained this year.

No one, whether in or out of the church, questions that celibacy has been a major cause of the exodus. Whether gay or straight, a human being who accepts a lifelong fast from intimacy thereby accepts a life of profound loneliness, at least in the earthly sphere. For many, the deprivation is too much to bear: of about 71,000 ordained Catholics in the U.S. today, 20,000 have married and thus barred themselves from sacerdotal duties.

The celibacy rule may once have been less demanding than it is now, as one *National Catholic Reporter* feature argued:

> Church law reserves ordination to men 25 or older, a rule that dates to the late Middle Ages when men were ordained at 25 and died at 32. Centuries ago, candidates were expected to have had certain life experiences by 25. Further, most envisioned only a few years of celibate life before expiring. "Hell, I could hold my breath that long," said one salty priest now expected to be celibate for a half century.

Times change, but in the last decade of the second millennium A.D., there is no sign that the Vatican might return celibacy to its former optional status. And by the autumn of his discontent, Father Don had long ceased to defend even the abstract idea of celibacy. The rule seemed "a rejection of Genesis 1," as he said privately after celebrating the Mass of Christ the King. "In the beginning, God saw right away that Adam was lonely, so he gave him someone to be with." Why, then, does so earthy a faith as Catholicism, where God is met sacramentally *in the flesh of everyday reality*, have such huge difficulties with everything to do with sex? It was a mystery to Father Don. "One of the worst things that ever happened to the church," he said, "was St. Augustine—how we canonized him *after* he had a chance to sow his oats. Now, everyone is supposed to be a hero in terms of their sexuality."

And yet.

Celibacy can also be credited with providing the church's most devoted mystics and martyrs through the centuries. Even today, around the globe, it is often celibates who, not being obliged to choose between duty to family and the call to self-sacrificial discipleship, most readily accept hardship, imprisonment, and death. Same goes for the plain inconvenience that is experienced routinely by pastors or chaplains whose availability to those entrusted to their care knows no reasonable bounds. Helen Prejean, the Death Row nun and author of *Dead Man Walking*, recalls being asked by condemned murderer-rapist Robert Lee Willie: "Don't you miss having a man? Don't you want to get married?" She replied that she had never wanted to marry one man or have one family—that she wanted "a wider arena for my love."

But intimacy means a lot to me, I tell him. "I have close friends—men and women. I couldn't make it without intimacy."

"Yeah?" he says.

"Yeah," I say. "But there's a costly side to celibacy, too, a deep loneliness sometimes. There are moments, especially on Sunday afternoons, when I smell the smoke in the neighborhood from family barbecues, and feel like a fool not to have pursued a 'normal' life. But, then, I've figured out that loneliness is part of everyone's life, part of being human—the private, solitary part of us that no one else can touch."

"What I miss most being here," he says, and I notice that he blows the cigarette smoke downward so that it does not drift into my face, "are the women and just bein' in the bars and listenin' to the music and dancin' 'til three in the morning. And I'm not goin' to lie to you, ma'am, I believed in doing it. Me and my lady friends, we'd get us a blanket and a bottle or a little weed and go into the woods and do it," and he gives a slight smile.

"Well, Robert," I say, "let's face it. If I had a husband and family, chances are I'd be there with them this afternoon, instead of visiting with you."

When Father Don told Nancy Piatkowski of his decision to leave, Nancy went to a friend's house and wept a bit. It wasn't just that she liked him immensely and would be sorry to lose him as a priest and a friend. It was the *work*—all they had achieved together since he arrived at St. Paul's in her second year as chair of the parish Liturgy Committee. Now, everything seemed at risk.

Half German, half Irish, full Catholic, Canisius College master's graduate in education, sometime craft teacher, sometime theater manager, sometime folklore researcher, Nancy had been engrossed in liturgy since 1978. In that year, she and her high school teacher husband, Dennis, both theater addicts with a shared love of high ritual and music, designed and wove a much-celebrated stole for one of the priests. As a result, Dennis and Nancy had been invited onto the diocesan Liturgical Commission.

With her daughter Beth in college studying theater arts, Nancy had taken on the St. Paul's liturgy chair and begun a second master's, this time majoring in cultural anthropology and American studies. Her thesis—"The St. Joseph's Table Among Western New York Sicilian-Americans as a Marker of Ethnic and Religious Identity"—would be a mammoth reconstruction of the origins and transmission of the St. Joseph's Day custom of opening houses to strangers and providing a table of cold foods. "Involves American immigration patterns," Nancy would explain—her crackly, especially nasal version of the Buffalo *e-yak-sent* issuing with few verbs and no periods, just a continuing series of barely detectable semicolons—"how religious and ethnic identity reinforce each other; a ritual that ties generations together and enhances a sense of rootedness; the tenacity of this belief; in any given family, the table is done the same way today as in pictures I have from eighty-five years ago; same foods; same altar to St. Joseph's statue at the same place on the table; or a picture of the saint, leaning against a wall; bread in the shape of a monstrance or of sheaves of wheat; breaded vegetables and fish . . ." and on, and on, until someone interrupted her or simply walked away.

Father Don was a soul mate. He and Nancy shared a theatrical aesthetic, an irreverent, sardonic style, and a round-peg-and-square-hole relationship with sober Republican Kenmore. Father Paul gave them room to maneuver and together they launched a campaign to modernize St. Paul's staid liturgical ways. Most controversially, the Nancy-and-Don team had succeeded in ripping out most of the altar rail to create a spacious open area around the altar, used the marble to construct a simple but stately lectern and lectionary stand, and accentuated the altar itself by moving the tabernacle from its former high and central place to one side. The next step would have been to move the baptismal font from its private room into the main body of the church, but with Father Paul's recent moratorium on interior renovations, this was now on hold. What else, Nancy wondered, would now go by the boards, without Father Don's advocacy in the rectory?

The resolute and sometimes caustic manners of Nancy and Father Don had made them a fair number of enemies, not all of them conservatives, but the pair had helped to attract a keen and savvy dozen or so core members of the Liturgy Committee—some joining because they sensed a variety and vitality in the parish's celebrations and liked it; others because they felt someone should stop the terrible twosome before they destroyed everything that was ancient and proper.

As well, the pastor's own firebrand self still glowed enough to ignite the odd liturgical ruckus. An instance had come this fall, when the Knights of Columbus had asked for clarity on whether or not they were welcome to provide honor guards at special celebrations in St. Paul's Parish. Few things irritated Father Paul as much as these honor guards—consisting of "knights of the fourth degree" who, rigged out in satin-lined capes and plumed hats, lined up at the altar step and loudly drew their swords in honor of the sacrament's consecration. Until Paul Whitney's arrival, the fourth-degree knights had been accustomed to strutting their stuff at confirmations and other special parish occasions; in recent years, they had been quietly discouraged from attending. But now someone had raised the issue anew, and the pastor, for reasons that remained obscure, requested a policy statement from the liturgy committee.

The discussion *started* harmoniously enough. When Nancy announced "New Business" that Wednesday evening in the rectory basement, Father Don made a short speech about the honor guard question, using words like "triumphalism" and "militarism" and "distraction." Nancy nodded approval. One committee member recalled being with his preschool son at Mass in another parish when the knights drew their swords and "the little guy yelled out, 'Look, Daddy, pirates!' " and everyone laughed. Another member confessed that her chief memory of her own First Communion was of being terrified by the men with their strange uniforms and clanging swords. It did seem "kinda archaic, you know, those swords in church, and all."

That was when Ray Krempholtz spoke up. Ray, chairman of the ushers, chief lector at weekday Masses, chief acolyte at funerals, eucharistic minister, counter of Sunday collections, former Holy Name Society president, former Parish Council president, retired store manager of Buffalo Hotel Supply, tall, trim figure in golf shirt and gold-rimmed glasses, who had attended Mass daily since 1973 in thanksgiving for his wife's recovery from a huge stroke, who had joined the Knights in 1960 principally for the bowling, had spent much of this evening's meeting chewing quietly and amiably. Until now.

"I'll say this," Ray said placidly. "Most of the Knights of Columbus members, at least a third of them here in Kenmore, come from St. Paul's Church."

Down-table, Coty-Ann Henk nodded. "Mm-HMM-huh."

"And many of the color corps, the fourth-degree knights, are from St. Paul's Parish."

"Mm-HMM-huh."

"And if we can't do our thing—I mean, if you're telling *them* that they can't be here, and that's all, then they'll go to some other parish."

There was a short silence. It might almost have seemed a subtle threat of feet-voting, if anyone could have imagined Ray Krempholtz leaving St. Paul's under any circumstances short of death. But he had certainly turned a rubber-stamp exercise into a debate. So Father Don said, in a more conciliatory tone than before, "I don't think the objection is to having them come here for a once-a-year Knights of Columbus function or something like that. I think the objection is specifically and only to the color guard."

Ray: "Because of the swords?"

Father Don and Nancy together, their heads nodding in unison: "Because of the swords."

Coty: "What is it, Father Don, that you said a few minutes ago—the reason why it isn't correct?"

Father Don: "OK. I believe that with the, ah, with all of the—ah, how do I wanna put this?—the redirection of Vatican II in the past thirty years of church history, there has been a move away from the triumphalism of previous generations which crept into the church."

Coty: "Meaning?"

Father Don: "Triumphalism? Like, even the Pope himself does not run around with that beehive hat on anymore. The coronation ceremonies have been changed. That kind of stuff. And certainly the swords in particular, ah, the swords have no liturgical function."

Bob Rivard said, with a big grin, "You should beat your swords into plowshares, I guess, eh?" But the others were watching Ray, and no one laughed.

"You know," Father Don started. "Um," Father Don continued. "Ah." Father Don stopped. There was a silence. Neither he nor anyone seemed to know where to go with this. Father Don himself might have let the matter drop, but it was the pastor who wanted a statement. But what do you do if the committee that's supposed to *make* the statement doesn't agree to what the pastor wants? Father Don scratched his neatly trimmed beard, tugged his earring, and began again. "It's just, in my mind, and I'm sure in Father Paul's mind, because he's the one who has the main objection to it, and I'm following right behind him, that triumphalism just does not seem to fit in with the whole idea of the liturgy, the Mass, the Eucharist. It just seems very foreign to it." He trailed off, bared his teeth and gritted them as a beaver might, looked around, and leaned back again, an unhappy look on his face.

"And especially," Nancy tried, "at a parish celebration such as First Communion or confirmation; or something like May Crowning; which is in my memory not the Knights of Columbus but the Knights of St. John; which is a similar organization with, like, all fuzzy hats and swords; and again that triumphalism; with military hats and uniforms . . ."

It fell to Maggie Denham, the committee's blond, curly-haired, pink-cheeked, pink-lipsticked, girlishly forty-something secretary, to interrupt: "I was just going to ask. What is the history of the Knights of Columbus? I mean, I know they have bowling alleys and you can play bingo, but . . ." She revolved her hands in the air as if reeling in a kite.

Ray beamed over at Maggie and delivered a condensed history: "The Knights of Columbus was an organization started by Father McGivney for the poor Irish people who had come over to this country and got no work and had no money. So when someone passed away they had no way of taking care of the widow. They had no way of paying even for burial expenses. So he started a sort of insurance company—that's what the Knights of Columbus is, an insurance company."

Questions burst from all around the table.

"So how did we get to—"

"But wasn't it also a Catholic answer—"

"—the swords?"

"—to the Masons?"

Ray: "No, nothing to do with the Masons."

Maggie: "No, but to have their own organization so that they wouldn't be taken in with the Masons?"

Father Don: "Well, it was like the Holy Name Society, it was set up to give the Catholic guys—the immigrants who were coming in—a social organization. Just like Ray described. It was a social organization."

"Insurance, right," said Ray.

Maggie, her secretary's pen clawed tight in the hand she was waving, a white sneaker wiggling at the end of a tightly blue-jeaned leg, persisted: "But then, how did they get to the swords? I mean, I thought you were gonna say it was to protect the Pope or something."

Opposite her, Rose-Ann Martin, as big as Maggie was slim, as disheveled as Maggie was dainty, inscrutable sleepy eyes under short gray hair, pallid and heavy-lipped with no trace of makeup, scratched at a vast forearm that emerged from her blue jacket and seemed to decide, after weighing the matter, to amble to the Knights' defense. "Well, look at the Masons. They have their whole thingy-thingy too. Running around with their aprons and so much crap."

Carolyn Pratt, small and quiet by Rose-Ann's side, touched her arm. "Excuse me, but my father was a Mason."

Rose-Ann, apologetically: "But you know what I mean. We're mocking the Knights out, but these other societies have their little ceremonies too."

Maggie: "No, I'm not mocking them out. I'm just trying to find out—"

Ray: "Well, the color corps, it's like Father says, militarism came into this thing. It's an honor society, it's a patriotic order, that's what it is. And remember, Christopher Columbus, in his day, they all wore swords, and this is the Knights of *Columbus*. They're venerating, or honoring, Christopher Columbus."

Father Don: "Which has no connection with the church!"

Nancy: "This is, again, why we've taken the flags from the church too; because" (at this, Ray exhaled a bit of air and pressed back in his seat) "to put the flag of a particular country in the worship space is contrary to the liturgy; because—"

Rose-Ann had been sitting quite still, shoulders straight, elbows out, and forearms parallel on the table, but now she leaned slowly forward, her big hands chopping into the air. "I don't think we have any right to tell them what to do. It's their organization and they can act the way they please. Our thing is to decide whether we want them here. If we do not want them, I think we should say so. But we should not criticize what they do."

Father Don, his voice rising: "We're not. We're *not* criticizing what they do. We're just saying, this part of what they do, do we agree with that in our church, as a policy?"

Rose-Ann: "Well then, we should just say we don't want them to come, but I don't think we should dictate how they should run their ceremonies." As Rose-Ann would readily confess if asked, part of her reason for being on this committee was that she did *so* enjoy a debate.

Maggie: "But you can give them an option—"

"No, I don't think you can. I truthfully don't."

Coty: "But you have to give them an explanation."

"Fine, but you can't say, 'You can come, but you do it the way we want it done.' "

Father Don, caressing his fountain pen like a Rosary, said, "But then we shouldn't be telling *other* people, like when people want to bring in their own organists for their weddings, we shouldn't be telling them that we have certain regulations regarding music, which they have to follow."

Rose-Ann: "No, that's not the same thing."

"Yes, it is."

"No, it's not, really."

"Oh yes, it is, yes, it is." Father Don's hands batted vertically at the air as if to return Rose-Ann's volleys. "Because it has to do with the *liturgy*. They want to come in and use their swords during the *liturgy*." He leaned back, spent, and crossed his legs.

"But if we don't want them," Rose-Ann persisted, "then we should just say, 'Please do not come.' We should never dictate to anybody. For that matter, I'd say to those people who want their own organist and their own music, to go somewhere that will let them do it. I don't think we should sit in judgment of everything and say we want it done our way. I don't think that's right."

Ray, seeming to think this had now gone too far: "But then again," he said soothingly, "that's the Catholic way, always has been."

"Most certainly has *not* been," Rose-Ann almost shouted. "You don't get it here, you go somewhere else where you *can* get it. *That's* the Catholic way."

"Nawwww," said Ray, but almost to himself.

W hen Nancy had dried her tears, she left her friend's house and went home to the house on North End Avenue that she and Dennis (downstairs) shared with her widowed mother (upstairs), daughter Beth having now moved to Springfield, Massachusetts, where she was interning as a scenic artist. A small sign posted next to the mailbox advised:

Warning:
This house is protected by killer dustballs

Inside, a visual cacophony proclaimed this the home of craftspeople, collectors, and cat lovers. In the hall/living room/dining area, tables, shelves, and floor were filled with weaving equipment, live feline specimens, hundreds of books, Russian matrioshkas, Ukrainian painted eggs, Polish wooden figurines, candles and crucifixes of every known style, puppets and ceramic miscellanies from all the earth. Piles of old newspapers vied for space with sewing materials. Even the ceiling was cluttered with origami mobiles. In the bay window, a loom jostled with a computer and printer. A sewing machine and assorted fabrics covered the dining table. The sofa sighed when sat upon, an event which first necessitated piles of documents being swept to one side.

Nancy had work to do, last-minute work for Advent Sunday. The priests' missal binders had to be restocked with the new season's prayers and propers; instructions had to be written for acolytes, lectors, and eucharistic ministers. An Advent Guide for Families had been circulated with suggested prayers for lighting an Advent Wreath candle at meals, and suitable games and activities for the season. (This had been pulled together by Father Don and Nancy and enthusiastically endorsed by the Liturgy Committee. The group briefly considered the idea of a similar offering for Lent, but could come up with no serious suggestions of kids' activities. "Keep all the rules for forty days and forty nights?" giggled Maggie. "Lock up your chocolates?" agreed Nancy.)

The church's Advent Wreath was ready to sit wide and sleek on its slim wooden stand, and Respect Life had, as usual, erected its Giving Tree, a bush whose leaves had been replaced by over 650 tags to be collected by parish-ioners. Each tag suggested a Christmas gift ("Girl 6 years: clothing or toys") for someone in need—a resident in an AIDS hospice; a member of a poor family in one of three parishes, including St. Paul's itself. Nancy had ironed the blue, purple, and white seasonal banners, which would blend into the royal-blue altar hanging and vestments. Folk ensemble leader and guitarist Tom Johnson (at the ten o'clock) and organist Aaron Grabowski (at the four other Masses) would provide variations on O Come, O Come, Emmanuel as a subtext through the liturgy. At the start of each Mass, a lector would an-nounce the theme:

> *The prophet Isaiah makes a universal plea today, not only for the people of his time but also for us. He prays for the Lord's return to ease their sense of abandonment. We too pray with Isaiah: ". . . Rend the heav-ens and come down . . . for we need, you, Lord our Father." And may you find us watching!*

When Father Don had written this theme statement to sum up the Liturgy Committee's careful reflections on the day's readings and prayers, the last sentence had been:

> *And may you find us doing right!*

But, as he had reported to the committee just before Advent, "it was sug-gested by someone that the idea of 'doing right' comes off as moralistic."

Rose-Ann Martin had snorted at that and raised her eyes to heaven.

"Well," said Father Don, his voice rising a key, "it could be interpreted that way, and that's not the way we're going with it." He shrugged and turned the page to the Christmas Mass schedule.

"When," Rose-Ann wanted to know, "will be *the real* Midnight Mass?" By which, as veterans of previous such discussions knew, she meant a tradi-tional Midnight Mass that featured, unlike those of some previous years, all the joyous trimmings—incense, a full fleet of acolytes and candles, and, above all, a sung *Gloria*.

Nancy giggled. "At midnight," she promised. "And we'll put a large notice on the organ for Aaron saying, 'Please do a very loud and joyous *Gloria*, otherwise Rose-Ann is going to come up there and beat the crap out of you.' "

Everyone laughed, except Father Don, who had had enough of Rose-Ann by then. Earlier that night, the simmering Knights of Columbus issue had returned to the table with a draft policy statement written by Nancy. The draft stated that while the Knights would be welcome to use the parish church for their own private celebrations—if they gave at least three months' notice and conformed to the parish's "liturgical norms"—the honor guard would participate at parish Masses only by special invitation, and its participation would be restricted to leading the entrance procession and the recessional. The committee dickered over minutiae for a while (why three months? what norms?) before Bob Rivard (he whose son had once yelled, "Look, Daddy, pirates!") came to the nub of the thing.

"The entire tone of this thing sounds like you're inviting them *out.* You just don't want them!"

"It does," said Rose-Ann, "it does have that tone. Father Don," she said, laying her hard blue eyes on the priest and flashing a wide girlish smile, "are you intending to invite them to anything, ever?"

"Nope."

"Well, that's what it sounds like."

"Well, that's what it's *meant* to sound like. Under the present administration, they will not be invited to any parish activity. If they need a parish to come and have one of their Masses, they are welcome, but we have some slight restrictions to that." (Rose-Ann drew in her breath to speak, reconsidered, and said nothing, merely putting her hand up to cradle her chin and peering down at her papers with a heavy sigh.) "They can come to our regular scheduled Masses anytime, just as anyone can. But we don't want them participating as an honor guard and that stuff."

"It's militaristic; it's warlike—" Nancy started.

"And it just doesn't fit into the ebb and flow of the liturgy as we understand it today," Father Don finished.

Nevertheless, Nancy promised to rework the statement to adjust the tone and bring it back yet again after Christmas.

Father Don's plans for departure were not yet known to any at the table except Nancy. His interview with Bishop Head had gone OK, he supposed.

The bishop had seemed sympathetic when the young priest described his vocational crisis and, to the request for a leave of absence, said he would grant it; as for the timing, he would have to consult Father Don's spiritual director. Father Don had told Nancy he expected to see out Advent and Christmas and be on his way early in the new year. He would start seeking an apartment and a job, preferably in western New York, where he had roots and family. As to what kind of job, all he knew was it wouldn't be counseling or social work or anything like that, and "definitely nothing to do with the church."

From the financial report enclosed in the St. Paul's parish bulletin for November 21:

YEAR ENDED AUGUST 31, 1993

Church income, excl. school	627,792
Expenditure, excl. school	483,028
Surplus (excl. school)	144,764
School income:	392,450
School expenditure	580,928
School deficit:	(188,478)
Total parish deficit:	**(43,714)**

Thanksgiving had come and gone, and attendance at Mass on the holiday had been, as usual, greater than on most holy days. The city of Buffalo, having elected Democrat Anthony M. Masiello as its new mayor, accepted philosophically the news that in the dying days of the Jimmy Griffin administration, at least a hundred vacant city jobs had been filled by the not-so-lame duck's fellow residents of the predominantly Irish-American South Buffalo. Dave and Claire Taylor, who were still unwelcome at Claire's parents', had run, as usual, in the Turkey Trot; afterward Claire cooked Thanksgiving dinner at home for just the two of them.

Dave was being haunted by a mysterious dream he had had on their honeymoon in Nantucket. He was holding an egg, a large heavy egg, holding it with both hands in front of him. The egg was very heavy, and he was afraid he would drop it. A crowd of people gathered; they accused him of betraying them; they had entrusted the egg to him and he had failed. When he looked down at the egg, it had grown a beard and a deep voice came from within it: *What's wrong, my son?* Dave started whimpering: *They're saying I betrayed them, but I didn't! I didn't!* When Claire woke him, he was still crying.

Whereas Dave's self-accusations remained something between him and his dreams, the situation with Claire's parents sat right out where everyone could see it. For Thanksgiving, therefore, Claire had set her heart on creating the perfect holiday dinner right in their own home. But by midafternoon, the turkey finally done, Claire's blood sugar was dropping rapidly. While Dave listened to the emptiness of his stomach, Claire fussed with candles and reheating. Dave muttered darkly, "Forget the candles, forget the platter." Claire suddenly went pale, and Dave pushed her down into a chair and stomped into the kitchen. Distracted, he grabbed a hot glass casserole cover in his bare hands and wound up eating Thanksgiving dinner with one hand in a bowl of ice, the tension broken as the two of them guffawed unceasingly through the meal.

The holiday had gone unobserved by the Forlenza family. Sammy's grandfather, Mary Ann's dad, died at 3:00 P.M. on Thanksgiving Day, which was precisely the same day and time that his mother had died, four years ago. Feverish, a blood clot in his left ventricle, a catheter in his heart, kidneys out of action, the fifty-nine-year-old had been floating in and out of comprehension for a few days. "Let me go," he would gasp from time to time. "I have to be someplace." On Thanksgiving morning, he asked his brother, again and again, "What time is it?" and he called out for his mother before he gave up the ghost.

"I'm not religious, of course," Mary Ann said afterward, "but I can't help seeing it as a sign that he is OK, that his ma is caring for him." She also recalled that her grandma died calling, "Mary, Mary." There was no one with that name in the family. Sammy, who had known that his granddad was dying, didn't talk much about it when it finally happened, but was quieter than usual for a few days. The funeral over, he set his sights on First Reconciliation.

"OK, kids," called Father Don on a cold, dark Advent evening in a thin imitation of a stadium announcer, "now's the time you've been waiting for."

The kids and their parents, having sat through prayers, Bible readings, and Father Don's thoughts on the parable of the lost sheep, rushed to form six lines for the various priests. Father Don was waiting in the face-to-face confessional, Father Paul in the reading room, Father Dick in the sacristy, three visiting priests in chairs spread out across the sanctuary. Meanwhile, a scattering of grown-ups waited outside the two screened confessional boxes, which were manned by two more visitors ("because, kids," as Father Don had explained, "adults get lost too").

Mary Ann signed to Sam Sr. to look after Allie and led Sammy to the nearest line, Father Don's. Chaos ensued for close to an hour as the lines snaked into one another and the church echoed with babble that was as effective as any soundproofing to protect privacy. Slowly, Sammy's line inched forward. As Father Don emerged from the face-to-face confessional to hand a child back to his or her parents, he would greet the parents of the next one briefly before priest and young penitent disappeared behind closed doors.

"Are you ready?" Mary Ann asked Sammy, and he nodded.

"Do you know what you're going to say?" He nodded again.

Then they stood quietly, Mary Ann behind her son, hands loosely draped around his head and neck. Through the open door to the reading room, Father Paul could be seen, in plaid vest and purple stole, hunched forward, elbows on knees, listening to a tiny girl with braided hair. He spoke and she nodded. He spoke again and she shook her head, swinging her feet between the priest's open legs. Then he smiled, extended his hand, and held it over the child's head. He made a wide sign of the cross, and brought his palm to rest for a moment on the child's forehead.

When Sammy finally reached the front of his line and disappeared with Father Don, Mary Ann leaned awkwardly on a pew until the door opened and Sammy kind of skipped the few steps to his mom. He insisted that she immediately attach his shining "JESUS MAKES ME NEW AGAIN" pin to his striped button-down shirt, and then raced off to join another line at a table in the center of the sanctuary. There, he wrote "Sammy Forlenza" in purple Magic Marker on a felt sheep. He instructed Mrs. Blum exactly where he wanted it pinned to the hanging green banner. With his sheep safely on the smiling brown Jesus' left shoulder, Sammy looked around for his mom, found she had disappeared, and spied his dad hurrying toward the back of the church. Allie had discovered a font of holy water and, thinking it a drinking fountain, pulled herself up to plunge her hand in for a drink.

What Mary Ann had done, somewhat to her husband's surprise, was to pop into the adults' confessional. Sam Sr. pondered this unusual turn of events. Mary Ann had been feeling pretty low since her dad died; maybe this was something she had to do to make her peace. He stood peacefully, hands in pockets, watching Sammy and Allie run and slide in the back vestibule, until his wife reappeared, blowing her nose.

Mary Ann was very quiet as everyone piled into the family Mazda and headed home for a late pizza dinner.

"Well, Sammy, how was it, your first confession?" his dad asked from the driver's seat.

"It was fun," said Sammy.

"Fun? How's that?"

"Um-ah, I told him my sins and he gave me a pin."

Mary Ann broke out of her reverie as they turned off Delaware Avenue onto Delaware Road. "What did Father give you for a penance?" she asked.

"Um-ah, the pin," Sammy replied, leaning forward in the back seat and pointing to his chest. "Ma," he chided, "you helped me put it on!"

"No, but for a penance, after you confessed. Didn't he tell you to say a prayer, or do something nice, or something?"

"Um-ah, my actofcontrition."

"No, but . . ." Mary Ann shrugged.

"Maybe they don't do that anymore," said Sam Sr. quietly as he turned into their driveway.

"Sure they do! I just . . ." She trailed off again.

"Well, maybe they don't do it for kids."

Faith

December: For twenty-five years, a week or so after every Thanksgiving, a Bethlehem manger scene had taken over the Kenmore municipal information booth at the intersection of Delaware Avenue and Delaware Road. This year, the holiday display had, in the words of Nan Morris, veteran assistant secretary in the St. Paul's rectory, "gone ecumenical." As to *why* the Christmas crèche must now be accompanied by a menorah, a Star of David, miscellaneous Dickensian statuettes, and a weeping Santa Claus holding a child, Nan was at a loss; perhaps the New York Civil Liberties Union, which had threatened a lawsuit before settling for the mixed religious metaphor, could explain. At any rate, on December 9, the second day of Hanukkah and the second Thursday of Advent, Christmas hymns were crackling willfully through the crisp morning air from two loudspeakers atop the Municipal Building as Judy Nice, Director of Adult Sacraments, drove by in her bright red Cutlass.

Judy was headed downtown to Canisius College. Today was the last of twice-weekly classes in the Development of Christian Doctrine, a small milestone in Judy's part-time progress toward a B.A. major in religious studies. Arriving in the classroom five minutes ahead of time, Judy squeezed into her usual place next to her friend Kathleen, another of the four religion majors in the class. (The rest were here in partial fulfillment of the Jesuit college's required minimum of three religion courses in general programs.) Slowly, the class filled with undergraduates—dreamy, nonchalant, studiously underdressed.

Enter Father Daniel Liderbach, S.J., a gaunt, bespectacled, thin-lipped man with a flick of gray in his dark crew cut. Neither in looks nor in demeanor did the small Jesuit professor give any hint of being a radical, yet that was certainly what some in the Vatican would consider him. Indeed, this class might almost have been in the Pope's mind when he called, in his October encyclical, for bishops to take tighter control of Catholic colleges.

"Good morning," Liderbach said quietly to the air, and then he turned his back to write on the green board:

What does the church need to discover the consensus of the faithful?

This was followed by a cryptic series of staccato headings (such as "The fidelity of the laity in the face of persecution" and "Newman's data"). The last heading was:

The church cannot expect the faithful passively to accept doctrine.

"A brief word about the test," Liderbach began. In a soft monotone, he recapitulated the ground covered in past weeks. True doctrine, Liderbach reminded his students, must emerge from the community of faithful people, rather than being imposed upon them.

"The whole course can be summarized in this," he said, and tapped the final heading before reading it aloud. " 'The church cannot expect the faithful passively to accept doctrine.' When the community says, 'We cannot accept that,' it's not because the community is unbelieving or disobedient. It's because the community is human." He stopped and said the last word again, as if savoring the sound of it: "human."

Suddenly, the professor took a peculiar crab walk to his left, stamping his left foot down hard, then dragging the right foot slowly across to join it.

"FOOT-note," he said as he again stamped and dragged until he stood near the door. "FOOT-note. I hear people say, 'The will of God.' I don't know what the will of God is, except for this: that God wants me to be a"—

he paused again—"a human being. *That*, I'm sure of." He began chopping the edge of his right hand into his left palm for emphasis.

"A priest?" He chopped. "Nya-ah, can't tell.

"Male?" He chopped again. "Probably.

"Celibate? Perhaps.

"But human! No question about that. So!" He ambled back from his "footnote" position to his regular spot just left of center, where he stood stock-still, hands hanging. "So, when doctrine comes along, we cannot give up our humanity."

And if the faithful were human, Liderbach repeated for good measure, they could not be expected "passively to accept doctrine." In stressing this point, Liderbach was referring his students back to a piece of required reading—an 1859 essay by John Henry Newman, a formerly Anglican theologian who had, late in his life, been elevated by Rome to the rank of cardinal.

Newman's essay cited twenty items of "data" that purportedly demonstrated how Christian laity had held to true doctrine through the Arian controversy, a devastating power struggle that split the fourth-century church. This schism came after Arius of Alexandria took issue with popular Christian wisdom by denying the divinity of Christ. According to Newman, it was lay faithfulness (rather than bishops' power) that ensured the survival of the doctrine that Jesus Christ is God.

A century plus twenty-five years after Newman published *On Consulting the Faithful in Matters of Doctrine*, it was the centerpiece of Liderbach's course; other texts included an extract from renegade German theologian Hans Küng's *Infallible? An Inquiry* and a historical overview by Liderbach himself entitled "Notes on 'The Rule of Faith.'"

Liderbach's essay made its stand on an aphorism of the fifth-century Pope Celestine: ". . . *legem credendi lex statuat supplicandi*," which the Jesuit interpreted:

The Rule of Faith determines the rule of doctrine. Alternately expressed, the Rule of Faith acknowledges that the mind of the community of believers reveals the doctrine for that community. . . .

In the fourth century, the believing community had come to acknowledge a new manner of interpreting its belief in its Lord:

because the community was praying to Christ the Lord as if to a God, the community recognized a need to confess that Christ the Lord is God together with God the Father.

That development was an experience of the psychological need to begin with the experience of faith, in order to formulate doctrine; an experience of the need for the Rule of Faith. . . . As a consequence of that methodical application of the Rule of Faith, Christ Jesus came eventually in the fifth century to be identified as fully man and fully God.

Despite the lessons of the Arian controversy and Celestine's "rule," Liderbach continued, later popes had often strayed from the idea that doctrine must stem from the community's experience of faith. It had fallen to John Henry Newman to restore the Rule to its former place.

. . . The consensus of the community is thus the voice of doctrine. Consequently, if the teaching church intends to discover the inspired mind of the church on any question, then the church needs to investigate the mind of the communities of believers. Newman argued that that mind was manifest in the communities' public acts, such as their liturgies, feasts, and prayers. Those acts are testimonies to that apostolic dogma that the Holy Spirit inspires the communities to hold in the bosom of the church. When the church so fashions its doctrine, its teachings will be well received by believers. . . .

In the cases cited by Newman's "data," the "sentiments" of the laity had remained doctrinally true even where local bishops had gone astray, even in the face of persecution, even on pain of death. Newman had concluded that the consensus of the faithful—the *sensus fidelium*—was an acid test of true doctrine.

"They were being persecuted," said Liderbach of the anti-Arian lay holdouts. "They were being driven out of their homes, out of their states, exiled."

Once more, the professor interrupted himself to stamp and drag his way over to the left side of the "U" of tables in what was perhaps a way to compensate for his monotone. "FOOT-note," he said again. Exile, he said— that was no small thing; it was a "terrible" thing. "When I was in Munich, I met a man who lives in Tunis, a wonderful, sweet, thoughtful, kind man." The Jesuit produced a cute woodchuck grin, then put it away. "But this man has killed Israelis, and he will kill again. Because they have driven him from his home." Liderbach walked back to the opening of the "U" to pick up his thread.

The church's classic doctrine, he said, was that a Council, a gathering of all the world's bishops, could not be wrong. Yet, the Councils of history had been known to contradict each other. So, even the Councils could not be trusted. The only true guide in the end, he said, was the *sensus fidelium*. The faithful had proved, by their steadfastness, that the Holy Spirit guides and strengthens the laity. Therefore, "the consensus of the faithful deserves at least as big a place in theology as scripture, or [Newman's fellow nine-teenth-century theologian] Denzinger, or the statements of the Councils."

"Newman's was a revolutionary thesis, and the First Vatican Council was persuaded by it," Liderbach told Judy and her classmates. "But no one talks about it much, because people immediately began saying it wasn't very important. And when you finish this course, you too will forget about it soon enough, because it doesn't have a place in theology.

"Scripture has a place, Denzinger has a place, the Councils have a place, even modern philosophers have a place, but hardly anyone ever argues from this . . ." The professor raised an arm, pointed vaguely at his scrawls on the green board, and brought it down to slap lightly against the side of his thigh.

If the authority of the *sensus fidelium* has been overlooked at the Vatican, as Dan Liderbach suggests, it has become a rallying cry for the many who dissent from Rome's less popular teachings. And the idea of what Newman sometimes called "the Consent of the Faithful" could hold special relevance to the status of Paul VI's encyclical on birth control. If, as Newman argued, true doctrine must be confirmed by the collective mind of the laity, the verdict on contraception must still be in doubt, to say the least. It has become commonplace for pollsters in Western Europe and North

America to report that most lay Catholics—or at least those who have achieved childbearing age in the past three decades—reject *Humanae Vitae's* teaching.

True, these polls tend to include as "Catholics" all respondents who identify themselves that way—rather than applying any test of faith or practice. It's doubtful that John Henry Newman would have set store by such a consensus. Yet there's no serious question that in industrialized countries, most Catholic couples who practice their faith also practice contraception, or have done so, or plan to do so. In the United States, according to the journal *Family Planning Perspectives*, only 4 percent of white Catholic married women were using natural family planning in 1988, down from 32 percent in 1965.

Advocates of the "natural" method point, with some justice, to underreporting of advances in the technique of anticipating a woman's time of fertility. The old "rhythm roulette" method, where Catholic couples were expected to place their trust in a moon-regular menstrual cycle, has been supplanted by the more scientific daily observation of changes in body temperature and cervical mucus. Not just religious adherents but patients of fertility clinics can testify to the relative accuracy of these methods. That fall, the *British Medical Journal* had cited a World Health Organization study which found that in Calcutta, India, almost 20,000 women who used the observation method had no more pregnancies than would be expected for users of the pill—0.2 pregnancy per 100 women yearly. Similar studies in Germany and Britain found failure rates of 0.8 and 2.7 percent—which was, the journal noted, better than condoms and comparable with diaphragms and coils.

But natural family planning has one big downside: abstinence relies wholly on self-discipline, and as such, it is sometimes tougher to sell to a partner. When an obedient Catholic woman is forced or coerced into sex, she must, in addition to the degradation, risk both unwanted pregnancy and lethal disease.

Desire, duress, and disease aside, theologians still debate vigorously whether there is any fundamental moral difference between the "natural" and "artificial" methods. But most laity merely shrug. As one layperson put it in a letter to the Jesuit weekly *America*:

The theologians and bishops continue to struggle over this document, which I thought was written for the laity. Meanwhile, the laity wonder what all the fuss is about. It is a lay issue and we have decided it. . . . I can only make sense out of all this in terms of power, the attempt of one group, primarily the Roman Curia, to exercise power over another, the laity. We who compose a majority in the church resist that.

Left to the laity, the issue might have been resolved back in the mid-'60s, when Paul VI, having convened a commission on birth control, was presented with a bound collection of letters from couples in the Christian Family Movement worldwide, mostly complaining about the sufferings inflicted by the rhythm method. By a massive majority, the commission's theologians, moved in part by this outpouring from the faithful, concluded that Pope Pius XI had erred in condemning contraception as inherently wrong. It was widely expected that Paul VI would bow to this consensus. Instead, he held his predecessor's line.

Pope Paul's position was based in part on the writings of a Polish theologian named Karol Wojtyla, who in turn, as Cardinal Archbishop of Krakow, strongly supported *Humanae Vitae*. Wojtyla is now Pope John Paul II, and he continues to urge Roman Catholic doctors, hospitals, and pharmacists to follow a "rigorous moral code" by refusing to have anything to do with contraception. That includes those involved in AIDS prevention, who would otherwise distribute and advocate condoms (and frequently do so anyway). The Vatican reportedly considers public dissent from *Humanae Vitae* an absolute impediment to selection as a bishop.

And thus the ultimate irony: with the upper hierarchy loyal to *Humanae Vitaes*'s teaching, the laity mainly apathetic to it, and most pastors, parish staff, and even bishops studiously avoiding the topic, the enduring legacy of the 1968 encyclical seems to be that it has effectively, and despite itself, given the faithful some experience with the idea of going against church teaching and instead being ruled by their own consciences.

The results go far beyond birth control. Kenneth Untener, Bishop of Saginaw, Michigan, in *Commonweal*, suggested that the encyclical had "contributed to an attitude among Catholics that authoritative teachings can be brushed aside, and that church discipline (e.g., Sunday Mass attendance) is less binding." It had, for example, become more difficult for the church to defend its position on abortion.

The logic of the encyclical, Untener wrote, was "not compelling," to the general population or to Catholic laity, or to many priests and bishops. He urged "an honest and open discussion, at least in acknowledging that after twenty-five years *Humanae Vitae* hasn't been accepted by the majority of Catholics."

To his Canisius students, Dan Liderbach was careful not to be misunderstood regarding the consensus of the faithful. Cardinal Newman had never advocated a system of doctrine by democracy. Judy's professor turned to the green board and drew a line under the phrase "the sentiments of the faithful."

"That," he said flatly and slowly, "does not mean sentimentality." Newman's idea of a popular "sentiment" had nothing in common with a pollster's. The true "sentiment" of the faithful, Liderbach told his class, was no mere statement of opinion, but rather a point of faith that conformed to clearly defined criteria.

Judy had carefully copied these criteria into her notebook during an earlier lecture; now, she could flip a few pages back to the entry headed, "Criteria for the Rule of Faith." Liderbach had said that for a belief to qualify as the authoritative consensus contemplated by Newman, it must pass five tests. First, did this point of faith assent to the "apostolic tradition" inherited from previous generations of Christians? Second, was it truly a "common instinct" shared by all, or were there splits or skepticisms? Third, were there competing explanations for the consensus or was it clearly a product of "leadership by the Holy Spirit"? Fourth, was this consensus shared by "those who pray" for confirmation from the Holy Spirit? And fifth, did the belief elicit "the faithful's response" in a natural way?

Liderbach had offered an example much remarked by Judy. He had said that he did not believe in hell; he found it impossible to reconcile the idea of eternal damnation to "the consistent Christian understanding of a loving God." Liderbach had explained that he could allow himself this disagreement both with traditional catechisms and with popular "sentiment" because this particular teaching did not seem to have been proved valid according to the five criteria. Judy could not remember which particular criteria he had cited concerning the afterlife, but it would be hard for anyone to make a case against artificial birth control based on the second, third, or fourth criteria. Or, especially, the fifth.

Now, however, Liderbach was doing a stamp-and-drag again, this time stamping his way into a *"big* footnote."

"To his great credit, Paul VI said about the document *Humanae Vitae* in July 1968, 'This is not an infallible doctrine.' And the second thing he said was 'Every conference of bishops has to interpret this.' And how did the Canadian bishops interpret it? They interpreted it as"—he adjusted his sedate speaking pace down a notch to dead slow—"a human doctrine. And they said, 'Take a look at it.' Clearly, they were saying, this is a doctrine that calls upon people to be obliged by their own conscience.

"In other words, it is a doctrine that calls upon people to be human. To be human, we are obliged to follow our consciences. To be human, we must be intelligent, we must use our own freedom, we must be responsive to our own consciences.

"So I like to say to people, if you work in Detroit and live across the river in Windsor, Ontario, contraception is a virtue; if you work in Windsor and live in Detroit, contraception is a mortal sin."

If this was a joke, no one smiled. Judy watched the professor seriously, elbows on table, chin in hands. Liderbach turned back to the board to point once again at his final heading.

"Newman says, you cannot expect the faithful to be passive. They are going to be angry and critical, responsible. They're going to be *human*. And if you don't consult them, they are not going to pay attention.

"And most of the time, the church has in fact been quite good about consulting the faithful.

"But not in this instance."

C*atechism of the Catholic Church*, paragraphs 2368 and 2370:

. . . For just reasons, spouses may wish to space the births of their children. It is their duty to make certain that their desire is not motivated by selfishness but is in conformity with the generosity appropriate to responsible parenthood. . . .

¶ Periodic continence, that is, the methods of birth regulation based on self-observation and the use of infertile periods, is in conformity with the objective criteria of morality. These methods respect the bodies of the spouses, encourage tenderness between them, and favor the education of an authentic freedom. In contrast, . . . "the innate language that expresses the total reciprocal self-giving of husband and wife is overlaid, through contraception, by an objectively contradictory language, namely, that of not giving oneself totally to the other. This leads not only to positive refusal to be open to life but also to a falsification of the inner truth of conjugal love, which is called upon to give itself in personal totality. . . ." [Pope John Paul II: *Familiaris Consortio* (1981)]

Your father will burn in hell!" If a similarly damning assertion had helped turn Judy Nice into the questioning believer who had now become a Director of Adult Sacraments, it set her kid sister Barb on the road to unbelief. Unlike Judy, who had taken her teacher's damning announcement straight to her mom ("Do you really believe that, Judy?"), Barb, in the first or second grade at St. John the Baptist, felt too troubled to talk about it to anyone.

The class was plodding their way through the 499 questions and answers of the Baltimore Catechism; while Barb has long forgotten the actual words that the nun read out, they were probably in Lesson 12, "The Marks and Attributes of the Church":

> Question 166: Are all obliged to belong to the Catholic Church in
>   order to be saved?
> Answer: All are obliged to belong to the Catholic Church in order
>   to be saved.

This burned Barb up. Protestant or not, she declared to the entire class, "My dad's good!"

That's when the nun pronounced her fiery verdict—or at least, that's the way Barb remembers it. (At the time, there was a wide gulf between official doctrine and popular belief on this matter. If the sister really thought Catholic teaching consigned Protestants to hell, she was misinformed. It's true that, until Vatican II, the church taught that Protestants were not true believers. But as to the eternal fate of any particular person—even persons as evil as Stalin or Hitler—such matters were considered best left in the hands of God.) Barb replied hotly: "If my dad goes to hell, I'll go with him." That day, Barb says, is when she started feeling there was something wrong with the Catholic religion. She had often knelt down to pray with Dad; once or twice, she had even visited his church with him and, on the whole, much preferred it to St. John's. The people singing vigorous songs and getting served little cups of juice in their seats instead of reciting in Latin and kneeling before the priests. Barb thought it was "real neat."

Three decades later, Barb Cribbs considers herself an atheist, except for those times when she thinks no, maybe she's really an agnostic. And yet religion—*Catholic* religion, of course—pops up all over the place in her childhood memories. The shrine to St. Anne in the backyard. And the holy people—nuns, novices, priests, seminarians—who always seemed to be visiting Mom. And playing Mary in the Christmas pageant, which had an upside and a downside: Mom had released seven-year-old Barb's long, dark hair from its braids for the occasion, but there was that problem with the doll— Barb didn't like dolls and didn't have any, so another kid brought the baby Jesus. The doll was huge, only an inch or two smaller than Barb herself, and she was so mad, carrying this huge "baby" down the aisle, "Joseph" walking behind whispering jokes about it.

Confession: she *hated* that. She would go in there and make things up. Well, what was she supposed to say? She hadn't committed any murders or robbed any banks; she didn't even know any good swear words. "I fought with my sister," Barb told the priest every week of her life for six years until she switched to public school. Never got more than five Hail Marys ever, so even her made-up sins couldn't have been too bad.

Bedtime prayers, with the words that terrified her: "Now I lay me down to sleep, I pray the Lord my soul to keep, and if I die before I wake, I pray the Lord my soul to take."

Nightmares about dying.

Little Susie, born in 1959, three years after Barb, seven after Judy. In those days, people called Down's syndrome mongolism and Susie mongoloid, but Mom called her "a little angel" since the little sister had no reasoning and therefore could not sin. Susie almost died when Barb was in the seventh grade: some rare blood disease. Barb told Mom it wouldn't be so bad if Susie died, since she was already a little angel. In heaven, she wouldn't have to miss out on any of the things she missed out on here.

"I was raped when I was fifteen," Barb says. "It was more or less a date rape, I guess, and I remember thinking that the only way to justify what had happened—my shrink loves this—was to marry this person. So at fifteen years old I'm trying to come up with some kind of plan to get the person to fall in love with me and marry me and make me clean. Obviously that didn't work.

"I didn't tell my parents. I didn't tell anyone. I felt disgraced. I felt like I couldn't belong to the church anymore."

Barb met her present husband, Tony, in her sophomore year at Kenmore West High School, where she had insisted on transferring from Cardinal O'Hara. Tony was a year older. His parents were Lutheran or something; he says he joined a Catholic confirmation program because that way he got out of English class, which he hated, and because there was a Catholic chick he adored. Barb says that's "probably crap," since Tony is "a pathological liar, though I hate to say it, and he's real good at it too. The woman who babysat for him a lot was a Catholic and I think she had a lot to do with his conversion. I know he believes in God because we have these discussions. I don't know if he prays. I know he doesn't go to church."

Barb and Tony and their friends played endless games of Monopoly, intricately modified, on her mother's living-room carpet. Forget houses and hotels: *bars*, especially on railway stations, were the money-spinners.

Barb quit school in her junior year and went to work as a waitress in a sub sandwich shop. That same year, she got pregnant, got married, and got out of the Roman Catholic Church forever.

"There was no question of abortion," Barb says today. "I'm not anti-abortion. I think it has a place in the world and it should be medically done. That is a choice that I feel a woman has a right to make. But *I* wouldn't make that choice. To me, I was having a child, and I would do the best I could to raise that child. Whether Tony wanted to participate or not, that was OK, and if he wanted to just hang around and not get married, that was all right too. Getting married was just to please my mother. It was important to her, so it was important to me. To her, it was a disgrace I was pregnant. No one should know. That's why we had to get married."

So Mom arranged for Barb and Tony to meet one of the priests at St. John's.

Barb remembers it vividly: a sunny afternoon in May 1972. A well-lit spacious office. Barb and Tony in armchairs; the priest—Barb doesn't remember his name—sitting across a desk. It must have been after a Mass because the priest still had his white robe on; Barb remembers him removing his stole and kissing it before putting it away. Perhaps he was in his forties; at any rate, he seemed old to the seventeen-year-old Barb. He was amiable enough at first.

The priest said Tony and Barb would have to enroll in a pre-Cana class and gave them some information about that. Barb said that would be fine, but she thought her mom wanted the wedding to take place pretty soon.

The priest asked, how soon? Like, maybe next weekend.

The priest asked, why? Barb allowed that she was pregnant; said she and Tony had been thinking of getting married sometime anyway, and this just made it sooner. Tony sat still and silent; as far as Barb recalls, he never said a word through the whole meeting, except hello.

The priest said Tony and Barb, at seventeen and eighteen, weren't old enough to take care of a child; they were children themselves. Barb said, that was why they wanted to get married, for the sake of the child.

The priest asked, why did they want to marry in the Catholic Church? Barb said, because her mother wanted it that way.

He asked, "But that's not what *you* want?" She asked, "What's wrong with doing something out of respect for your mother?"

The priest said that everything was against a couple starting out in marriage so young. That having a child to raise might be their downfall. The baby would be a burden to them; they wouldn't be able to take care of themselves and to grow and become adults. Barb noticed that Tony was shifting around a lot in his armchair, and hoped he wasn't going to lose his temper.

The priest said he happened to be on the Catholic Charities adoption board.

He said there were lots of couples out there who wanted to have children and couldn't, and this was a good opportunity for him to give the child to someone who could take care of it and give it a better life.

He said he would not marry Tony and Barb unless they first agreed to give it up.

He said, "Good white babies are hard to find."

Tony got out of his chair and took a swing at the priest. Barb was quick: she jumped up and reached out to kind of hook the swinging arm, enough to force the clenched fist off course, and pushed her betrothed out of the office without saying goodbye.

A couple of weeks later, Tony and Barb Cribbs were married in an Episcopalian chapel. Two decades and two sons later, still happily married although much troubled water has passed under that bridge, Barb occasionally goes to a Catholic Mass for a family occasion or such. She never receives the sacrament.

When Barb's first son was born, his cousin Becky Nice was thirteen months old. Judy had married Rick Nice at eighteen, straight out of high school. They met on an ice rink; he was a quiet, easygoing lad who somehow, nonetheless, reminded her of Mick Jagger; his father was a former Catholic, but Rick had had no formal religion in his childhood, so he converted because, besides Judy, all his friends were Catholic too. When he left school he was drafted: Army Corps of Engineers. Everyone had a friend or brother in Vietnam; the death count was everywhere. Rick and Judy decided to get married quickly.

"Rick and I really wanted to be together," explains Judy, "and I was raised to believe that good girls got married first, so it was kind of that kind of thing. Although, well" (giggle), "I won't go further than that." Rick hoped for a posting in Germany, dreaded Nam, got Korea. While he was away, Judy worked at a neighborhood drugstore. Rick returned in November 1970, unscathed but for nightmares. They took a small apartment; Becky was born the following October. Judy, then twenty, quit work; Rick worked the line at the Chevy plant, like his father and brothers.

Judy kept her blond hair long and wild, wore love beads, and sang her daughter lullabies from *Hair*. Both Becky and her younger brother, Danny, were baptized at St. Paul's, but the Nices were not churchgoers. All the same, Judy wanted her children to go to St. Paul's, as her parents had done. The parochial school wasn't then charging tuition, so Rick said, "Why not?"

When Alicia was born in 1978, Becky was in the second grade, preparing for her First Reconciliation, and Rick and Judy had started taking her to Mass occasionally—it just seemed right. Now they wondered if they were doing enough. "It was like truth time," Judy remembers. "Either we were raising these kids Catholic or we weren't. It was stupid to keep going to these sacraments if we didn't believe in them." Besides, they liked what Becky was being taught at school; the child didn't seem frightened by religion, as Judy had been.

"Bless me, Father, for I have sinned," Judy said a short while later. "It has been ten years since my last confession."

"What took you so long?" said the voice on the other side of the screen, a smile in the voice. Judy was home.

Judy got involved with the Home School Association, and joined a group agitating for better teachers' salaries. They went to see Father Crotty, who had taken over after the dreaded Monsignor Ring's stroke. They pointed out that a certain teacher had to have three jobs to feed her family. He said, "But look at the healthy glow in her cheeks."

Father Crotty died, and the new pastor, Paul Whitney, appointed Sister Sandy Makowski, S.S.M.N., to get adult education groups going. Judy joined a Bible study group. Alicia—Lee—was now in kindergarten; Becky headed for O'Hara. Encouraged by Sister Sandy, Judy enrolled at Villa Maria College, started work on a two-year certificate. In religious education.

For her internship, Judy worked for Sister Sandy, who was by now a firm friend and a role model well suited to Judy's inclination to an ever-questioning kind of faith. Four years older than Judy, she had followed her twin sister Jean into the "Marys" who had taught them grade school. When Jean got killed in a car accident, Sandy realized she had never in her life felt anything without sharing the feeling with her twin, had never considered a thought complete until she had told Jean. Sister Jean was dead; Sister Sandy had lost part of herself. Leading Bible studies at St. Paul's, she was obliged to speak about the loving compassion of God, but failed to believe it. She spent much time immersed in the book of Job, and was carried for a while by the simple faith of some of the women studying scripture under her, who had seen their own tragedies, and (despite them? because of them?) believed.

When Sister Sandy learned to believe again, it was not in a God who had killed her sister, but in a God who wept over the death of a friend. By 1987, when she left the parish to study canon law and become the first woman officer of the Buffalo diocesan marriage Tribunal, she had helped form something of the same kind of faith in her friend Judy, who had by then finished her religious ed course and was ready to step into the gap.

"Director of Adult Sacraments," was the job title that Father Paul offered Judy, and it both thrilled and intimidated her. The title didn't seem quite to fit a laywoman; the work neither. RCIA. Parents' preparation for baptism. Pre-Cana. Programs for returning Catholics. Annulment support. Scripture group. Seasonal lectures. Magazine rack. Adult Formation Committee. Diocesan catechumenate team. Judy started a B.A. at Canisius. Surprise—she could do it all.

1988: Becky and Danny both at O'Hara. The classes were mixed these days; Judy, visiting her alma mater, always felt funny going in the boys' door. Then: Becky pregnant at seventeen, just like her Auntie Barb. Shame, rage, and tears; the entire family in counseling. Thank God for General Motors' health plan. Judy, the self-condemning mother, needing help most of all. Becky left O'Hara, moved out of home, later married the young father. Danny transferred to Kenmore West. For Christmas, Rick gave Judy a little red Cavalier, down payment made, and the payment book. Thought it might help cheer her up. It did.

Baby Nicholas smiling up at his thirty-seven-year-old grandmother. Then: the shame over the shame. Judy recovered; they all did. Surprise—life went on.

By that December 9, the second Thursday of Advent, the day of Judy's last Development of Christian Doctrine class, word of Father Don's decision to leave the priesthood had reached the ears of most. Bishop Head had decided to send the young priest to St. Luke's Hospital in Washington, D.C., for a psychiatric assessment before making a decision about the requested period of leave. Father Don was impatient to get a date of departure, but considered the delay a mere formality, as did the pastor, who had to remind him more than once that, for now at least, he had a roof over his head and a salary, and the younger priest himself didn't own, as Whitney put it, "a pot to piss in."

The pastor had placed his own plans for departure on hold until the parish settled down a bit. The second parochial vicar, Father Dick Sowinski, was not the kind of man who could run the parish alone, even temporarily; nor would he want to. Father Dick was a decent man and prayerful priest in his forties, whose sympathetic ear and quiet advice were often sought after, who would take long walks, sometimes up to four or five hours a day, to keep body sound and soul centered. Administration, management, and liturgy were not, as he would readily acknowledge, among his strengths.

Whitney figured the chances of replacing the departing Father Don were slim. The shortage of priests in the diocese of Buffalo was already legendary, and churches—beginning with underpopulated downtown parishes—were closing or merging at a depressing rate. Everywhere, laity were having to pick up responsibilities that priests and nuns used to handle, and even a big parish like St. Paul's could no longer automatically expect three priests.

The pastor would advertise the vacancy when it became official, but he wasn't expecting much, unless it was yet another in a long line of parochial vicars troubled by booze or sex or emotions—priests looking for a place to heal. Frankly, Whitney didn't think he had the energy anymore.

As expected, three newcomers had been welcomed into the catechumenate shortly before Advent—two women in their mid-twenties and a thirty-year-old man.

Maria (single, serious, and open-mouthed; scraggy brown hair falling absently from a black head band) had wanted to be a godparent for the child of an old school friend, but, although she came from a Catholic family, had never been confirmed. Father Paul had said she could stand up for the baby, but only if she promised to be confirmed; unlike many, Maria took the promise seriously, so here she was.

Debbie (vivacious, tall, dark, big-haired with wide white-teethed smile) had been confirmed in the Presbyterian Church (Judy thought) and planned to marry a Catholic guy at St. Paul's in June.

And Mike (bottomless blue eyes, Roman nose, short dark hair, quiet commanding voice), who was something quite unusual. Mike Merrill, a graduate of Dartmouth College (English), the University of London (literature), and Columbia (journalism), had briefly been a cub reporter before switching tracks and returning to school for a premed course. Now a first-year medical student at UB, he was married to a Polish-American and just-short-of-lapsed-Catholic occupational therapist named Melanie Mary Graban (long legs, curly blond hair, an endearing way of squishing up eyes in concentration), who sometimes came along to the group for curiosity's sake.

If Debbie and Maria were pretty sure they wanted to be Catholic (or, if not, kept it to themselves), Mike was hugely ambivalent. For Mike, who couldn't seem to help examining every proposition, including his own thoughts, from every angle, ambivalence was an old friend. At thirty, he sometimes considered himself "a prisoner of my own intellect." In long but self-effacing and always meticulously constructed musings, he tended to use two phrases a lot. One was "on the one hand." The other was "but then."

On the one hand, the Catholic Church seemed as good a place as any for Mike's endless search for spiritual truth, a search whose previous ports of call had included Presbyterian confirmation class (as a teen) and Buddhist meditation (since his undergraduate days), lately mixed in with Christian prayer much influenced by T. S. Eliot.

But then, large chunks of Catholicism made no sense to Mike—worse, often seemed nonsense. Contraception, for instance. Mike happened to consider almost all the world's evils—"violence, war, poverty, despair, depression, several forms of insanity, social alienation, homelessness, and racism"—to be side effects of overpopulation. So contraception struck him as an absolute necessity, the very opposite of sin. Then there was the church's patriarchal authority structure, and the way the hierarchy could make massive mistakes—the Inquisition, Galileo—and take centuries to admit them. (The year 1992's revelation to Rome: Galileo was right!)

But then again, no religion was perfect. A priest he and Melanie had known as students in Boston, the one who married them, used to say that being Catholic was "sort of like living in a house with a crazy aunt in the attic. You hope she won't come downstairs when there's company, but even if she does, you love her as one of the family."

Mike wondered if he would really be able to love the crazy aunt, not having been born into the family.

Meanwhile, he had resolved to keep the worst of his doubts to himself. Leastways, until he saw the lay of the land. While the ethos in the catechumenate seemed markedly tolerant of disagreement, Mike had a feeling there was a wall out there, a limit to the field of acceptable opinion. Trouble was, he couldn't see where the wall was.

Mike already knew there were different walls for different Catholics. One of his eclectic group of friends, a Jesuit named Father Marty Moleski, was a case in point. One time, Mike had mentioned to his friend that he didn't believe anyone would be condemned forever—that in the end God would gather up everybody and all things would be made whole. Well, Marty had come right out and said what Mike had said was *heresy*. Mike had never heard the word used seriously in conversation before. Marty said if human beings were truly free, then it would always be possible to separate yourself from God, through a willful act, an act of pride. "Well, I kind of agree with that," Mike would later say privately. "But then, where I turn into a heretic again, I guess, is I also agree with Blake: 'Eternity is every hour.' And time is circular, not linear, so even if you were separated from God 'forever,' for now, you could always come back to him later. If you see what I mean?"

Heretic or not, here he was, a catechumen. Melanie only partly understood. She told Mike one Saturday morning while spreading peanut butter on a bagel, "I'm as Catholic as I am Polish, it's just something I was born with and can't shake. But someone like you, making an informed adult decision to join . . ." She shook her head, puzzled.

But as Mike had told Judy some weeks before: "I want religious coherence in my family—like people say, 'I want my children to be brought up Catholic so that they have something to rebel against later.' I see something in people who are brought up Catholic: they have a real sense that there's something out there beyond a physical plane. At least at one point in their life they had that shiver, that sense that there is something larger than themselves."

But again, the children (thus far purely conjectural) were only part of it. Mike also felt he needed that shiver himself, something to deal with the gloomy part of him, the part that sometimes used to wake him up in the morning feeling, for no apparent reason, desperately lonely on the earth.

For Judy, Mike presented a problem. She liked him—a lot. His serious-ness, his way of arguing with himself, while those blue eyes pierced you unblinkingly—oh, Mike was "real precious." Although, of course, for Judy, everyone was "real precious" in some way. The trouble was, she now had among her catechumens a huge range of aptitudes and interests, from Tony, whose thoughts were strictly his own but whose background and interests were practical and traditional, to Mike, to whose questioning instincts she had to allow free rein without letting the whole catechumenate get sucked into cerebral mind games.

Judy blamed this heterogeneity, in part, for a problem that had begun to worry her: the way discussions tended to stay in the shallow end of the theological pool. Too often, those sitting around the rectory dining table would get within sight of a big question, and then veer away, often with a joke. They seemed to be following some unwritten "keep it light, be *nice*" rule, as if this were a dinner party in polite company.

One Sunday, for instance, the Gospel had presented Christ's challenge to materialism: "I was hungry and you did not feed me." The group had almost, but not, got into one of those classic debates between the socialist and the capitalist versions of Christian ethics. Someone confessed that while homeless people roamed the streets, he was considering whether to get cable: "I've got this beautiful new TV and it seems like it's going to waste."

Mike's hands were folded, his elbows on the table, his cheek resting on one hand, very still. There was that sense about him, in the way he played with his pen in nearly imperceptible half-inch movements, of a tightly controlled restlessness. "Mm," he said, "I'm having a real moral problem with the fact that in a few years, as a physician, I'm going to be making big money out of people's sickness."

Judy: "Will you balance it somehow, Mike? Will you find ways to—?"

Mike: "Well, sure, but—"

The man with the beautiful new TV: "Sure, just think of it as your chance to give back to society. Think of all the taxes you'll be paying."

Judy giggled.

Mike (smiling): "Well, thank you—that's really good!" And they moved on to something else.

On another Sunday, the Last Judgment came *this* close to provoking a debate about the interpretation of scripture. Tony had told his small group that what "challenged" him in that day's Gospel was the thought that "God could come at any time and find me unprepared."

Ken Monaco: "But you don't want to focus on that. Then you believe out of fear."

Dennis Hurley, who believed the End was near, cited worldwide floods, earthquakes, and the progress toward the unity of Jerusalem. But "I agree with Ken. Better not to focus on it."

Another Sunday, another troublesome issue avoided. At the time of the big fire in Malibu, California, Judy had referred to the TV news footage showing a lone house standing surrounded by devastation and the owner thanking God for sparing her home.

"It confuses me," Judy had confessed. "Does that mean all the houses burned were burned because God so decided? And shouldn't we place our confidence in the building code, rather than in God rescuing us?" She looked around the table. People nodded, looked troubled, but no one picked up on her question.

The same went for sex and sin. Judy said, "I don't remember a time when Jesus preached against sexual sin. I should have looked this up more carefully, but—"

"He was no Doctor Ruth," said the man with the new TV.

"So what does that say to you?"

"Well, I don't know. It tells me he was God. I mean, he wasn't preoccupied with it, and us sinners sure think about it a lot."

"But as a man, Jesus had sexuality."

"Right, we don't wanna estimate what he did with Mary Magdalene. He almost got out of hand there." Giggles all around. "Just kiddin'."

Sometimes, that fall, Judy went home Sundays wondering if her group was never going to venture past the humor barrier into deeper waters. She was seriously reconsidering a decision she had made early in that fall to dispense with weeknight evening "catechetical" sessions of previous years. She had made the change after attending a seminar for leaders like herself, at which it had been suggested that maybe two meetings a week was too much to expect of candidates. But, as Judy reflected later, the weeknight sessions in previous years had often provided a time to focus seriously on "the issues of Catholic teaching," as she put it. Not (she hastily added) that she would ever allow doctrine to be "crammed down the throats of the candidates." But as the fall progressed, she continued to worry about the chattering quality of Sunday mornings.

Judy did consider many of the avoided theological questions to be "sidebar issues." But she was more concerned about the unwillingness to deal with social justice. For her, the biggest issue was, as she put it once: "What is your response to the word of God? The word of God in your own heart, as an individual, sure, but in the communal heart too. Because if it's not communal, the community, then you go back to fundamentalism. And that's not what we're trying to do here."

Even more discontent with the "keep it light, be nice" rule was Ken, although he had different ideas about "what we're trying to do here." The Pope's main man had been doing some homework lately on the purpose of the catechumenate. He had, for a start, got hold of a book, *RCIA: What It Is, How It Works,* by Patricia Babernitz, published by Liguori Press ten years before. The author promoted a balance between recognizing, nurturing, and welcoming "the whole person" of the catechumen, on the one hand, and, on the other, studying the church's doctrine and presenting a thorough "overview of what it means to be a Catholic." Ken had drawn a big thick arrow pointing to the latter phrase, and another to a paragraph that urged "a well-planned teaching schedule which gives sufficient attention to all the essential aspects of faith—not just the parts we find easy to teach!"

The final chapter of Babernitz's book named worrisome "trends in the catechumenate," including the following:

Statements like the following are often heard: "The RCIA is a process." "You can't program conversion." "We must react to the felt needs of the catechumens." These are true statements, but they need to be balanced by the church community's need to pass on what it means to be Catholic.

On a Saturday morning some months later, when Ken had made up his mind to take a stand against relativism in the catechumenate, he would sit back after an especially splendid pancake breakfast and use Babernitz's analysis to launch one of his great speeches:

"Judy's *always* saying, 'It's a *process*, not a program; you cannot program faith.' You know what? I *agree!* It *is* a process. But it should *also* be a program. You need *balance.* Judy's so into this process—process—process, but without some kind of program, we're like travelers without a road map. If I want to go to California, and I don't have a compass, don't have a map, OK, maybe I'll make it there somehow, but I may go to Canada first.

"And I know there are other RCIAs that *do* have a program. St. Gregory the Great, in Williamsville, has a *fantastic* program. They have this introductory class, they talk about *revelation;* another week, they talk about *faith.* And here's *human life. Prayer.* Personal *conscience.* You get into the catechumenate itself and they talk about the *Bible,* they talk about *church,* they talk about *morality,* the *sacraments,* each one in turn.

"Do we go over the sacraments? Yeah, we *go over* the sacraments. This past week, we talked about baptism, confirmation, and Eucharist *all in one session.* It's like 'It's a requisite, we have to do this.' But do you know how much time you can spend on just baptism? Just the Eucharist?

"It's a lack of balance. I'm not asking for straight catechesis, straight doctrine, the straight-dogma kind of teaching. What I'm in favor of is presenting what the church is all about, presenting the teachings of the church, and discovering practical applications. Sharing experiences is very important. *Very* important. And in terms of sharing experiences and so forth, there's nobody better than Judy. Jamie Shaner too. They're *excellent,* in terms of that. They're exceptional! *Exceptional!*

"But they always downplay the teaching. It's like they're encumbered by it. It's like it gets in the way of true conversion.

"And I think the formation of personal conscience is hurt by it. To the point where it's, like, 'How do you see this? And how do *you* see this? And how do *you* see this?' That's important, to get those feelings, but it's necessary to bring it back in and hear what the church teaches about these things. Otherwise, we get nothing more than a group therapy session, as opposed to a journey of faith. As opposed to *sound teaching*. In other faiths, people have to learn what the church teaches. In RCIA, it's 'Let the Spirit move you.' It's 'What do you think? OK, and what do *you* think?'

"It becomes so there's no objective moral truth. It's 'How do I *feel*, am I right with God?' But what do I *base* this on? It's important to believe, but it's just as important to be asking, 'What am I believing?' We need guidelines. We need guides. Why do you think God gave us the *Bible*? Why do you think God sent us *Christ*? Why do you think God sends us Christ's *mother*? We need guides.

"Why did Christ say to Peter, 'Upon this rock I will build my church'? We have a shepherd. You can join the flock or reject the flock, but if you're gonna join it, then it's 'Come, follow me.' The Pope is Christ's vicar, Christ's vehicle on earth: 'Whatever you bind on earth will be bound in heaven.' "

A breakfast guest interrupted. "Ken, aren't there *any* church teachings that you have problems with? Like, what if, at the RCIA table, someone said, 'I really don't believe there's anything wrong with masturbation, and prohibiting it imposes a load of guilt on—' "

"So join the Lutherans!" Ken shouted with a laugh.

"That would be your answer?"

"No," he considered, "it would not. I'd say, 'The church teaches this, and, like a lot of things we talk about, we have to accept it on the faith level. You use your free will to accept or reject that teaching, but *you have heard here what I believe to be the truth.*' "

On December 9, the Thursday of Judy's final doctrine class, the Buffalo *News* reported on an inside page:

LOCKPORT PRIEST ACCUSED
OF SEXUALLY ABUSING BOY

Charges denied: diocese will contest lawsuit

The story said a $2.9 million lawsuit had been filed by a couple and their fourteen-year-old son against Father Bernard M. "Corky" Mach, fifty-five, pastor of St. Mary's Catholic Church in the town of Lockport. The plaintiffs alleged that Mach had molested the boy two years ago in the rectory.

The boy said he had stayed overnight at the rectory to look after Mach's two dogs because the pastor had expected to be out late. Frightened by a TV show, the boy had been invited to sleep in Mach's bed. The priest had then showed the boy pornographic movies before fondling him, exposing himself to him, and then forcing himself on the boy.

Allegedly, Mach had afterward comforted the crying boy, hugging him, saying, "God forgives us for all our sins," and assuring the boy that what had been done was normal.

The plaintiffs charged that diocesan officials and the bishop "knew or should have known" about the behavior, which was "tolerated and thereby sanctioned" by the church.

The newspaper said a Niagara County grand jury had investigated the boy's claim two months previously but had chosen to issue no indictment because the police, after interviewing parishioners and colleagues of Mach, had found no corroborating evidence.

Similarly, the diocese of Buffalo had investigated the case and, finding no verifying evidence, taken no action against Mach, a popular priest associated with the Mission movement, which runs eight-night spiritual exercises in parishes. The diocese had therefore turned down a settlement offer from the family.

A police investigator was quoted saying, "There is quite a Corky fan club out there. Some of his conduct, I would say, is untraditional, such as his language and the off-color jokes he tells, but that does not make him a child molester."

A lay friend of the priest said that it was common for the priest to hug and kiss people "as a warm and loving gesture" and that he would trust Corky with any of his seven children and five grandchildren.

And Mach's attorney expressed confidence that his client would be exonerated on the civil action just as he had been before the grand jury.

Perhaps the story's inside placement was a reflection of a similar hunch by someone on the desk at the News. Or perhaps it was merely a sign that alleged sexual abuse by a priest was no longer big news. Since the 1985 conviction of Louisiana's Father Gilbert Gauthe, who had molested thirty-five youths, sexual assaults by priests had hit the (ever-smaller) headlines almost weekly. Corky Mach was not the first western New Yorker to be so accused, and he was, after all, a mere parish priest. Nothing as newsworthy as the then-unresolved allegations against Chicago's Cardinal Bernardin, or the resignation of Santa Fe's Archbishop Robert F. Sanchez after 60 *Minutes* acquired videotapes of women who claimed to have had sex with him when they were in their teens, or with the numerous allegations of abuse by entire communities of teaching brothers. A month earlier, Bishop John F. Kinney of Bismarck, North Dakota, chair of the U.S. Bishops' Committee on Sexual Abuse, had stated that the bishops were currently relying on a study which indicated that most such charges were true, and only 5 percent were without substance.

Media outlets had recently trumpeted "estimates" by novelist-sociologist Father Andrew Greeley, who thought that between two thousand and four thousand priests might have abused as many as 100,000 underage victims in the past twenty-five years. An editorial in the New York *Times* had juxtaposed Greeley's figure against that of New York sociologist Father Philip Murnion, who "estimated" 15,000 victims over forty years. "Either figure is shocking," the *Times* commented, "but it should matter that one is more than six times the other, or that one suggests 375 victims a year compared with 4,000. (Conservative estimates are that each year adults sexually abuse some 200,000 children in the United States.)"

Counting the financial cost was slightly easier. A lawyer for the U.S. Catholic Conference had told the press that dioceses had spent at least $60 million in sexual abuse settlements, not including legal and medical fees. Greeley put the figure at $50 million *a year*, when therapy for the abusive priests was included. According to the Associated Press, the archdiocese of Chicago alone had reportedly spent $2.8 million on sexual misconduct cases in 1993, a year in which it ran up a nearly $4.5 million deficit.

Even the Pope had finally spoken up publicly, calling for better screening of seminarians. "These failures of a small number of clerics make it all the more important that seminary formation discern scrupulously the charism of celibacy among candidates for the priesthood," the Holy Father had said during the past summer. "These failures are tragic for the victims and for the cleric involved." The training and formation of priests should therefore take into account cases "where a culture of self-centeredness and self-indulgence has made inroads," the Pope said.

Yet, in the coming weeks, the case of Corky Mach would turn into a big story after all. Making the difference would be, first, the TV extravaganza that played out in St. Mary's Church the day after the news broke. Arriving for Mass at St. Mary's that Friday, Corky Mach would be accompanied by two fellow priests and greeted not only by hundreds of loyal parishioners but by TV cameras and lights, for which the occasion appeared orchestrated. "I am innocent and the forthcoming trial is going to prove that," Mach said in his homily, occasionally reaching out to grasp a crucifix as if for support. He added: "I may need some of you to testify on my behalf that I am a good priest and a good person." Then he choked back some tears.

After the TV phase, the campaign would hit the letters column of the *News*.

FATHER MACH SHOWING
WAY TO SPIRITUAL GROWTH

said the headline over the contribution of one St. Mary's parishioner:

> Father Bernard Mach and the spirit-filled community he has helped
> to create are the reasons I returned to the church and, for me, are a
> great source of spiritual growth and learning and a contributing
> factor to the degree of peace and happiness I have. Father Mach is
> an honest, direct, and loving priest. He leads with integrity, con-
> viction, and compassion.

Later, the beloved pastor would go into hiding, having announced that he had received a death threat, even as Bishop Head penned a letter to his flock cautioning people not to jump to conclusions over unproven allegations:

> There is a real danger that people will generalize, blaming or
> suspecting many because of accusations regarding the few. Even

worse, there is a danger that our many, many good priests and religious will consciously or subconsciously alter their attitudes and actions toward others—become more distant, less compassionate, less willing to be living examples of the love that the Lord has for all of us.

My dear friends, just as it would be a mistake to ignore the accusations that have been publicized in the media, so it would be a mistake to generalize based on those accusations. Just as it would be a mistake to take no action in response, so it would be a mistake to overreact. Just as it would be a mistake not to take some corrective measures when the allegations are warranted, so it would be a mistake to blame the many for the sins of the very, very few. . . .

"When I saw Corky on TV holding the cross," Judy said, "something about it didn't seem sincere. And then, after it had all come out, I remembered that scene, and I thought, 'I couldn't defy God like that.' I would expect lightning to come down and strike me dead. Really."

But more shocking to Judy would be the entry into the story of Father John Aurelio, Corky Mach's best friend, who was a national Catholic figure, a rising star in the diocese, and a priest whom Judy had come to respect deeply.

SOURCES SAY PRIEST
ADMITS ABUSING BOYS
WITH REV. MACH

By Lou Michel
News Staff Reporter
LOCKPORT — The Rev. John R. Aurelio has told Niagara County law enforcement officials that he and the Rev. Bernard M. Mach sodomized young boys 15 to 20 years ago in an East Aurora house they once shared.

Father Aurelio, the spiritual director of Christ the King Seminary for the Catholic diocese of Buffalo, told authorities that he and Father Mach drank alcohol and smoked marijuana with young boys and then participated in acts of sodomy with them, according to three Niagara County sources close to the case.

Both priests today were placed on leaves of absence. . . .

Niagara County investigators recently approached Father Aurelio, 56, because of accusations about his friend, Father Mach, 55. During that interview, Father Aurelio told law enforcement officials about the incidents 15 to 20 years ago. He said that the boys, whose ages ranged from 12 to 14, "came on to them" and that he and Father Mach initially refused to participate in the acts, according to sources close to the investigation.

Father Aurelio, who is well known for writing children's Christian storybooks, explained to law enforcement officials that he and Father Mach were just out of the seminary at the time and "sexually naive," a source said. . . .

But Father Aurelio also told Niagara County investigators that Father Mach did not sexually abuse the Lockport boy.

Father Mach has adamantly maintained he is innocent of that claim and said he is willing to take a lie detector test. . . .

The two priests sold the East Aurora house about 10 years ago, but they now jointly own a cottage on Lake Erie.

Father Aurelio admitted the acts after authorities told him that the five-year statute of limitations for felony charges had run out and he could not be prosecuted for acts that occurred 15 to 20 years ago. . . .

While Judy neither knew Corky Mach well nor particularly cared for him, John Aurelio was nothing less than a role model. He was a "children's liturgist" known across the United States for what a *News* profile later called his "almost magical ability to weave the Catholic Church's gospel into stories that speak to people's lives." One of his several books had won the Catholic Press Association's National Catholic Book Award.

The profile would quote Assistant U.S. Attorney Lee Coppola, described as a longtime friend of both Aurelio and Mach and a parishioner of St. Catherine of Siena Church in the suburb of West Seneca. Coppola told of Aurelio's monthly "Story Sunday" at St. Catherine's:

> "He calls all the children up to the front, and they look up at him with their mouths open," Coppola said. "The parents look at each other and marvel, talking about what a wonderful job he does, the simplicity with which he relates the message. Anyone would understand, especially children. That's the only time my kids would look forward to going to Mass." . . .

The profile described Aurelio as a brilliant organizer, and a winner of several awards for his work with migrant laborers, unwed mothers, minorities, and especially handicapped people.

"I really admired John Aurelio," Judy would say weeks after the dust had settled. "That's what hurt so much for me. If John could do it, then . . ." She trailed off, then began again. "So, my immediate thing was adjusting the trust, again. Every time you go through something like this, you have to adjust the trust. I would have trusted John with anything—my children, my life.

"So, yes, it makes you suspect your own instincts. It's like hearing your father was responsible. Or maybe worse, because some fathers aren't as good as John. He would get down on his knees and hug a handicapped child rather than talk down to them. He seemed like the most caring, sensitive man. I think the people would have canonized this man, he was that loved.

"He absolutely believed in heaven: he told these wonderful stories about families losing children and them coming back to tell their parents that they're all right.

"This has cost me a lot of thinking and sorting out, and I'm not through it. I'm really still kind of beat down by it.

"There are people who want to forgive and forget, but this is about children. That's harder to forgive. But you know, I think I could even forgive John himself on a one-to-one kind of thing, if I can work through this. I'm not there yet, but I could. But I don't know if I can forgive a system that allowed him to keep going and keep going.

"Could I give you cold hard proof that the system did that? No. I can't do that without naming names or things I've heard in confidence. A lot of people knew what was going on, and I have a harder time forgiving the people who were silent than I do the two men. But I know lots of priests who shared houses. Why were *these two* told to sell theirs? Apparently the bishop told them to get rid of it. Why them? There had to be something that someone had an inkling of.

"And I don't know too many priests that I can talk about it to, right now. They're so defensive. They're, like, 'This is our hurt, our pain.' But I'm here too, I'm part of this church. Priests seem to think it only affects them. They don't realize it affects all of us. It affects my authority as a church teacher, and it affects me as a Catholic in the pew."

If John Henry Newman lived still, might he find some "data" here? The faithful standing true in time of trial as, about them, robed men fall?

At Canisius College, on that second Thursday in Advent, the final class in Dan Liderbach's Development of Christian Doctrine course was drawing to an end. To test his students' mastery of the material, he moved about the room, throwing questions out.

"Jeff. Why did Newman insist that the church must consult the faithful?

"Good. Brian. What did Newman foresee in cases where doctrine was developed without consulting the faithful?

"Good—they *will* ignore it. Max. Why did Newman so expect the faithful not to accept doctrines without consultation?"

Max, sleepy and unshaven under thick black eyebrows, clearly had no idea. Liderbach waited.

"The Spirit," Max offered finally, poking at the back of his flat hand with a pen.

"The Spirit, good. What about the Spirit?"

Max said nothing.

"Is it guiding them?"

Max agreed this was well put.

"Good. Well, sort of good. Can you give me another reason? Jim? Randy?"

There were no answers. Liderbach prowled the tables, looked hopefully at Katherine, then at Judy. He sighed very slightly and moved back to his usual position at left of center. "I *told* you," he complained. "And this is an important matter for the test. I stood here," he said, walking over near the door. "I stood here like this, and did this," he said, chopping his right hand into his left palm. Judy shook her head as if to clear it.

"I know," Liderbach said, chopping hand into palm, "I am absolutely certain of one thing . . ."

"Right," Judy said.

"Judy."

"That you are human. That God expects you to be human."

"Good! God expects me to be human. It's extremely important! So, Randy. What does it mean to be human? Why does being human mean that I won't accept doctrine passively?"

Randy shrugged.

"Anyone else? Kathleen."

"To be free."

"Good! To be human means to believe in yourself, to think for yourself, to make your own decisions. To be free. That's it. Good luck."

Winter into Spring

Saying No to Father

When he gets mad, Jamie Shaner's husband, Dick, doesn't yell, doesn't even raise his voice; he just talks faster. The angrier Dick gets, the faster the sentences crowd into one another. On the Sunday before Christmas, in the sacristy after the noon Mass, Dick Shaner's blood boiled.

"We decided . . ." Father Don had shrugged, and Dick's sentences or, rather, questions tumbled. *Who* had decided? Who made that kind of decision? Father Don? The pastor? Nancy Piatkowski? And why? *Why* decide not to announce an evening of Christmas carols? Because it's not "liturgically correct" to make announcements in Mass? According to whom? Dick leaned closer, all but spitting in the parochial vicar's gold-studded ear, and asked again, *"Who* 'decided'?"

Who decides? For the Shaners, the question would become something of a theme for that Christmas, meaning the season that had officially begun (by decree of the St. Paul's Liturgy Committee) two days before, on December 17. Certainly, it was destined not to be altogether a time of joy and goodwill. Not for Father Don, who, unbeknown to Dick Shaner, had life-transforming decisions on his mind. And not for Jamie and Dick Shaner either, for their season had started out tarnished by grief before surging into disappointment and wrath. Before the holly was off the Shaners' front door, matters would cascade into something akin to a power struggle, with a startling whiff of venom.

A day into Advent, Jamie had answered the phone to hear that Tommy Hamed was dead, two weeks shy of his fortieth birthday. Tommy had been Dick's best friend since they were both freshmen at Archbishop Walsh High down in Olean; he had been best man at the Shaners' wedding. He lived in Rochester, was married, and had three children. Tommy had lacked Dick's passion for sports and music, but they had shared many long youthful nights, and had often poured young hearts out to each other. It was to Tommy that Dick confessed his unrequited love for Kathy Kelly, on whom he turned his shy smile one night at a Walsh dance and then, at last, actually kissed her, sitting in the darkness high in the gym bleachers while the kids danced far below them (but he was so drunk that night that the thrill of her touch went to his stomach and he threw up on the floor in front of her). Dick and Tommy and their crowd, guys too big to worry about the drinking age, would take six-packs down to the river dikes and wander the town streets ripping out a mailbox here and picking a fight there, just for the laughs. At the Back Room Door bar, they'd take turns biting down on a glass and drinking the beer down, no hands. If the glass broke, they would chew and swallow the glass too. Dick himself was famous for eating lighted matches.

Dick Shaner: future Parish Council president, young and free as the '70s dawned, his head full of beer, later a little grass and, occasionally, speed. Scraping through graduation, but prouder of having made the football and basketball teams. Mumbling a confession from time to time, skipping some of the details under the heading of "all my other sins," and going to Mass every Sunday, because not to do so was a mortal sin.

Circumstances separated Dick from his best friend. Dick settled down somewhat at state college in Geneseo, grew taller, lost weight, studied harder. Started noticing Jamie, a slim, dark, quiet, delicately desirable presence on the edge of the Olean crowd. Took her to a Burt Reynolds movie one summer, began dating her seriously the following fall. Spent less time chewing glass, more time with Jamie cruising the back roads at twilight listening to rock music, cracking a few Budweisers or a bottle of cheap wine, munching pork rinds and red licorice, waiting for Dick's dad to put the bedroom light out and then sneaking into the living room to watch TV, or whatever. It became official: they were in love. Jamie graduated from business school, managed her retired dad's rental properties, and worked in a bank. Baptized Greek Orthodox, confirmed Episcopalian, she started going to Mass with Dick. Out of respect for his parents, she went to catechism class and was received into the Roman Catholic Church.

Tommy became a schoolteacher, married, and moved to Rochester; Dick, having graduated with honors, drove with Jamie to Buffalo to interview for a PR job in a savings bank. Jamie sat wide-eyed downstairs watching big-city pimps issuing orders to women in leather. Dick got the job.

After the Shaners had Scotty, they attended Sunday Mass at St. Margaret's in North Buffalo but didn't otherwise get involved. They moved to Kenmore and joined St. Paul's. When the unborn Cory died, Dick and Jamie, sustained by their pastor and succored by their evolving faith, slowly grew into pillars of the church. Dick won the pastor's nomination to the Parish Council; Jamie became a mainstay in Judy Nice's catechumenate; together, the couple led the Adult Formation Committee. By then, the family had been completed by the birth of Tyler.

Now that Tommy was gone, Dick felt bad about the times he had put other things ahead of getting together. He remembered spring weekends when Tommy had wanted the Shaners to come up to Rochester and Dick had pleaded St. Paul's activities or Scotty's soccer or Little League. After Tommy announced he had leukemia, he had said, "Promise me that if Scott has a soccer game the day I die, you'll miss his soccer game." Dick had said, "Promise me that if it's a big game, you won't die that day."

Tommy had loved spring; had longed to see just one more. He had promised to take care of little Cory in heaven. At the Requiem Mass, Dick delivered the eulogy. And saw to it that Tommy's requested songs—Eric Clapton's "Tears in Heaven"; Bette Midler's "Wind Beneath My Wings"— were played at the wake brunch (the local priest having vetoed them as Mass music).

Almost every night in Advent, the Shaners lit a candle before dinner on their brass wreath and read a seasonal meditation by popular spirituality writer Edward Hays. (*O come, O come, promised One of the ages. Come into our homes, sit at our table . . . Emmanuel, set our hearts on fire.*) They collected used clothing and toys for a transitional housing program, and filled the gift orders on tags that Scotty and Tyler had picked off the Giving Tree: "Toy for girl, 3" (a picnic basket set); "Socks for older man" (a box of them). But Tommy's death had driven Dick into a damp sand trap of emptiness. For some weeks, he kept rolling back in, even after moments on a slippery green.

The weekend of the seventeenth was a case in point. Dick and Jamie had got the tree up Friday night, with its mementos of Christmases past (for Scott, a Crayola box with five little elves sticking out of its top; for Dick, a miniature Cleveland Browns helmet; for dead little Cory, a praying angel on a cloud). After a pizza dinner, Dick had opened a bottle of wine and settled down with a pajamaed Scotty to watch the Sabres-Kings game while Jamie puttered about cleaning up. "It's the best game I've ever seen," Scotty announced after the first period. A few minutes later he was asleep on a pillow against Dick's leg. Stroking his son's hair, Dick looked around the living room—the tree, the lights in the window, the wooden manger he had carved with his own dad's help—and felt there was, after all, magic in his world.

Saturday evening, they had taken the kids and Dick's parents to visit the Shrine of Our Lady of Fatima at Youngstown, New York, a half hour's drive away on Lake Ontario. They walked from the parking lot through gray snow and a sea of glistening angels, Magi, shepherds, camels, asses, stars, tablets of law, a Sacred Heart, an alpha, an omega, an anchor, a sheep. A carillon somewhere chimed "O Holy Night," while, somewhere else, loudspeakers blared "Hark! the Herald Angels Sing." Near the shrine's blue dome, they shushed the boys and entered a grottolike pod, its air wet and hot with the smell of beeswax, its rocks lined with votive candles ("OFFERING $2.00 U.S."), a statue of Mary with children. Kneeling at her feet, Scotty wrote a note to squeeze into the stones—"Help me in school, please"—and lit a candle before heading outside to attack a wide metal stairway. ("Climb to the top of the Basilica, where you can have an ANGEL'S VIEW of 15 acres of spectacular Christmas lights," the ad in the diocesan paper had urged. "View the Avenue of Saints and the Spirit of Christmas.") At the top, a giant blue-robed Mary, the planet Earth under her bare feet, looked out over a razzmatazz of fairy lights. "Pretty cool, huh, Scotty?" said Jamie. "You can even tickle Mary's toes." Tyler demonstrated.

But Dick couldn't stop thinking about Tommy, and death. It didn't help that he had entered a period of disillusionment at St. Paul's. His Adult Formation committee's "Advent Evening of Reflection" had attracted a pathetic crowd of forty from the parish's three thousand households. The Parish Council had become a tedious affair in which an apparently aging pastor's leadership lately consisted of reciting financial, baptismal, and funereal statistics. To make it worse, the Bills seemed to be headed for yet another Super Bowl berth; for Dick, a Browns fan since childhood, the thought of another Bills-manic January was too much to bear.

And so it was unsurprising when, on Sunday the nineteenth, Dick's Christmas spirit crashed on the sacristy floor. Adult Formation would be hosting a carols program that night and had invited an inner-city youth choir to lead the singing. To supplement bulletin notices, a committee member had delivered to the rectory an announcement meant to be read at all weekend Masses. At Sunday's noon Mass, Father Don presided and Dick was lector. After communion, the parochial vicar stepped to the center of the sanctuary and Dick waited for the announcement; instead, Father Don went over the Christmas Mass schedule and berated parishioners who telephoned the rectory rather than checking the bulletin for Mass times. When the recessional reached the sacristy door, Dick, still holding the lectionary aloft, looked over his shoulder at the bearded priest behind him.

"Father Don, did we screw up? Didn't we get you a notice about the carols program?"

"Um, we decided not to make that announcement."

Dick seethed while the priest shrugged his way out of his chasuble, then exploded. *"Who* decided . . . ?"

"I'm sorry," the parochial vicar said after that. "I just forgot."

"But you just said you *decided*—"

"Look, I'm sorry. I apologize, OK?"

Later, Dick learned the announcement hadn't been made at *any* Mass. Had *all* the presiders "just forgot"? Dick knew the problem wasn't just Father Don; the pastor himself frowned upon church announcements, which he considered a disruption to the worshipful atmosphere during Mass. This infuriated Dick. Here a few people were working their buns off to build some sense of belonging in the parish, but the priests—who spoke so often about "community" and about laypeople being called to "lay ministry" and comprising "the Body of Christ"—were standing in the way. Laypeople were ready to take responsibility, but the clergy clung to power, making their *decisions* and expecting everyone else to say, "Yes, Father, thank you, Father." It seemed to Dick that it would be a good thing if laity said no from time to time.

So, when only about a hundred carolers arrived on the front steps of St. Paul's on a mild evening that was perfect for a fine family occasion, Dick was ready to kick butt. The turnout seemed just one more sign of the parish's apathy toward Adult Formation's efforts to "build community," and the priests' liturgical fastidiousness hardly helped. The following night, he and a fellow committee member hooked up by telephone to draft a letter to the Parish Council.

In doing so, they unwittingly set in motion a chain of hostile letters and pivotal events. These events, while neither earth-shattering nor even parish-shattering, would manifest the ambiguous power balance that besets Catholicism today.

Looking back on that winter, Jamie would insist, and Dick agree, that the season's friction was little more than a matter of personalities—Father Don's personality, and Judy Nice's, and Ken Monaco's, and Dennis Hurley's, and the pastor's, and yes, certainly, Jamie's and Dick's. But power struggles are inevitable in today's Catholic parish, given the profound shifts in attitude and governance over the past quarter-century or more. The declarations of Vatican II had sharply defined the church in a way that placed laypeople rather than priests at its center. Then came *Humanae Vitae* and the rebellion of the laity over contraception. Then, in parishes around the developed world, came the consequences.

When adult Catholics matter-of-factly denied to their popes and priests the right to tell them what to do in bed, it was akin to a teenager's first defiance of her parents' curfew. That first battle marks the beginning of an exhilarating and relentless downward shift of power. And as power shifts, a point is reached where the child stands confused, awed by her own independence and disillusioned by her parents' feebleness. The parents too are left unsettled. They may welcome the epoch or merely acknowledge its inevitability, but they still consider the child a child.

The child will always be the parents'. Her values, understanding, and foibles are formed by her roots. But so long as the power ambiguity lasts—maybe just until the child is indisputably "grown up," or maybe until the parents die—the confusion grows, giving birth first to regret and then to rage.

Christmas came, with the usual snow, crowded malls, road deaths, reminders of loss, and the occasional small miracle.

Dave Taylor had not seen his estranged parents-in-law since before the August wedding. Claire had had the occasional strained conversation with her mom, usually on the phone; her dad had hugged her when she turned up, alone, at his birthday dinner in September. No one had mentioned her black husband; there had been no dinner invitations either. Dave and Claire had decided not to push it.

But after their solitary Thanksgiving dinner, the thought of Christmas pressed silently on Claire. She longed to spend Christmas Eve with her husband at her parents' home, as would her sisters and brothers with their spouses. After weeks of deliberation, she and Dave agreed on a bold move. On Christmas Eve, they would arrive without fanfare at Claire's parents' front door as if it were the most natural thing in the world. If no one answered the door, or if they were otherwise made unwelcome, they would "go home and deal with it." But Claire had her money on the Christmas spirit and old-fashioned politeness.

On the twenty-third, the day before the planned assault, family custom called for Claire and her siblings to go bowling around four in the afternoon. Throwing gutter balls in the deserted alleys for an hour and a half had long ago proved an effective way to relieve tension before the intensity of the holiday gatherings. Afterward, the siblings usually went to their parents' house for a light supper, where they were joined by their spouses; they moved on to visit each other's homes to check out the trees. Claire joined the others for bowling, and decided she would just pop in at her parents' place to say hello.

In the kitchen, her mom said, "You're not staying?"

"Can't. Dave will be home from work at six."

"Well, why don't you call him up at work and tell him to come over here for dinner?"

Claire froze, not sure she'd heard right. Her mom, who had, it seemed, arrived at her own private resolution about this holiday, looked Claire firmly in the eye but kept her voice matter-of-fact. "Or, if you like, you could take a plate of food home to him."

Suddenly, the ball was in Claire's court. She called Dave at the office: "Wanna come over to my parents' house for dinner? I don't know where it came from, but you're invited." An hour later, Dave was standing nervously on the doorstep. Inside, the dog barked but no one in the house full of people heard the bell, so he just stood there in the snow for a while until Claire's mom, noticing the dog, came to the door.

"Merry Christmas," Dave said, and held out his hand. She took his hand, and, to his astonishment, kissed him on the cheek.

"Merry Christmas," she said quietly, and led him into the house.

Father Dick Sowinski's Christmas card was a prayer printed on parchment stock, with calligraphy by Rose-Ann Martin, self-appointed thorn in the Liturgy Committee's side:

> Child of Bethlehem
>   house of bread
> Man of Jerusalem
>   city of peace
> You have loved us
>   without limit or condition
> In our greatness and
>   in our misery
> In our folly and
>   in our virtue
> May your healing hand
>   be upon us
> And your light
>   within us
> So that we too
>   may become bread and
>   peace for each other

*L*et this be a sign to you,' " Father Paul read at 12:30 A.M. as wind blew and snow fell outside. " 'In a manger you will find an infant wrapped in swaddling clothes.' And suddenly, there was with the angel a multitude of the heavenly host, praising God and saying, 'Glory to God in high heaven, peace on earth to those on whom his favor rests.' My brothers and sisters, the good news of the Lord.

"Well, a merry Christmas to you all. Well, thank *you!* I love this Mass for lovers and other strangers. Midnight Mass. Some churches canceled it; for those of you from St. Andrew's, a special welcome to St. Paul's.

"We have had a bad week, as you well know. I'm not going to dwell on it a great deal because I expect to speak to you about it later. But somehow in trying to make sense of what to say tonight, it was very difficult not to somehow deal with the experience of these past weeks, the media situation. For those of you who came to us from out of town, there was discovery this month that two of our priests were engaged in pedophilia. Two very popular priests.

"And as a result, the media had a field day with it. And our bishop has been rather mute. But the situation is such that all of us are suffering, not just us, the priests, but you, the people of God. In fact the church has probably suffered an almost irreparable amount of damage in the western New York area because of this situation. This kind of scandal is one that rocks the very foundations of our faith.

"And so, somehow, in thinking about what to say tonight—and Lord knows I had enough time to think about it because I was shoveling snow three times today—well, how do you make sense out of a beautiful feast day like this, when you and I, as Christians, celebrate our salvation and the birth into the world of our savior? How do you somehow relate it to the frailty, the weakness and the vulnerability of our human nature?

"We could go on for a long time talking about the human nature of Jesus that Mary gave to him, his enfleshment, if you will. But I found some things that somehow tickled my fancy and I'll share them with you.

"Look, two contrasting images. Here to my left, the manger. There, behind the altar, the cross. It's not a big distance, is it, between them? Physically in this church, it's about thirty feet. And for some people, it's a very short time. I buried an infant this past week who lived twenty-four hours. Born with a bad heart at Sisters' Hospital, transferred to Children's Hospital, and flown to Cleveland. And in twenty-four hours, little Eileen was dead.

"And on Tuesday, I was with a forty-seven-year-old woman with cancer who had just been told that she had just a week to live. She desperately wants to live, and she hates to give up life.

"I think the important thing here is that we cannot separate this scene here, the manger, from that scene there, the cross. Sometimes I think when you and I get so excited about this scene here, we sentimentalize it, we make it into something that's merely cute. And we don't relate it to that scene there. Somehow, when you and I live out this Christmas mystery, we need to keep the two of them together. We need to live both of these mysteries together, because this mystery here leads to that mystery there.

"So let's think a little about the mystery of Christmas. It's a reflection and a foretaste of an event that we're going to celebrate here in a very few short months, the Easter mystery. At that time we'll be talking not only about death but going beyond it to resurrection. And that is our glory, our victory, our crowning glory.

"We use holly to make wreaths at this time of the year. Noticed that? It's tough stuff, that holly—prickly, with red berries. The thorns remind us of the thorns that were put upon Christ's head, the red berries of his blood. And the poinsettia too reflects the blood of Jesus. So you see, the mystery of Christmas is tied to the mystery of Easter.

"Joy and death, together; and that death leads to resurrection. Christmas to Easter. The moment we are born, we begin to move away from our mothers, and move toward that other mystery. . . ."

It *was* the real Midnight Mass after all, Rose-Ann Martin decided with satisfaction as she plowed her feet through the thickening snow in the early hours of the twenty-fifth. Maybe her tireless bleats at Liturgy Committee had had some effect—the incense, the candles, the sung *Gloria* with that absolutely fabulous crescendo into the *Amen*, the three priests concelebrating. OK, the canon wasn't sung, but face it, the pastor was no Pavarotti anyhow. Rose-Ann's bulldog scowl, too deeply etched and too tinted by irony to signal her moods, scrunched up as she peered through the murk to cross a silent Victoria Boulevard, heading home. Now, if only Whitney would quit preaching about death.

Rose-Ann Martin, Ph.D., M.L.S., M.A., linguist, classicist, sometime librarian and calligrapher, could have used a more upbeat message tonight. Niagara University, in a financial crisis, had canceled, effective January, the two courses she taught as adjunct professor in French. At fifty-three, Rose-Ann had no idea how she would scratch together $495 a month for the mortgage in the new year; certainly, calligraphy shows, wedding invitations, and her single elementary French course at Canisius College would not be enough. She supposed she would try the school boards again for a librarian's job, although it had been more than a decade since she'd left Riverside High. Everyone wanted computer skills these days. Maybe she'd have to stuff envelopes for a while. At her age, with four degrees and six languages.

Rose-Ann trudged into her driveway, the evidence of her afternoon's snow-pushing now obliterated, and opened the kitchen door to return the raucous Christmas greetings of her two black retrievers, Ariane and Tippy. She threw her coat onto a kitchen chair, lit a Virginia Slim, and walked over to the VCR to hit the rewind button. She had recorded the Midnight Mass on EWTN, the Eternal Word cable network, from Our Lady of the Angels Monastery in Irondale, Alabama.

Now, *there* was a Midnight Mass! The celebrant flanked by deacon in dalmatic and subdeacon in tunicle. Mother Angelica's sisters, in full pre-Vatican II habits that hid both foreheads and necks, receiving communion (on their tongues) through a hole in a screen behind the high altar. Huge clouds of incense glistening in the floodlights. The Latin *Kyrie* and *Sanctus* and *Pater Noster* and *Agnus Dei,* with violin and organ accompaniment. The chants seemed to echo down the decades from Sister Elmira's choir at St. Mary's grammar school in East Islip on Long Island in the mid-'40s. Rose-Ann sat back and smoked for a while, gazing at the TV set and ignoring the scene behind it, a vision part living room, part warehouse, part apocalypse. The remodeling of her study arrested midway for lack of funds, boxes of books and papers were piled crazily high, separated by a maze of impossibly narrow paths. Where, she wondered, could her teaching certificates be?

"I guess I'm discouraged, depressed," she admitted to an acquaintance some days later, her last Niagara semester over and no new job in sight. "And panicked. And *angry!* I'd like to see her head roll in the dust."

"Her head?"

"Sister Mistress."

Meaning, the Mistress of Novices who had kicked Rose-Ann out of the Sisters of Charity of Halifax, in Nova Scotia. In 1961.

Rose-Ann had wanted to be a nun ever since the first time she sang Gregorian chant in Sister Elmira's kindergarten class the year of Hiroshima. Rose-Ann lived with her mother and German-American grandparents, who ran the town bakery. Rose-Ann doesn't care to talk about her father. Her memories are filled up with church.

Walking a mile to church with her grandfather, who was a near-daily communicant. Watching her mother and aunts (who worked as maids or as clerks in Karp's Stationery Store) launder the altar linens and robes. Staring at Sister Elmira and the other nuns and thinking how wonderful it was for someone to give their whole life to God. Sitting in the locker room after a field hockey game at Seton Hall Catholic Co-educational High School in Patchogue, thinking, "I have only one life to give to God."

And then, three years in the novitiate in Halifax, with Sister Mistress.

"I never liked her," says Rose-Ann, letting big tears of rage fall three decades later. "She was nasty. Uncharitable. She ridiculed people. She made everybody feel like they were dirt under her feet. Especially the poor ones, the uneducated ones. I didn't like them either, I admit. But at least I didn't mock them out. And when someone left, she'd tell how that person had got married, and was divorced, as punishment. She was kind of . . . aristocratic. She'd walk around like this"—Rose-Ann thrust her flat nose into the air—"all the time.

"I heard she's dead now. I hope she's paying a little bit. Not much, but a bit.

"She didn't like me; I don't know why. She would hear some other Sister walking along the corridor and yell out from her office, 'Slow down and don't walk so heavy, Sister.' Meaning me. Even when it wasn't me out there. She accused me of things all the time. We had twenty minutes to do our chores every morning, and she assigned me to clean two lavatories at opposite ends of the building—the toilets, the showers, the floors. I couldn't ever get the floor dry in time, so I would leave the windows and doors open. And I got into trouble for that. And I never had the guts to tell her, 'Lady, *Superwoman* couldn't do that in twenty minutes.' And twice she caught me in my free time reading textbooks in the classroom. She yelled at me and called me 'worldly.' Her idea of free-time activity was mending underwear."

In June 1961, Novice Catherine Dennis, twenty, was called to see Sister Mistress just before going on retreat to prepare to take temporary vows. Sister Mistress had decided novice Catherine Dennis didn't have a calling. Exit Catherine Dennis, with no further explanation, just a ticket home in the plain old name of Rose-Ann Martin, a young life's only ambition crushed.

"No, it wasn't devastating," Rose-Ann says, blowing her nose. "It was . . . cold. I didn't react for twenty years. It was as if someone had dropped something and broken it. It was as if Sister Mistress had said, 'Go get a dust mop and sweep this up.' It was just like that. I never reacted. It was like being just totally . . . I don't know.

"I never spoke about it for twenty years. Never spoke to my family about it. They never asked me. I think I didn't want to face my feelings and get angry. Ask me another question."

"What happened twenty years later?"

"I got a little more sure of myself."

"How?"

Rose-Ann cleans her cheeks; shrugs. "Probably watching all that women's lib stuff, during college. I'm not a feminist; I didn't believe all the stuff they doled out. But I could see that a lot of what they were saying— about the way women were treated—was true."

The Sisters of Charity had not, altogether, cast Rose-Ann loose. They had enrolled her in St. John's University, where she applied to study Latin. No one told her that "the women of the college" were not permitted to do this. When she arrived to take the Latin entrance exam, for which she had spent the summer preparing, a functionary explained the situation and asked if she had another language. Rose-Ann said French, and was sent off to take that exam instead. She trotted off down the corridor without protest. "If someone told me today that I couldn't sit an exam because I was a woman," Rose-Ann says, "I would look back at them and say, 'Who ya kiddin', lady?' " She passed the exam, spent most of the next fifteen years in full-time study (doctoral thesis: "Nature and the Cosmos in the Works of Rémy Belleau") and most of the rest in academia. Until now.

Nancy Piatkowski and her colleagues on the Liturgy Committee could be excused for thinking of Rose-Ann as a conservative, but that's not the sum of her. Labels don't come in her size. Enigmatic, perhaps. Combative, certainly. A stumbling block to the stereotype-enamored. She wouldn't dream of quarreling with the Pope's massive new catechism, but nor would she dream of standing in judgment over the cluster of gay male friends with whom she has eaten many boisterous meals over the years. She is a lay associate (or Third Order member) of the Dominicans, and her favorite TV shows are *Murder She Wrote* and Bills football games. She's revolted over the epidemic of child sexual abuse, but she also feels "bad" for the priests who, "ya gotta believe, have been fighting and falling, fighting and falling, for most of their lives."

She thinks it's a scandal that hardly anyone goes to confession between the biannual parish penance services, but admits she herself has gotten out of the habit, Saturday afternoons being inconvenient, with craft shows and what have you. She thinks there should be more "devotions" at St. Paul's, but personally finds the Stations of the Cross interminable and never says the Rosary. She votes Republican, wishes the U.S. bishops would steer clear of politics and economics in their pastorals, and adores Mother Angelica. Yet she feels quite at home with the liberal clergy of St. Paul's, loves the ensemble singing at the ten o'clock Mass, and, when traveling, would sooner attend a plain-clothes hand-holding Mass at a Newman Center college chaplaincy than the ancient but stuffy Tridentine Latin rites offered at selected churches in most major cities.

And while she's always ready for a good fight about liturgy, she thinks liturgists take the niceties too seriously. "It's not for *the people!*" she exploded after one Liturgy Committee meeting that winter. "It's for *God*, for crying out aloud. It can be the stinkiest lousiest liturgy you've ever seen in your entire life, but if it's a valid Mass, it makes present to us the death and resurrection of Christ; he has completed it but the Mass is our way of being present at it. It is the one point at which time and eternity meet. It is the total union of the Body of Christ. It spans time and space and unites the church triumphant in heaven, the church suffering in purgatory, and the church militant on earth. I know that's an old-fashioned way of saying it, but that's precisely what I believe. So, *who cares about the details?"* She delivered all this with the impassable glower she drops only rarely for a boyish smile that flashes up the sides of her lips and briefly warms her eyes from their usual metallic blue.

Perhaps, talking to Rose-Ann in her kitchen on a winter's afternoon when she's comfy in her XL Georgetown U. sweats and picking at a noodle casserole with an eye on the Bills' playoff game, you might be bold enough to suggest that, like many people who enjoy the sheer mental exercise of an argument, Rose-Ann habitually chooses the more provocative side, which just happens, in the St. Paul's Liturgy Committee, to be the right wing. And if you did, she might look up and issue a wheezy chortle that rocks her shoulders mightily, and whisper, "Oh, I'm a cream puff, really."

And then she might confide that the above-mentioned contradictions do not exhaust the paradoxes, that there are things she has done in her life that she simply won't talk about. Things that, if her best friend Marian read them in a book, she would never talk to Rose-Ann again.

"I don't know too many people who have had a priest come out of the confessional to apologize to them."

"What was that about?"

"I can't tell you that."

"Then why say anything about it at all?"

"Because . . . Because I wouldn't want you to think that everything I believe I learned in kindergarten and have believed ever since. For years, I believed differently."

"For example?"

"I won't tell you."

"Not even one example?"

"OK, one dumb example. A *clean* example. The ordination of women. I used to think they should change that. I still know there's nothing *theologically* against it. Even the church will tell you that. Otherwise, they'd be saying there's one baptism for guys and one for women. But it's not important to me anymore. It's tradition, and as long as the Pope says no, I think we should just go with it. It's not a big deal. It's peripheral."

"Compared to what, for instance?"

"OK, compared to the Real Presence of Christ in the Eucharist, for instance. I mean, look at these kids today and the way they behave at Mass. They have no idea what's really happening there. No idea, really. I'm sick and tired of hearing about the people of God, the people of God, the people of God. I'd like to hear about *God*, once in a while, for crying out loud."

"What difference would it make? If they understood the Real Presence?"

"A *lot*. It makes a *lot* of difference whether that's Christ you're holding in your hands or just a piece of bread in his memory."

"But *what* difference? Will they go to hell if they get it wrong?"

"Oh no, no, no."

"What, then?"

"OK. You . . . You can be a little less dishonest with yourself if you're really receiving Christ than if it's just a piece of bread in your hands. I never hear that talked about anymore. We are Catholics, not Methodists. We aren't better than those other people, but we shouldn't lose what we have. You cannot believe what you want and say you're a Catholic. To be a Catholic means to believe the Creed."

"But can't two Catholics believe the Creed in two different ways?"

"No."

"You believe it in the same way as everyone in the parish?"

"I hope so. I really do."

"But, seriously, do you think that?"

"No."

"Do you think you believe it in the same way as your priests do?"

"I hope so."

"But do you think so?"

(Pause.) "Yes, in fundamentals, I do. They teach straight doctrine, generally. Although I once heard Father Don say to a bunch of little kids, explaining the Mass to them, that during the Offertory they can doze off or go to the lavatory, as long as they wake up for the collection. I told him afterward, that was a dumb thing to say to kids.

"I go to the ten o'clock Mass Sundays because of the singing, but I'm telling you, one day this guy Father Bagley is gonna get punched out. I'm tired of hearing about his last week's agenda and all the people he saw and what he did. I mean, I don't give a damn, I really don't. On Trinity Sunday, his whole sermon was 'I kept thinking all week about what I was going to tell the people of St. Paul's about the Trinity.' He said it twenty times, going on and on about who he'd met and who he'd had lunch with. I wanted to shout, 'If you don't have anything to say about it, shut up and pray the *Glory Be* or something.' He could have said, 'It's a mystery, so let's just pray the *Glory Be*.' I mean, do your damn homework, and come in here and say what you're supposed to say.

"And I haven't heard them say anything vaguely on the subject of morality in years. I don't ever hear them talking about sin."

"And you think you should?"

"I *damn well* think we should."

"That's what the Pope seems worried about . . ."

"And he *damn well should* be worried about it. Especially in this country. My girlfriend, she was telling me, so excited, about how for the confirmation class she teaches, the kids are going to go to homeless shelters for a project. I said, 'Bullshit, Marian. Are you teaching them what they're supposed to know? Do they know their *doctrine?* Do they know what the *sacraments* are about? If they do, then, great, they can go to all the homeless shelters they want. But don't substitute all this crap for real doctrine.

"I teach in a *college*, for crying out loud. These kids don't know their faith. They don't have the slightest idea that abortion could possibly be wrong! They think everything's up for grabs! And I'm saying, if people don't know what it means to be a Catholic, you can have all the happy little things you want, and it's nothing."

"All these moral teachings—from abortion to masturbation, all that. Do you have to believe them all to be a Catholic?"

"You most certainly do, baby. *Or you do not belong.*"

"Is birth control on that list?"

"At my age, certainly!"

"But seriously?"

"OK. Philosophically, it is something you should believe. The rationale for it—the *rationale*—is true, I think."

"You're hedging."

"Because it's hard to explain. The contraceptive mentality leads to too many things. It leads to an attitude of 'We don't want to be inconvenienced, so let's get rid of it.' And so we get the whole mind-set. Unwanted children today, unwanted older people tomorrow. We have bought into secular thinking, and I think our young people are brainwashed because of it. And I think contraception is the start of it, because it's a way of not accepting responsibility."

"Yet you don't feel a need to condemn your gay friends?"

"Of course not. I wouldn't judge anybody, about anything." (Pause.) "Although I'm a little better about that now. There are certain questions I am more likely to take a stand on."

"For example?"

"Abortion. Euthanasia."

"And before?"

Long pause; ice-blue stare.

"How much of what I tell you will be in the book?"

"Everything, maybe."

Silence, then: "Look, I want to tell you something profound."

"OK."

"I could never conceive of myself as not Catholic. Not because I was born that way, but because I am baptized, and I have a relationship with the Trinity. And I couldn't conceive of living without that. I can't conceive of myself not receiving the Eucharist. I see these kids going off to the Hare Krishna and Zen and stuff, and that's fine for them, but we've been given all these treasures as Catholics and it breaks my heart that they can't see it.

"I've been badly treated by some people in the faith, but to me, that's not the church. There isn't a religion in the whole world that could possibly hold a candle to it. It sounds like I'm being snooty, but I'm not. I really don't care what the Muslims or the Buddhists believe, and I think it's quite possible that God would accept them all, but for myself, I can't conceive of believing anything else.

"It's like Mother Angelica says: 'You've only got one job, and that's to become a saint.'

"Or like this says it." And she hands over a text on parchment stock, her own calligraphy declaring in black and red a credo of John Henry Cardinal Newman, which she remembers reading as a young child:

God has created me to do him some definite service. He has committed some work to me which he has not committed to another.

I have my mission—I may never know it in this life, but I shall be told it in the next.

Somehow I am necessary for his purposes, as necessary in my place as an archangel is in his. If, indeed, I fail, he can raise another as he could make the stones children of Abraham.

Yet I have a part in this great work. I am a link in a chain, a bond of connection between persons. He has not created me for nothing.

I shall do good. I shall do his work. I shall be an angel of peace, a preacher of truth in my own place, while not intending it, if I do but keep his commandments and serve him in my calling.

Therefore, I will trust him. Whatever, wherever I am, I can never be thrown away. If I am in sickness, my sickness may serve him. If I am in sorrow, my sorrow may serve him.

My sickness, or perplexity, or sorrow may be necessary causes of some great end which is quite beyond us.

He does nothing in vain. He may prolong my life. He may shorten it. He knows what he is about.

He may take away my friends. He may throw me among strangers, he may make me feel desolate, make my spirits sink, hide the future from me—still he knows what he is about.

The carpet stretching north beneath old Ruthie Hemerlein's window was a speckled white now, and, like everyone at this time of year, Ruthie had been reminiscing a fair bit. As children, she remembered, she and her siblings had gathered twigs and branches during Advent in order to fashion crude "cradles" for the Christ child. On Christmas Eve, they would put these cradles under the tree for him to sleep in, safe and warm. And after the days of Christmas, the cradles were put away until Holy Week, when the kids tore them apart and fashioned a cross from the remains. Ruthie would place her cross on the orange crate that served (with a cover hand-sewn by her stepmother) as her bedside table, briefly replacing the statue of the Holy Mother that usually stood there. "The wood of the cradle makes the wood of the cross possible," her stepmother used to say, "and the wood of the cross makes the wood of the cradle viable."

Ruthie had often needed to ask what "viable" meant, and always forgot the explanation. But she got a vague sense that Christ "shares my suffering, which gives me hope that new life will come out of it." This hope had survived even through the dark time after her divorce, until an advertisement for a day of "renewal" for divorced and separated Catholics led her to make her confession and receive communion again for the first time in three years. A brief involvement with the charismatic renewal followed, reawakening an interest in the church that led her to join and lead groups of divorced and separated Catholics, during which period her renegade views about the indignities of church annulments earned her a stern talking-to at the diocesan Chancery. Ruthie stood her ground. "I said it wasn't in my game plan to marry again, but that if it were, I would get married any way I could get married, and I would remain as a practicing Catholic whether they liked it or not. Because *God's* the guy who judges me, not the Tribunal."

But Ruthie's encounter with Christian joy had also sparked a search for spirituality that, in time, led her to visit the town of Medjugorge in what used to be Yugoslavia but now belongs to war-torn Croatia. In Medjugorge, before and during the war years, many claim to have seen and heard the Virgin. Ruthie loses all traces of her usual ironic overlay when she talks about her prewar visit to Medjugorge. "I truly believe that I was in the presence of the Blessed Mother there," she says. "I didn't see her or hear her, but I really believe it.

"I didn't go over there with the idea of seeing or hearing exceptional things. I just figured I wanted to be on holy ground once in my life. They had a six o'clock Mass there every night, celebrated in Croatian, and I sat there in the pew and the sermon during Mass was by a Croatian priest and he must have talked for forty-five minutes. I didn't know a word of the language but inside of me I felt he was talking about love and forgiveness and repentance. And the next day we got the translation and that's what it was all about. Now, I couldn't have known that all on my own, could I?

"The next day, the others walked up a rocky hill called Cross Mountain, above the parish church, and it was like ninety-five degrees, and I was thirty pounds heavier than I am now, so I thought, 'I'm going to die if I go up,' so instead, I sat and prayed in a big meadow behind the church. And this little old lady came over and sat next to me. She was Italian, from Italy—you could tell because she smelled of garlic—and she yabber-yabbered in Italian and then the two of us sat there praying the Rosary, and all of a sudden, I don't know why, I started to cry. And the old lady put her arms around me, and I tell you, it was like the Lord had his arms around me. I'm going to cry now. This is silly. I just felt like I was in a very holy place. And I promised him then that I would do what I could to spread my faith—not to promote Catholicism, but to promote the message of repentance and prayer and loving."

Jamie Shaner's New Year's resolution was: "I will have fewer regrets." During Advent, she had found time almost daily to read and to reflect on the state of her life, and this thought had kept occurring to her. Too often, when leaving a doctor's office after a meeting about Tyler's asthma, she would pepper herself with accusations: "Why didn't I ask . . . ? Why didn't I press him on . . . ? Why do I feel too intimidated to change doctors?" And how hesitant she had been to confront Scotty's third-grade teacher over her reliance on handed-out dittos instead of activities that might test and stretch kids' minds. Even that time when the pizza she'd ordered to be delivered between Dick's arrival from the office and his and Scotty's fast departure for a Sabres game had arrived three quarters of an hour early, Jamie had said nothing, and everyone ate oven-dried pizza.

True, Jamie was capable of cutting remarks—as Father Don had discovered when she made her "What's in a name?" speech concerning the RCIA-versus-OCIA business at Mass last September. But that had been a momentary impulse—a passive-aggressive gesture perhaps, but not a conscious statement of opposition. Jamie had grown up in a house where raised voices and dissension were unthinkable. She had always been awed by people who spoke their minds freely and confidently. Surely, if she did the same, her world would not fall apart.

Fewer regrets, Jamie promised herself. Next time someone delivered a pizza early, back it would go.

Jamie's quest for assertiveness was immediately clothed with religious fervor. For Jamie was a worldly kind of mystic, who considered ordinary maturity a part of true spirituality. Not that she would use the word "mystic" about herself; Jamie was still, at times, self-conscious even about the word "spirituality." Such words had been foreign to her a decade ago. Before Cory.

Three weeks after the stillborn Cory's quiet burial in the Garden of Angels—an event of which Jamie, still in shock, retained only a cloudy memory—Father Paul had presided over a memorial Mass. From the options offered them, Jamie and Dick had chosen readings from Lamentations—*It is good to wait in silence for the Lord God. . . . The favors of the Lord are not exhausted, his mercies are not spent*—and the Gospel of John, where Jesus weeps over the death of his friend Lazarus and promises: "Did I not assure you that if you believed you would see the glory of God?" Tom Johnson, the ensemble leader, had suggested a new hymn composed by himself, which always afterward would bring Jamie's tears: *As the sparrow finds a home in you / and the swallow makes a nest in you / so my soul yearns for you / the living God. . . .*

It was true: now that she lived in the shadow of death, Jamie's soul yearned. The memorial service behind them, she and Dick tried to get on with their lives, and Dick had somewhat more success—taking up golf that summer helped him a lot. But Jamie seemed fused with death. She visited Cory's grave once a week, and paged through the album she and Dick had carefully filled with mementos (the first sonogram, the pregnancy calendar with which Scotty had awaited his baby brother, the hospital ID tag, the "fetal death" certificate, the snapshot—tiny face emerging from receiving blanket, closed eyes, Jamie's delicate overbite). Someone gave them a copy of Rabbi Harold Kushner's *When Bad Things Happen to Good People* and Jamie read it, found it wise, gentle, and ultimately unhelpful.

She felt she had to find some meaning in her son's death; only years later would she come to think of death and pain as something that happens despite, not within, God's meaning. She and Dick paid one visit to a support group for parents who had lost a baby, and Jamie was repelled by the sound of people sobbing out their grief four or five years after the death. She was determined not to be like this, yet slowly she felt doors closing in her mind, leaving her trapped in a black and empty room. Her doctor referred her to a psychologist, and the talking helped, some.

It was more than nine months after Cory that Jamie—now pregnant again—felt the doors in her mind opening again. She found herself pointed toward God. She would sit in church waiting for Mass to begin and when

Father Paul came out in his robes, she would be overwhelmed by his presence; she felt there was an aura around him. Or Tom Johnson's ensemble would play a song and sometimes she would feel raw sadness, but sometimes an awareness of something else, something better. From then on, she was prone to unheralded waves of gooseflesh, a feeling of movement deep inside her that she could not comprehend. It felt as if (she could find no better way to describe it) her soul were dancing. Before, she had believed in God and heaven and so forth, but she had believed it, as many do, for want of having thought about it much. Now, she *felt* it. God shared her sadness, and God would help her understand.

Even so, the mental pain remained huge. Jamie was just coming out of her despondency, and Dick was settling into his second golfing summer and his first on the Parish Council, when she miscarried. "God damn it," Dick said when she started bleeding, "enough already." His wife was being tormented by nightmares about death, and the nightmares increased when she got pregnant again. After Tyler was born, Jamie remained terrified to be alone with the boys at home when Dick worked late. She pictured herself being bludgeoned to death by an intruder; she feared the pain less than she feared death itself.

Jamie's nightmares began fading around the time Tyler began crawling; now, it was Dick who stayed home nights with the kids, at least on Thursday nights. For Jamie had at last found a niche at St. Paul's, having heard a Mass appeal for RCIA sponsors and started going to Inquiry sessions. She was struck, more than anything else, by the ordinariness of the people in the catechumenate, both searchers and guides. It suggested the possibility of being "spiritual" without being a fanatic. An evening might be devoted to exploring forms of prayer, or to discussing what kind of man Jesus was. One time, they just played a tape of the sound of a brook while looking at a picture of Jesus, and then talking about what each had seen or felt. Thursday nights at the parish center became partly a peaceful refuge from a confusing world and partly a place to grapple with the confusion, to figure things out. And Judy Nice became a model for Jamie's nascent spirituality.

Jamie's first year as an RCIA sponsor was a time to discover the magic of liturgy. It began with the Rite of Welcoming—signing her catechumen's ears, eyes, lips, heart, and hands, Jamie was flooded with intense, unnameable feeling. On the following Holy Thursday, when a young priest went on hands and knees to wash her feet, it was as if she were in the Upper Room with Jesus himself. Dick too grew more serious about his faith, but it was Jamie who was now moved to tears even at an ordinary Sunday Mass, and Jamie who, when the tears had passed, would look around at people in the adjoining pews and wonder how it was possible for them to sit there filing their nails as if nothing was happening.

With two young sons, a part-time bookkeeping job, and all this dancing going on in her soul, the last thing Jamie needed was another pregnancy. For years, she had known vividly when she was ovulating, and after Tyler, she used her diaphragm at those times. She felt ready to have her tubes tied, but wanted to be totally sure before taking the step. Many couples she knew had decided on vasectomies, but Jamie, who was clearest about two being enough, wanted to be the one to do it. Except, she *wasn't* sure. There might be no essential difference in church teaching between the mortal sins of voluntary sterilization and day-to-day contraception, but there was something about the surgery, something indefinable, that troubled Jamie's spirit. It had to do with the irreversibility; with making a permanent alteration to her body for what seemed "purely selfish reasons." She didn't think this had anything to do with being a newly reborn Catholic; she just wanted to know it would sit right with God. For now, she would stick with the diaphragm.

And then came the one night, in the winter of 1991, when things moved too fast. Jamie knew what time of the month it was, and when her period didn't come, she fell apart. Another baby, now, seemed too much to cope with. Jamie started spending hours sitting at home, doing nothing but mouth, over and over again, the words "I can't do this."

For days, she kept going over it in her mind, not fully understanding what her dilemma was. She couldn't see herself having an abortion. Not after Cory. Her circumstances were certainly not terrible enough to justify it. But right then, she could understand more clearly than ever how a woman could make that choice. And what if she was *not* pregnant? She couldn't keep going on like this from month to month. And then again, what if she *was* pregnant? "I can't do this." The circle was unending. Even when her period came a week later, Jamie felt unable to move on. Still, she delayed making the move to sterilization. She seemed to have a permanent headache.

Her friend Leslie called. Leslie had endured a long struggle both with infertility and with the sensibilities of the clinic of a Catholic hospital whose intricate compromises with the church's teaching against artificial insemination had included making a pin-prick in a condom which was then used during intercourse for sperm collection. (The pin-prick made it possible, theoretically, for conception to happen naturally.) Jamie poured out her confusion, and Leslie said, among other things, that she was sure that Jamie would make the best decision a thinking and spiritual person could make. When she put down the phone, Jamie no longer had a headache, but felt no closer to a decision. That night, at Inquiry, she decided to tell the group what was going on in her mind.

It all came out like a steam train, but without the rails. Finally, she came to her point: the church had its teachings, about birth control for instance, and abortion for that matter, "but sometimes a person has to do what's right for you." What followed was the most excruciating evening Jamie ever spent in Inquiry. The group polarized at once; some were sympathetic, some outraged. People pounded fists. Did Jamie know what an abortion *was*? Of course she knew, she was just saying that maybe you have to look at life's decisions in the light of life's situations. That maybe, in the end, people have to answer to their own consciences and their own relationship with God; maybe they didn't need any extra guilt. The fist-pounding continued; anatomical descriptions of fetuses were provided. Later, in another room, a member of the group asked Jamie if she could talk, and sobbed out a confession of having had an abortion some time before.

Three years later, Jamie still thinks people should be allowed to follow their own consciences. She still has not made an appointment to have her tubes tied. She says she no longer sees an aura around Father Paul, and believes that "people like Dick and me are the church too, with or without Father Paul." She still can be moved to tears by a Mass, but it happens less often. She says she no longer fears death. "Before," she says, "my whole focus was what I did and what I had. It wasn't that I didn't believe in heaven, but I feared leaving the here and now, because all this"—a sweep of her slim wrist taking in the house, her things, the city—"was all I knew. Now it just seems like there's so much more than this, so it's not so scary to think of losing it. Because there's more to me."

It was quite a month, that January, for the writing and receiving of letters. Ken Monaco, the Pope's main man, wrote to the editorial page of the Buffalo *News*, adding to the burning correspondence ignited by Father John Aurelio's confession that he had had sex with minors. "The real source of scandal," Ken wrote, "is the moral relativism implicitly and explicitly found at all levels of moral education, in almost all denominations. The pedophile and the homosexual certainly represent a serious moral/sinful disorder, but this tendency would be eradicated if religion and society together shaped a culture that made sexual responsibility and control the norm. . . ."

Competing explanations for unpriestly misconduct abounded. Most of the *News* letters followed the well-beaten path of blaming either homosexuality or celibacy or both. Church leaders responded that celibacy had nothing to do with it. (Didn't most abuse occur in families? Hadn't nearly 2,000 scoutmasters been removed by the Boy Scouts of America in the past two decades because of suspicions of molestation?) Gay advocates pointed out that many pedophiles are heterosexuals, and most gays don't molest children.

Few laity at St. Paul's asked Paul Whitney what he thought; to those who did, he confessed to being mystified about the epidemic's cause, but made no secret of his scorn for bishops who had routinely covered up allegations of misconduct for as long as he had been a priest—and who sometimes went on to recommend the culprits for the papal honorific of Monsignor (which was one reason he himself never used the title).

"It's a deflating and excruciating time to be a priest," the pastor said in early January. "It makes me want to cover my collar when I go to the bank. I think I've kept my own personal life pretty clean. I'm not totally free of slips here and there, but I'm happy to say it's women I love—nothing like betraying the trust of children."

Whitney thinks priestly celibacy should be made optional, as it was until about the tenth century, but he does not think celibacy has much to do with the rash of abuse. "It's not just priests," he points out. "Lots of doctors, psychologists, teachers, and lawyers have been called into question. But I'll grant this: it'll be even tougher to defend celibacy in the future, to bring it out as a virtue and a gift." He grants too that when celibacy was made synonymous with the priesthood, a caste was established that became attractive to men with sexuality problems. "It's a place for a man to hide," the pastor says.

Jamie Shaner agrees on all counts, but what bugs her is the failure of most bishops and priests, including Father Paul, to address the enormity of the crisis head-on. Jamie is clear in her own mind that the real meaning of the epidemic of molestations has less to do with sex and celibacy than with the imbalance of power in the church. Where power is concentrated in a few, she says, it is likely to be abused. The solution, in Jamie's mind, is to diminish the power of the clergy—and to allow all baptized people to be considered for ordination. "Letting women in would help a lot," she says with a sardonic smile that makes it difficult to gauge the intensity of her seriousness. "We'd be a good influence on the guys. Maybe they could learn something from us."

What of Rome's sacramental argument—that only male priests can fully represent Jesus Christ at the altar? Jamie's only response is to turn up her eyes like a Valley girl and say, "Like, I'm SO-rry, I don't THINK so."

You can never be sure which Jamie you'll meet next. The Valley girl makes only rare appearances alongside the sardonic critic, the sensuous young mother, the occasionally coarse bookkeeper, the nascent mystic weeping as her soul dances to God's music. But that January, the Jamie most in evidence was the fighter. "No regrets."

After Father Don "forgot" to announce the Christmas carol event, Dick had taken the draft letter of protest to the Adult Formation Committee, which had duly endorsed it:

. . . We would like further review of the policy and procedure for making announcements after Mass, to publicize parish-wide events and programs. Although we accept Father Don's apology that the failure to read what we had prepared was inadvertent, we believe that a clear, written policy with an established procedure would help avoid this from happening in the future. . . .

The letter was presented to the Parish Council by Dick Shaner on Wednesday, January 19, a day the snow was so heavy and the temperatures so low, at minus 20, that even in Kenmore, which prides itself on clearing the streets and sidewalks, the schools were closed.

The timing was not brilliant. Early in the meeting, Father Don had stood up to announce his impending leave of absence. He had expressed his growing doubt in his own vocation and said that while the exact period of leave had yet to be determined, it would begin sometime in February. He carefully stated that this development had nothing to do with recently revealed "improprieties" by two fellow priests, and finished by asking for prayers, "that I may find happiness and fulfillment whatever the future holds."

Perhaps because Father Don's news had already leaked out quite widely, no expressions of shock followed. A few minutes later, Dick Shaner presented the Adult Formation Committee's report and its letter to the Parish Council—a letter that just happened to address the departing vicar's chief area of responsibility and pride—liturgy. In the verbal brawl that followed, it seemed everyone present had a gripe about parish worship—from the limits on announcements to the Liturgy Committee's insistence that anyone reading a lesson at Mass should attend a training session first. The rule, in the view of some councillors, was insulting to a parish with a more than adequate degree of literacy.

In Father Don's mind, there was no doubt as to who was behind this final assault on his work: Jamie Shaner. The young vicar had been reserving a special rage for "Miss Bitch," as he thought of her, ever since hearing her "What's in a name?" speech. That September morning, Father Don had only barely fought down the impulse to stand up in church and respond to her presentation. "I was ready to rip her face off," he would remember with heat more than a year later. "I didn't really know Jamie well, but until that day I'd respected what I'd seen of her—how involved she was, how committed and everything. But when she did what she did at that Mass, I said to myself, 'She's got a mean streak—I'll stay away from that.'"

But the former parochial vicar sees more than the clash of personalities that the Shaners speak of. He sees a fundamental conflict over authority.

"Let's face it," he says, "the church talks a good act about the people being in charge, but in reality it's the priest who's in charge. In the documents of Vatican II, there was this sense of empowering the people, but in practice the clergy still have the last word. We're groomed in seminary to the idea that we, the priests, are always the instructors. We bring the people along in our vision, according to our mind-set, rather than letting them follow their own.

"In the same way, especially for financial matters, the buck stops with the pastor. Downtown, they're not thinking, 'What are the people doing in that parish?' They're thinking, 'What is *he* doing?'

"But it only goes so far. Gone are the days when the priest's word was the ultimate. Because of Vatican II and the '70s, the people don't trust the clergy. Many of them think they got screwed over. They're, like, 'The clergy changed everything on us, and we've gotta keep an eye on them or just as we start getting comfortable they'll pull the rug out from under us again.' You see that very much with the conservative laity, who think they're now the watchdogs of faith and orthodoxy, as if they have been ordained. And they certainly make you feel as if they're the true Catholics and you're a piece of doo-doo.

"And of course, on the other hand, the clergy have never trusted the people. Because part of our ordination is that *we* are the ones charged with upholding the faith.

"In a parish like St. Paul's, the way we had it set up, the way we envisioned a parish where the people are being empowered, there was obviously more of a tendency for that tension to exist. Whereas in some parishes, where the pastor has all the power and everyone knows it, there's no tension. So we almost set ourselves up for power struggles."

What, then, was this tumult that had beset St. Paul's, this squall of hostility whose waves were, even now, still building to full height? A clash of personalities? Absolutely. An organizational power struggle? That too. But perhaps it was also something more central to modern Catholicism—something specific to the celibacy of the priesthood.

It starts with inexperience—the fact that the average celibate priest knows little of the give-and-take that the rest of us must exercise daily in relationships at work and at home. But there is also a more crucial difference of perspective. Even the most liberal-minded celibate looks at the church from a point of view many miles from that enjoyed by even the most committed lay leader. For any priest, the parish is much more than a job—it is his life. For lay leaders like Dick and Jamie Shaner, it is closer to, well, a hobby.

Imagine how politics would change if the law obliged the President of the United States to forsake spouse and family. Even the most liberal commander in chief might be forgiven for saying, if only to himself, "What does Congress know about what this country needs? I gave up my life for my people, and those schmoes on the Hill go home every night to eat with their spouses and play with their kids and make love to whomever." Likewise the "celibate" manager of the Yankees, the "celibate" CEO of General Motors, and the "celibate" minister at First Presbyterian: they too might justifiably question the commitment of first basemen, middle managers, and church elders. Sooner or later, whether it's a question of liturgical order or financial control, there will come a time when a priest has had enough of being second-guessed.

Thus, Father Don: "I mean, if Jamie were putting on an addition to her house, she wouldn't do it herself—she'd go to an expert. But she doesn't allow for the same kind of thing in the church. There are certain areas where we, the priests, have the training, and sometimes you have to rely on the experts to make judgments for you.

"I think when Jamie hit out at me she was using me subconsciously as a scapegoat for the hierarchy in general. Because I would say our theologies are very close, mine and Jamie's. But I represented the authority of the church, and Ken Monaco, for example, even though his theology was *very* different from hers, well, he was just some dumb fuck who didn't make a difference."

Personality did, of course, come into it. Dick and Jamie directed their anger not at the saintly Father Dick, nor at Father Paul, who had nursed her through grief and recovery. It was in the junior vicar, so free with his opinions and so quick to sarcasm, that they found a central-casting bad guy.

"I admit that I brushed Dick off when he raised it," Father Don says of the omitted carols announcement. "I had forgotten it altogether, and then remembered just before the noon Mass, and a lot of people were wanting my attention just then, and then I just kind of decided quickly not to put it in. And then when he raised it with me I just wanted him off my back. Because it was part of the truth: I *had* decided. . . . But the other part was true too: I had forgotten. And yes, I didn't like announcements. *None* of the three of us priests liked announcements. And here was this big deal about a stupid little announcement.

"It wasn't until the Parish Council that I realized it was still a big deal. And at the meeting, I had basically spilled my guts to that group, and that didn't seem to matter.

"That night, it took everything in me to stop myself from getting up and saying to Dick Shaner, 'Ef you, I don't need this shit anymore,' and leaving right then."

By now, the disillusioned Dick Shaner, despite his personal affection for Father Paul, had expressed to a few fellow parishioners his belief that St. Paul's was being run by a "lame-duck pastor" with his eyes on the door and little enthusiasm for anything but the restoration campaign. As if to support this thesis, Paul Whitney was not present at the Parish Council that frigid January night. The pastor's planned New Year's in Florida had been ruined by several inconveniently timed funerals and instead he was taking a brief holiday at a friend's home in Middleport, New York. Housebound by a blizzard, the pastor spent the evening morosely watching coverage of the latest California earthquake.

A tremor of a different kind shook Judy Nice's mail tray the next morning:

Dear Judy,

I may be slow but I eventually get the point.

After my public humiliation by Jamie at that 10 o'clock Mass in the fall, after Dick's blowup and accusations after the noon Mass in December, after the letter to the Parish Council from the Adult Formation Committee regarding my having the announcement canned, I now realize there is a conspiracy against me and my ministry and my judgment.

If you and your committee feel I have slighted you in any way, I'm sorry, for that has never been my intention. It is a real crime and shame when innocent human error is blown so out of proportion as to be turned into a personal attack.

All I can say is that I am glad I am leaving because it would be impossible to continue to work under these kinds of circumstances with people like that.

Don

When Judy showed the departing vicar's note to Jamie, the latter's equal and opposite fury sent her home to her computer. There, she issued a three-page piece of her mind, addressed to Father Don and encrusted with an edge of bile so thick as to surprise even herself.

Jamie read her draft over once, then read it again:

> . . . If you found this "public humiliation," I question your ability to assess a situation for what it is. . . . To accuse me of conspiring against you is perhaps the most ludicrous idea I have ever heard. . . . I have had very little personal contact with you. All I know of you is what I have heard you say in your official capacity as a priest. Let me cite for you some of the things that I have heard you say in that capacity as a priest that have led me to the opinion I have of you. . . .

Jamie listed a half dozen ill-considered utterances she had heard from the provocative young priest's lips on various occasions since his arrival in the parish—concerning, among other things, his own unenthusiasm for the sacrament of Reconciliation, the Pope's incompetence, and the U.S. bishops' collective lack of "balls." She concluded:

> I cannot begin to count the number of times I have overheard you speaking unkindly—no, maliciously—sometimes about people I know, and other times about people I do not. . . . These are but a sampling of the reasons why I dislike you, distrust you, and disrespect you. But to accuse me of conspiring against you—you grossly overestimate your influence in my life. On the other hand, you really underestimate my abilities. If I had conspired against you, my efforts would have been far more tenacious than what you have imagined. . . .
>
> To say that you could never work with people like us—I'm sure you are very right about that. Our center is our God; our focus is community, sharing, and giving.
>
> I personally feel you have made a very wise decision. Hopefully your time away will bring you clarity about your future, whatever it may be.

"No regrets" being the order of the year, Jamie wrote Father Don's name on an envelope and delivered her letter, uncensored, to the junior curate's mail tray in the rectory. She also left copies for Father Paul and Father Dick.

Father Don had that morning left for Washington, D.C., where he was to undergo his psychiatric assessment—and where, ironically, he would meet up with a man with whom he would experience uncompromised romantic happiness for the first time in his life. Sunday evening, Jamie read over her letter, found some typing errors, and decided to switch the letter she had left in the mail tray for a clean copy. But when she went back to the rectory on Monday, she found the original letter missing from Father Don's pile. She went home and right away called the pastor. She knew, without asking, that Father Paul, acting as peacemaker and head of the "family," had pulled the letter from the tray after receiving his copy.

"Yes, dear, I have it right here," the pastor drawled, his calm voice betraying nothing of the astonishment he had felt in encountering the fiery, smug version of Jamie in her letter.

"Well, Father," Jamie said, "we need to talk about this, because I do want him to have that letter." They set a date for talking: Saturday afternoon, the twenty-ninth, at the Shaners' place.

"What you said in that letter is very, very true," Father Paul said after the Shaners' boys had been greeted and dismissed. "And I know it's not your penchant to write this kind of tough stuff. Don probably needs to hear it too, but whether he will be ready to hear it the moment he comes back from his screening in Washington, I'm not sure. I would hope that you trust me enough to make sure that when I sit down and talk to him about the contents of this letter, he'll be ready to hear it."

Jamie noticed that the words used by the pastor were not exactly a promise to pass on the letter itself. This seemed out of line; Father Paul had no more right to screen the mail than did the U.S. Postal Service.

This time, even for Father Paul, she was not going to say, "Yes, Father."

Instead, she said, "Maybe Father Don *needs* to see that letter. If he's leaving, he's not gonna have you running interference for him out there. And if he thinks it's tough where he is now, good luck to him in the real world, where he doesn't have a nice warm house and a maid that cooks and cleans and vacuums. And maybe my letter will let him see for just a moment how he affected someone."

The pastor nodded, agreed once again that Jamie had a point. She looked at him searchingly and he gazed back at her with his placid hazel eyes. He *still* had not said he'd release her missive.

"Father Paul, you have to promise me that you will give him this letter."

"Don't worry, I'll take care of it, dear," the pastor said, and Jamie knew, for sure, that his idea of taking care of it was very different from hers.

On the thirtieth, when Jamie saw Father Don at Mass, back from Washington and still in his priest's robes, she suddenly felt more angry at her pastor than she had ever thought she could be. "I'm not on his staff," she exploded to Dick after Mass. "He's not my boss. I'm a person who wrote a letter. He had no right!" So she went back to her computer, printed out another copy of her letter to Father Don, and sent it off again—in the mail, this time, without a return address. She added a covering note:

> This letter was pulled from your box by Father Paul with the understanding that he would choose the way to best handle this with you. I need to know without a doubt that you have seen my letter in its entirety.

A few days later, Jamie heard that Father Don, having finally received Bishop Head's permission for a leave of absence, had moved out of the rectory. Jamie has not seen or heard from him since. She never discussed the second letter with Father Paul, but has heard through Judy that he was furious with her for defying him.

What Jamie still does not know is that Father Don opened her letter in the rectory kitchen on a day when he was busy packing his personal effects. He read the covering note only, and handed the letter to Father Paul.

"Um, do I need to see this, Paul?"

The pastor folded the letter into a pocket. "It can wait," he said.

One Note Too Many

In Rapids, neither water nor rock gets damaged, but swimmers beware. That February, Judy Nice, flung between current and stone, felt bruised all over. The inner peace of last summer's retreat—*Is your God so small . . . ?*—had been churned by the storms of winter. She could have endured December's toppling of the previously esteemed John Aurelio. She could have withstood January's rage-laced letters. But within weeks, Judy had been caught in a maelstrom around the issue that she perceived as her weakest spot as a Catholic teacher: the freedom of Catholic conscience. When Ken Monaco and Dennis Hurley simultaneously determined to make stands for the authority of Rome, Judy floundered.

Father Don's accusation of conspiracy, with the hint of assigning blame for his own career change, had stung. The letter cast her, not for the first time, on the wrong side of an "us-them" divide in which—despite Judy's official status as a member of the ministerial staff—"us" still seemed reserved for men in black. On the Sunday after that letter showed up in her mail tray, Judy felt tears unaccountably welling up during Mass. Later, in the rectory dining room, she had to leave the catechumens three times in hastily convened discussion groups while she went off alone to gather herself.

It became an open secret that Judy was "losing it," although no one,

Judy included, really understood what was going on. Many times, she said to Jamie Shaner, "I don't know, I just don't think I can go on doing this." In a series of painful interviews with Father Paul, Judy had laid out her feeling of confusion and anger. After the Christmas carols fight, she had pleaded for better communication among the parish staff; after the Aurelio confession, she had urged the pastor to address head-on the epidemic of abuse; after Father Don's letter, she had simply poured out her heart. Each time, she had tried and failed to stem the tears, and then hated herself for being "unprofessional." Each time, the pastor offered his usual smiles, hugs, and supportive words. And each time, without Father Paul's letting slip a trace of judgment or complaint beyond the near-constant look of tiredness around his eyes, Judy went away feeling vaguely guilty for bothering him, and vaguely ashamed for not having turned the other cheek. She also felt, rightly or wrongly, that the pastor was sparing his most heartfelt sympathy for his fellow clergy. He kept saying lately that this was a hard time to be a priest. Judy saw this, but wished Father Paul would acknowledge with equal passion how hard it had become to be a Catholic laywoman.

By the first week of February, when Father Don was moving his things from the rectory and beginning his search for a job in hotels or restaurants, Judy was fantasizing daily about writing a letter of her own: quitting her job and, with it, all official involvement in the Catholic Church. Wherever she looked these days, she saw a church in decay. Judy wanted no part in it, or certainly not a leadership part. She compared being in the pay of "Institution Church" (as she had begun calling it, as distinct from the grass-roots "People of God") to being married to an alcoholic. To stay in the "marriage" and remain silent about the problem at its core, she felt, was to tolerate and foster the problem. More and more, she doubted that Christ had contemplated "Institution Church"—with its finery, its laws, its secrecy, and its all-male power structure—when he sent his disciples out to spread the Good News.

Did God want her to stay in the job? Judy had stopped asking the question that way. Along with her doctrine teacher Dan Liderbach, she knew only one thing about "God's will" for her: that God wanted her "to be human." She doubted God cared whether she stayed in her job or quit it, just so long as she was true to herself.

And yet. She loved the rituals as much as ever, loved the healing that she had seen the sacraments effect in people's lives, and the part she herself played in delivering that healing. Just the other day, Jeff Tredo had finally received his annulment; that made seven adults eligible to be grafted into the church this Easter. How could she not be there with them? How could she explain it to them?

But. That was like staying in a dead marriage for the sake of the kids—no great favor to anyone.

But again, her own life had changed profoundly since she had left her former aimlessness and joined in the annual cycle of healing, repentance, rebirth, and growth that is the sacramental year. Some women she knew spoke of getting the same sense of belonging and meaning, or better, from house churches that were led by and for women. But Judy couldn't imagine forfeiting the liturgical richness that she had come to love, or dropping the Mass-going habit of a lifetime. Nor could she easily discard a job that—when she was actually doing it rather than talking about it—she still loved with her whole heart. And for what? To return to housewifeliness? To look for a secretary's job?

It seemed impossible—at least as impossible as staying.

She would hang in, Judy decided each time she worked her way through the questions. Until Easter anyway. Then, if things were no clearer—well, she would have to wait and see.

Such was Judy's state of mind as February dawned. Of course, she had no clue what Ken Monaco had up his sleeve for Sunday morning, February 6, when he was next due to lead a session of the catechumenate. And neither Judy nor Ken knew anything about the letter that Dennis Hurley planned to deliver that same morning.

What Ken had was an article in the latest issue of *The Catholic World Report*. It was printed under a triumphant banner. "Start the Presses!" it read. "After months of delay, aggravated by sharp controversy, the English translation of the universal Catechism is ready for publication."

What followed was a short introduction followed by an interview with Monsignor Michael Wrenn, pastor of St. John the Evangelist in Manhattan and special consultant for religious education to John Cardinal O'Connor.

The introduction noted that the new *Catechism of the Catholic Church* had been available in French for over a year, but that the English translation originally produced by authority of a committee headed by Bernard Cardinal Law, Archbishop of Boston, had been delayed amid reports of "heavy opposition." This was an understatement—the Vatican had rejected the translation and ordered it heavily revised. Resistance was futile: the *Catechism* was, after all, nothing less than the crowning glory of John Paul II's pontificate—the first "universal Catechism" since the Council of Trent produced an authorized summary of Catholic doctrine during the Counter-Reformation of the sixteenth century. Wholly unlike the Baltimore Catechism of 1885, a series of simple questions and answers about dogma aimed at semiliterate American immigrants, the new document was a nuanced and complete description of official doctrine, intended mainly as a reference for generations of church leaders worldwide and as a source book for teaching materials well into the next century.

Monsignor Wrenn had, as the magazine put it, "taken a keen interest" in the production of the 698-page *Catechism*—keen enough for him to co-author an article alleging "hundreds" of errors in the first English translation. The final version of the *Catechism* had corrected these "errors."

Ken Monaco drew a large arrow in the *World Report* margin, its head pointing at "hundreds of errors," which Ken underlined. He added a thick, stubby arrow with a circle around it as the Manhattan monsignor explained:

> Quite a few of the errors were *not* minor points. There are places where elements have been dropped from the French original, places where new elements have mysteriously appeared, and quite a few places where the "error" in translation turns out to be a bit more serious than a simple mistake—places where a careful reader can see a theological bias at work.

Another thick arrow pointed to "the most persistent problem of that sort," which involved the first translation's use of sexually inclusive language. Monsignor Wrenn ascribed this effort to "feminist ideology," and said the rejected translation had taken "extraordinary liberties with the text in order to avoid criticism on these ideological grounds." He went on:

As it turns out, that situation arises three times within the very first paragraph of the *Catechism* itself. If the original translation had been approved, we would have been taught that God created "the human race," that God is "close to us," and that God "gathers the human race." In each case, the French uses the word *l'homme*, "man." . . . God became incarnate not as a genderless "human being," but as a male—a "man" by any definition you choose.

Beyond inclusive language, Wrenn said Cardinal Law's committee had, at times, gone beyond "authentic Catholic teaching" to offer "its own new and unauthorized version of that Catholic tradition." As examples, he cited the committee's avoidance of the words "sacred" and "obedience," of the terms "mortal sin" and "grave sin," and of all references to "Holy Mother church."

Ken Monaco marked that paragraph too, with a long and gracefully curved arrow. Turning the page, he framed with not one but two arrows a barbed exhortation from the Pope:

> I pray that the church in the United States will recognize in the *Catechism* an authoritative guide to sound and vibrant preaching, an invaluable resource for parish Adult Formation programs, a basic text for the upper grades of Catholic high schools, colleges, and universities.

Ken underlined the papal phrase, "an invaluable resource for parish Adult Formation programs." It seemed to Ken that, with an opportunity before him to lead that very week's catechumenate program, it would be a great shame not to tell the candidates about the *Catechism*. Had not the Holy Father also described the book as a "precious, splendid, profound, and timely gift for all"?

On February 6, Ken decided, he would present the gift.

When the *Catechism* finally hit America's bookshelves, David Briggs, the Associated Press religion correspondent, would write:

Muslims can be saved. Paying low wages and cheating on taxes are sins. Artificial insemination is morally unacceptable. This is not your old-style Roman Catholic catechism. . . .

Gone are the Council of Trent's anathemas hurled at non-Catholics, replaced by declarations that God's covenant with Jews is irrevocable and that Muslims are included in God's plan of salvation.

In addition to upholding the authority of the hierarchy and bans on sex outside marriage, the new catechism catalogs a list of modern sins such as tax fraud and the payment of low wages and declares the arms race to be "one of the greatest curses on the human race." . . .

The new catechism incorporates many of the revolutionary changes in the church since Vatican II, and even delves into the latest questions of medical ethics.

Discontinuing burdensome medical procedures on dying individuals is legitimate, the catechism declares, but an act intended to cause death even to eliminate suffering is considered murder. . . . Prenatal diagnosis is gravely opposed to moral law when it is done with the thought of possibly inducing an abortion.

But scholars and many U.S. prelates say the real significance of the catechism, taken along with the papal encyclical *The Splendor of Truth* released last fall, is its unapologetic effort to uphold church teaching in an age in which individual values and beliefs often supersede doctrine.

Ken Monaco says he never felt a need to ask Judy's opinion on his plan to tell the catechumens about the *Catechism*. He had had enough of dining-room chatter that steered clear of every troubling question of faith. For Ken, if these gatherings were not a place to study the teachings of the church, then they were missing the mark. This was a *catechumenate*, after all—how could the *Catechism* be out of bounds?

And so, on February 6, it was Ken Monaco who led the catechumens to the altar step after the homily and received the book of the Word of God from Father Gary with the dismissal: ". . . and may the Lord be with you there."

As usual, the group left by the sanctuary door and went quietly through the sacristy, where Pat Blum was leading the children in their version of the prayers, the solemn biddings and ragged falsetto responses coming from all corners of the sacristy carpet.

"Pray for, um-um, for my mom."

"OK, for Mrs. Mayfield, we pray to the Lord:"

"Lord, hear our prayer."

"I pray for my uncle who died in a war."

"OK, we pray for all of those who died during a war. We pray to the Lord:"

"Lord, hear our prayer."

"For my grandma who died."

"OK, for *all* those who have died, we pray to the Lord:"

"Lord, hear our prayer."

"My favorite dog died."

"Mmm. OK, for, ah, for all our favorite pets that may have died, we pray to the Lord:"

"Lord, hear our prayer."

"My grandma died too."

"OK, for *all* who have died—ah, we prayed that already, OK?"

"Um, for the poor."

"Yes! We pray for the poor:"

"Lord, hear our prayer."

"And, um, for those who are sick?"

"Mm-huh, we pray to the Lord:"

"Lord, hear our prayer."

"And patients in the hospital?"

"Well, I think that's kinda covered by 'those who are sick,' don't you? . . ."

In the dining room, when the catechumens had filled their mugs and the Word of God had been placed on the big table along with a candle and doughnut boxes, Ken explained that Judy was taking a rare opportunity to attend Mass with her family and would join the group later. He asked someone to read that day's second lesson, from the first letter of Paul to the Corinthians: *Preaching the gospel is not the subject of a boast; I am under compulsion and have no choice. I am ruined if I do not preach it! If I do it willingly, I have my recompense; if unwillingly, I am nonetheless entrusted with a charge.* . . .

Ken said that, like the apostle Paul, every Christian was under a compulsion to speak the truth, even if it was not accepted by many. His mandate thus identified, Ken launched into his presentation, talking fast and loud with his usual sweeping hand movements. Hunched over an impressive pile of books and papers, he quoted frequently from *The Catholic World Report*, summarizing the difficulties over translating the *Catechism*—inclusive language, mortal sin, Holy Mother church, and so on.

Ken looked around the table and slowed down for emphasis. "The *Catechism*," he said, "is a book that Catholics of all descriptions should read, and own, and digest." Then he said that the Pope himself had prayed "that the church in the United States will recognize the *Catechism* as an authoritative guide to sound and vibrant teaching."

"Excuse me," said Melanie Graban, seated between Ken and her husband, Mike Merrill. "What's a catechism?"

Ken explained, and Coty-Ann Henk and Dennis Hurley put in their cents' worth, but afterward there were still some blank looks around the table.

The point, Ken said, was that a universal Catechism was a *really important* document. Even though many people would probably reject the Pope's gift. "Which brings up the question of 'Should church teaching be a matter of people thinking whatever they feel good about thinking or believing, or has the Word of God definitely been handed down to us?' Remember we talked about the encyclical? *The Splendor of Truth!* Remember I had a disagreement with Judy on it? She had a real problem with it and I was very accepting of it. Do you think Christ would have had this problem? What would Christ say about the *Catechism* if he were sitting at this table? Would he endorse it? Would he endorse the encyclical? Would he say, 'Follow the Pope'? Would he say, 'Follow the shepherd of my flock'?"

Two dozen eyes stared. In the margin of her parish bulletin, Melanie wrote a note to her husband: "Do you get this?" Mike shrugged. Melanie, who, as a child in the '70s, had been sent weekly to Mass and "Religion" class, felt kind of stupid to have to ask what a catechism was, but it was not the first time she had felt she was "not a real Catholic." Despite the explanations from the team and the silence from the candidates, it was clear that Melanie was not the only one who remained unclear about the purpose of the new book from Rome or its relevance to Kenmore. Did it mean Catholics were no longer allowed to think for themselves? It seemed a long time since she had heard anyone saying anything like that. Melanie looked around the table: no one met her eye and still no one said anything, except Ken. His voice bounced off the walls.

The tension was relieved, somewhat, when the gathering split up into small groups to ponder a sheet of Ken's questions, the first of which concerned the day's Old Testament reading, which was a lament of Job:

> . . . Is not man's life on earth a drudgery?
> Are not his days those of a hireling? . . .
> My days are swifter than a weaver's shuttle;
> they come to an end without hope.
> Remember that my life is like the wind;
> I shall not see happiness again.

"It was," Mike Merrill would say, "a very depressing day." But as his group plodded through Ken's questions ("How do Job's words fit your life? When have events in your life taken you beyond what friends can help you understand? How have you experienced God or Jesus with you in times of suffering or loss?") Mike pondered Ken's speech. He wished he himself hadn't merely sat through most of it, staring at Ken so dumbly.

"I'd have liked," Mike recalled later, "to say something like 'You think the Bible is the literal word of God and all this stuff—well, why don't you and I go out and stone some adulterers after church, because that's what it says in Deuteronomy.' But I didn't. I thought to myself, 'You should be nice about this; this is a civilized gathering.' "

Mike felt uncomfortable, almost disloyal, about not having argued. He felt that, by implication, Ken had launched an attack on Judy and the way she ran the catechumenate. He wished Judy would show up, and hoped that when she did, there would be a chance to get Ken's follow-the-Pope view back on the table.

Just then, at about 11:30, Judy did slip into the room, grabbing a seat near the door. She had had a chilly encounter with Father Don before Mass but had managed to keep a lid on her emotions and now—still ignorant of Ken's opening remarks—she was glad she had nothing more to do than sit quietly while Ken gathered in the small groups and drew the session to a close.

As the groups were breaking up, Melanie walked by on her way to the coffee urn. Judy smiled absently at her. "How're you?"

Melanie stared back, eyes wide. "Disturbed," she said, but at Judy's quizzical look, she just shrugged and turned away.

It was Ken who now deliberately summarized his points about the *Catechism*. (He said later that he had wanted to make his full presentation in Judy's presence, and had been disappointed by her absence.) Judy sat there feeling ambushed and more than a little angry, but she kept her counsel. It was Mike who interrupted Ken's spiel.

"Ken," Mike said, "I think a lot of this stuff that you said today was in contradiction with something that Judy said earlier. You're saying that the ultimate source of all moral authority is the church, but Judy says that the ultimate authority is the individual's conscience. So, like, who's right?"

"That's a good question," Ken said, "and I'm glad you brought it up." A brief, confusing discussion followed, involving Ken, Judy, Mike, Coty-Ann Henk, and Dennis Hurley. Judy reminded Mike that it was "informed" conscience she had been talking about. Dennis said the highest authority of all was the Bible. Someone noted, regarding personal conscience, that "Hitler probably thought he was doing the right thing too," which made Melanie even madder, to be compared with Hitler because she dared to think for herself.

But, as usual, almost everyone in the room steered clear of discord. The carillon rang out the Angelus: it was noon, time to pack it in. Melanie peered out from under her eyelids at the restless bodies around the table. They were mostly *bored*, she realized, and she suddenly felt weary herself. She nudged Mike and muttered something about a lunch date.

Judy said the conversation would be continued on Thursday night (a month earlier, she had begun leading private sessions for the group of candidates, her own attempt at achieving depth). People chuckled and chatted as they collected their coats and headed out into the snow.

On a shelf in the reading room, a tunnel's length from the dining room where Ken gathered his papers and Judy gathered her wits and Dennis Hurley stood by holding an envelope with Judy's name on it, a two-month-old copy of *Commonweal* gathered dust. It contained, among

other things, the text of an open letter sent to all U.S. Catholic bishops by
Father Joseph P. Breen, pastor of St. Edward's parish in Nashville, Tennes-
see. The letter spoke about the growing gulf between the hierarchy and the
parish:

> . . . the vast difference between what is said in Rome and what
> actually happens and is espoused in Catholic parishes and institu-
> tions. All this without significant response from the bishops. One
> devastating effect of this development is that the authority and
> credibility of pastors is weakened. A sort of indifference to these
> authorities has set in and it is abundantly clear that an incalculably
> large portion of Catholics, people who consider themselves in good
> standing in the church and who are treated as though they are, are
> making their decisions without reference to what the established
> representatives of apostolic authority are saying to them. Such in-
> difference . . . will become habitual and will be at work across
> the board in moral and doctrinal matters—if indeed that is not
> already the case.

Among the issues needing to be addressed urgently, Father Breen wrote,
was the shortage of priests. He called on the bishops to address "squarely
and publicly" the issue of celibacy. It was "evidently and absolutely necessary to open the priesthood to . . . men who have arranged their lives in
such a way that their lives, and their families' lives, might touch their
parishioners' lives at many points."

Shortly after the letter's release, Father Breen's bishop, the Most Reverend Edward Kmiec, ordered him to sign a pledge not to speak publicly again
on the question of mandatory celibacy.

Even if she had wanted to, Judy could not hang about to chat after
the tense session in the dining room; she had to meet with Tony,
the most silent of her RCIA candidates, together with Tony's sponsor.

With Ash Wednesday just ten days away, it was time to finalize the list
of those who would be preparing for their entry into the church at Easter.
On the first Sunday of Lent, these men and women would be enrolled

formally as the "Elect" and their sponsors would "witness" publicly to each candidate's readiness for membership in the church. Tony did not know it, but his place on that list was in doubt.

Despite having known Tony for nearly nine months now, Judy considered him an enigma. Even the reason he wanted to be confirmed in the Catholic Church remained something of a mystery; both on Thursday nights and on Sunday mornings, he spoke mainly when spoken to, and not much even then. About the most animated he had got all year was one Sunday morning when the subject was not faith but furniture. Mike Merrill had mentioned, in passing, his recent move, on the coldest day of the year, to a new apartment.

"Stairs?" Tony had asked. "Freight elevator?"

"It's the upper floor of a house, up a narrow stairwell."

"Oh, that's complicated. *Very* complicated. Couches are the worst, flipping them over to save an inch"—suddenly, Tony's hands were waving, his voice veering from its usual shy monotone—"and headboards! . . ."

The only memorable clues to Tony's feelings about religion had come on two occasions when the scripture readings touched on life after death or the Second Coming of Christ. Tony had volunteered that there was something pretty scary about the idea of the Last Judgment. Judy was left with a feeling that Tony wanted to be confirmed mainly as a kind of insurance policy against eternal damnation.

Well, this wasn't exactly her bag, but she didn't regard herself as a judge over catechumens' reasons. She did, however, feel a need to hear him say clearly what he was seeking in the sacrament—whatever that might be. Neither Judy herself nor Tony's sponsor had yet heard him express this, despite repeated gentle probes. The team had discussed the list of candidates at a meeting at the end of January, and Tony's sponsor had confessed a reluctance to "witness" for Tony.

"I just don't know who he is," the sponsor had confessed.

"You too?" Judy had replied.

This was not, in itself, an insurmountable problem. Tony's sacramental sponsor on Easter night could be any confirmed Catholic in good standing, not necessarily a member of this team or even this parish. But it was customary for a parishioner to "witness" at the start of Lent, and for Judy, this rite was no mere formality—it was a way to ensure that "the community" had accepted the seekers. She had never before encountered a sponsor who declined to give witness.

The team had chewed the problem over for a while. Ken Monaco had wondered aloud whether the mystery around Tony's faith didn't reflect a certain insubstantiality in the catechumenate's proceedings. ("What are we feeding these people?" Ken had asked, but no one had replied.) The team had come close to deciding that Tony should be "invited" to take a little longer in preparing for his entry into the church, but Tony's sponsor had volunteered to buy the silent man lunch and try hard to draw him out.

The team had gone on to tick off the other candidates; without debate, each one was approved for the coming Rite of Election at the beginning of Lent. The only doubt had been whether Janet Ehrensberger would *want* to go forward, and, characteristically, she had yet to commit herself. Judy had had a short but intense talk with Janet after one memorable Inquiry session, at which everyone had been invited to "share your experiences of God." There had been some surprising and some emotional responses: people had spoken of meetings with angels, strange dreams, and feelings of being protected in times of danger or sickness. Mike Merrill, hitherto cautious about revealing his more unconventional religious ideas and practices, had talked openly about his Buddhist-style meditation, and no one had fainted.

Janet had said little, but when someone mentioned the word "heaven," her tears had flowed without relief. Janet, whose attendance record at sessions had been almost perfect and who had become so comfortable in the group that she could usually chat unemotionally about her husband, Michael, whose death would soon be two years distant, remained unsure whether she was ready to make her conversion official. Janet wished she knew for sure whether she actually believed or just *wanted* to believe; she longed for some hard proof that there was anything real behind all this talk of faith and heaven and what-have-you.

When the Thursday session had ended with an exchange of the sign of peace, Judy had enclosed Janet in a great hug. Quietly, Janet had asked her, "What does the church say about someone who is not baptized? Can they be saved?"

Judy took a breath. "Well, *I* think," she began, and stopped, thinking to herself, *Here I go again.* "Well," she began again, "I'm not sure *what* the church teaches. Part of me thinks that the Pope would say, 'If you're not baptized you're not saved,' but I know that the Vatican II documents say, you know, that there's a real respect for other faiths. . . ." Judy trailed off, realizing she was not helping much. Judy thought Janet should be baptized only if she *wanted* to be baptized, and not out of a fear that she would never see Michael again if she didn't. Janet said she had two more questions. If she was baptized, could she continue coming to the catechumenate meetings? And if she wasn't?

Those questions were easier. "Yes, absolutely," Judy had said, "on both counts." A week later, Janet had decided she would go forward to the Rite of Election—although she was careful not to commit herself just yet to the baptism itself.

Now, at noon on February 6, while the others headed off to Sunday lunches, Judy beckoned to Tony and his sponsor and they went downstairs to a private room. The meeting was a pleasant anticlimax, because over lunch with the sponsor the previous day, Tony had somehow, at last, managed to reveal something of himself. He had talked about feeling intimidated when surrounded by people who knew the Bible and who read books generally; he had also talked about the broken home of his childhood and the need he felt, now that he was engaged to be married, to found his own family on something firm and dependable—something as stable as the sacraments of the Catholic Church. Listening to candidate and sponsor present a brief summary of the previous day's conversation was enough for Judy to be sure that Tony belonged on the list for Lent. "Finally, our hearts spoke to one another," Judy said later, "instead of me being this 'teacher' figure, miles above him. It was the only thing that happened that day that I felt good about."

Part of Judy's mind was still rehashing the discussion upstairs—what Ken had said, what she had said, what she *should* have said. At this moment, she felt more vulnerable than she had in the fall after the subdued contretemps with Ken over *The Splendor of Truth*. Ken might have seen his morning's work as a small matter of saying his piece, of voicing the orthodox view, of balancing things out, but to Judy it seemed that Ken had declared war.

And it was a war that she felt bound to lose. In the war between liberals and traditionalists for the American Catholic soul, soldiers in both armies typically see themselves as part slaughter lamb, part persecuted elite. This sense of victimhood comes despite the fact that *each* side brings to the battlefield substantial numbers of troops, ample money for projects and conferences, powerful friends in episcopal places, and impressive tools of propaganda. Much of the time, organs like *The Catholic World Report* and *The Wanderer* seem to exist solely to provide ammunition for those who identify with Rome, and *National Catholic Reporter* and *Commonweal* for Catholics with a more liberal-democratic leaning. Ken at the catechumenate table had clearly considered himself part of an endangered orthodox minority— but when Judy had looked across the table at him, she felt as lonely as the commander of a besieged Gaulish outpost might have, looking out at Rome's gathering legions.

Judy said goodbye to Tony and returned to the dining room to collect her things before heading out into the snow. Contemplating the ideological struggle that had finally broken out openly in her little domain, she felt shaky, exposed, and solitary. And weary.

A letter sat on the pile of books that Judy had left on the dining-room table. Judy picked up the envelope and looked at it: no return address, just her name on the envelope. Recalling her encounter with Father Don before Mass, she assumed it was some kind of parting shot from the former vicar, now officially on leave of absence. A line from a song went humming through her head, a song from *Phantom of the Opera*, which Judy had seen in Toronto a year before: ". . . far too many notes for my taste."

Given her present state, there was a fair chance that any note from Don would bring either rage or tears. Having done enough crying within the confines of the rectory of late, she stuffed the envelope unopened into her purse and went on clearing up. *That's funny*, she said to herself when she noticed a sleek slate-gray-and-white volume on top of her pile, right under where the envelope had been. It was an annotated copy of the Rite of Christian Initiation for Adults. *One of the team must have forgot it.* Judy shrugged, and looked for a name. It was Dennis Hurley's.

The letter, which Judy opened as soon as she got home, had been printed out by a computer and consisted of two and a half single-spaced pages. Too long to be from Don. "Dear Judy," it began. "After much reflection I have some things I must say about the RCIA at St. Paul's." Judy sighed, sank into a chair at her kitchen table, and flipped to the ending, which, in retrospect, surprised her a lot more than it should have:

. . . *Please be sure of the course you are taking: I have great fear for you.*

Thank you for the pleasant and wonderful moments we have shared. I won't forget them.

Your Friend in Christ,
Dennis Hurley

Dennis? *Dennis* now?

Judy knew there were differences between Dennis's version of Catholicism and her own. Dennis quoted from the Bible with the verbatim ease of one inclined to read it literally, and tended to speak of Marian apparitions and the Rosary and suchlike in a way that suggested a more simple and old-fashioned kind of Catholicism than you'd expect in a thirty-seven-year-old man of the '90s. And don't get him started on the Millennium. But kindhearted, amiable Dennis—chubby, balding Dennis with his self-effacing chuckle and his endless struggle with his own verbosity, who had offered her his services so tentatively less than a year ago, who had ever since helped with doughnuts and driving and been a constant and loyal team player—had never even hinted, so far as Judy could remember, that he was unhappy with, well, anything.

Perhaps she had not been paying attention.

Dennis Hurley's religion was a half-and-half blend of a '50s Catholic childhood and a born-again self-taught religion that would have been, give or take a Hail Mary, at home in many fundamentalist chapels. One of the eight children of a Du Pont factory worker and a future bakery manager, Dennis was baptized at St. Margaret's on Hertel Avenue. When he was four, the family moved to Kenmore, and Dennis attended catechism class at St. Paul's; at the appointed times, he achieved his First Confession, First Communion, and confirmation, and he well remembers the terror of Monsignor Ring's visits to the auditorium to examine candidates at random. ("Father's coming," Sister had warned, "and you *better* know the answers.") The family had always said grace at meals; the children prayed a decade of the Rosary at bedtime. Dennis grew up believing that Jesus was his guardian and friend, and when he and his buddies watched *Time Tunnel* on TV and his friends fantasized about going back in time to meet George Washington or Paul Revere, Dennis dreamed of traveling further, to first-century Nazareth.

In high school, Dennis's churchgoing declined. After graduation, long-haired, mustached, sharing a West Side apartment with buddies and working as a general laborer at the Outokumpu American Brass alloys factory (where he rose to crew leader a decade and a half later), Dennis, like everybody, spent most of his off-work waking hours with a glass, bottle, or can of booze in hand, except when he was, as he puts it now, "chasing women." Well, what was being young in the '70s *for?*

He says he never stopped believing that God was protecting him and his family. "Jesus was watching and waiting, waiting for me to come back to him," says Dennis today. And come back he did. After Dennis married Lynne Yusczyk at Holy Spirit Church, where her sister Shirley was a member, the young couple's weekends were marked off by Saturday-night parties and the ten o'clock Mass next morning at "Spirit." Later, they moved to Kenmore and transferred their attendance to St. Paul's.

The Catholicism to which he returned in the mid-'70s was markedly different from that which he had left. Latin was gone, and with it the hellfire sermons, the single-minded focus on the individual's pursuit of heavenly salvation, and the expectation of unquestioning belief. The new Catholicism was a modern, social, ecumenical affair; many homilies were odes to tolerance and social conscience. God, previously found chiefly in reception of the sacraments and obedience to church law, was now supposed to be worshipped not only in church but in the workplace, in the struggle for justice, and in everyday life and love. None of which mattered much to Dennis—Mass aside, he was not a praying man, except for a Hail Mary or an Our Father when someone got sick or died. It was just that, in his book, a family (Holly Ann arrived in 1977, the twins Dan and Joe three summers later) was supposed to go to church. Dennis's family was everything to him, his job wholly tedious. He lived to come home to his kids, to take them on outings, or to horse around with them in the yard.

Around when the twins were beginning to walk, Dennis's dad had a severe stroke. Combined with high blood pressure, it weakened the fifty-eight-year-old man's body desperately. On the day Dennis's sister, a nurse, confided that she believed her father was dying, Dennis went home, buried himself in pillows like a child, and, for the first time since he really was a child, prayed with all his heart. The face of Jesus came into Dennis's mind and he held it there, pleading, "Have mercy on my dad." Toward the end of about twenty minutes of praying and weeping, Dennis says it occurred to him to ask what, if God would grant him this gift, he could do in return. And then he heard a voice saying, clear enough to make him shiver all over, two words: "Worship me."

A fortnight later, Ellen Hurley reported that her husband's blood pressure was down and he was off all medication except water pills. She said things had started turning around about two weeks before.

Dennis remembered the voice he had heard, and set out to learn about God so he could worship him properly. He got hold of an easy-reading version of the Bible called *The Book* and took it to work with him, reading passages in ten-minute periods between his having to shake new fragments into casts of molten metal. He would read some Old Testament, then some New Testament, until he had read the whole book in ten-minute slices. By the time he was done, the margins of every page were black with factory filth.

And he changed. He drank less, found he had less and less in common with most of his expletive-addicted co-workers, and talked about God and the Bible with two factory buddies, a black Baptist and a white Catholic. When they or others recommended Christian books, Dennis got them from the library; he also browsed in religious bookstores a lot and watched EWTN and evangelical programs on TV.

He and his buddies—as well as the TV evangelists—talked about the Second Coming quite a lot, and Dennis made that a subject for special reading, arriving at the conclusion that many of the prophecies of the apocalyptic book of Revelation were coming true in the last years of the twentieth century, especially as the Middle East faltered its way toward peace.

They talked about Creation too, but when Dennis read up on this he came to the conclusion that here some of the fundamentalists had it wrong: the world must have been made in seven "days," as the Bible said, but in the light of modern fossil-dating techniques it was clear that one of God's "days" was not the same as an earth day. After all, on that first "day," there wasn't even an earth yet, so how could God's "day" mean a twenty-four-hour rotation? It followed that in Genesis, Chapter 1, a "day" merely meant a particular time frame for God.

For ten years, Dennis read, pondered—and worshipped, as the divine voice had asked. Apart from the liturgy, he didn't get involved in any parish activities, and didn't feel called to do so. At home and work, Dennis made prayer a part of his daily routine, and the walls of the Hurley front room came to resemble the homes of much older Catholics; a large portrait of Mary with the child Jesus playing among pigeons, a head of the bearded Jesus, a large carved Rosary, a mounted statuette of Our Lady.

Dennis's father got sick again in 1993. This time, it was cancer, and when Dennis again prayed for his dad, the answer seemed to be: "Get ready, his time has come." Near the end, Dennis called a priest, who administered the last rites and told the dying Michael Hurley to say, as often as he could, "Jesus have mercy." Michael had not been a churchgoer since the late '60s, but he did as the priest said, and when he gave up the ghost, Dennis at his side, the old man had a scapular on, and mouthed, with his last breath, "Jesus have mercy."

It was soon afterward that Dennis told his confessor that he felt a need to help others find faith, as he had helped his father do. The priest suggested he consider helping out with the RCIA, so Dennis approached Judy Nice at a coffee hour that May. Soon he was there every Thursday night and every Sunday morning, talking up a storm about God and his infinite gifts, smiling and nodding and helping any way he could, and loving it all. Loving the Bible discussions especially. He was the "new boy" on the team, but he could quote scripture better than anyone there and, with all the reading and thinking he had done, he often had an answer to a question that puzzled everyone else. He felt everyone kind of looking up to him as he explained things he had read, his fingers always flashing semaphorically, twisting this way and that, outward, forward, inward, flattening and clenching. He missed maybe two weeks altogether between May, when he joined the team, and January, when he began writing his letter to Judy.

The Inquiry sessions that Jamie Shaner led Thursday nights were often less satisfying to Dennis than the Sunday Bible studies led by Judy herself; when people "shared" so freely and questioned so broadly with no firm answers being provided, they were, in Dennis's view, prone to lose direction. When Janet Ehrensberger spoke of seeking comfort from a psychic in the wake of her husband's death, Dennis waited for someone to warn of the perils of such things, but everyone merely listened sympathetically. Again and again, Dennis watched similar opportunities for teaching and correction go by—on Sundays as well as Thursdays. With time, he began to feel the catechumenate was more like a "therapy" group (he had heard Ken Monaco use the analogy at a team meeting and found it apt) than a time to learn and grow in the faith. "Anything goes" seemed to be the watchword, and Dennis began to wonder if they would ever move from questions to the wonderfully clear answers that he himself had found in God's Word.

With others, Dennis placidly teased Judy for her habit of referring to the Holy Spirit as "she" and, occasionally, to God as "Mother." But it slowly became less funny to him. It seemed to Dennis that Judy and her team were actually putting in jeopardy the ability of souls to win eternal life. "Because," he explained later, "if they're taught wrongly and accept it, and then subsequently come to find out the truth and reject the truth, then they're in jeopardy." He says this fear was confirmed by books and articles that he was reading, and programs on the EWTN Catholic TV network, which convinced him that some feminists were trying to take over the church. He liked Judy and didn't believe she intended any harm, but he was certain that her "feminist theology" was dangerous—dangerous, above all, for Judy herself, who was, as Dennis saw it, "throwing away her eternity. If you're teaching someone wrong doctrine, that's very, very serious."

For nine months, Dennis says, he kept these thoughts to himself. At first he felt it wasn't his place, as the newcomer, to criticize, and then he didn't want to start arguments in front of the catechumens and wasn't ready for a major fight among the team. He says, "I didn't want to be, like, the fanatical Catholic where people would say, 'You see? This is what we're trying to fight against.' So I stayed quiet. Because I'm not fanatical, in my opinion. I try to be very open-minded about people. Because the way I've lived my life, I'm no angel myself."

Dennis says he prayed about the matter, a lot, and the Lord said to him, "Don't leave; not yet; hang in there." And when he felt he was ready to speak out, he says, he prayed about that too, and the Lord said, "Be quiet, and don't leave yet."

And then, in January, he started writing his letter. This was too important to talk about. He wanted to get the words just right. It was, both he and

Ken say, pure coincidence that he delivered the letter on the very Sunday that Ken made his stand.

Dear Judy,

After much reflection I have some things I must say about the RCIA at St. Paul's. When I first joined, you and I talked about how much active participation I would take. I told you that I wanted to learn what is going on. Well, I found out. Ken asked you at the last team meeting: "What are we feeding these people?" It appears that they are being fed a Women's Spirit/Women's church/New Age/Feminist diet. I have done my homework and I understand what many religious and lay leaders have in mind for the Catholic Church. I know about the attitude among many in the church who feel this change is necessary and unavoidable. I have kept quiet when I should have spoken up and pointed out what is grave error being promoted as Christian Catholic faith. I didn't speak because I wanted us to appear as a team and not as people who couldn't get along. But you and others managed to get your opinions in, no matter what the consequence. I cannot keep quiet any longer because people's souls are at stake!

We are told that God could be a woman, could be a goddess or whatever you conceive God to be. People speak about going to psychics, palm readers, tea leaf readers, and other such things. They are also not discouraged because you feel it is perfectly acceptable. It is not allowed in the Bible and it is not allowed in the Catholic Church. People are to get their revelation from the Holy Spirit, the Bible, and church-approved methods (mystics, Mary, etc.). The Holy Spirit doesn't charge $25 a reading either. . . . Satan and demons can come as angels of light and have done so. St. Dominic dealt with many of these incidents, as did others.

That is of course if you believe Satan exists, which a great many learned people do not. They believe there is an evil force but that's about it. Where does this evil come from? All evil comes from humans? No. Jesus calls Satan by name, is tempted by him, talked to and cast out many demons. If these spirits aren't bad, why cast them out?

That is of course if you believe Jesus, which a great many learned people do not. A great many of these great many people who don't believe in Jesus teach in colleges. Even teach in Catholic colleges. I hope you aren't learning from such as these! . . .

Remember what Mark, Luke, and Matthew said: "It would be better if anyone who leads astray one of these simple believers were to be plunged into the sea with a great millstone around his neck." . . .

I cannot go along with the indoctrination of these people into this church that you are trying to create. Correcting men on their supposed sexist language, telling people that maybe the wise men could have been women, saying Jesus probably didn't say this or that, and other such things. Yet you play down Mary—THE MOST IMPORTANT WOMAN IN THE UNIVERSE FOR ALL ETERNITY! I don't understand—yet I understand. Mary is the lowly handmaid. Feminists don't like that image. They want the powerful goddess. You have said that we want change in the church, what kind of change? Into what kind of church? . . .

I feel bad because you are making yourself so unhappy. We are all oppressed, not just women. All are in chains until Jesus sets us free. And where does this freedom occur? In the kingdom of God. We won't be physically or emotionally free until we rest in God. There is no freedom or equality in this life for anybody. The only way is to let Jesus give you his peace. I will be praying for you and saying one of the most powerful prayers I know for you: the Rosary. You look like you are spiritually troubled, and have for a while now. The last couple of weeks it has really shown and if I saw it, others did too. . . .

"Enough," a dazed Judy muttered to herself. In a winter already despoiled by doubt and rancor, in the immediate shadow of Ken's presentation of the Pope's gift, this was—what? Not a deathblow, certainly; hardly a flesh wound; she could shrug it off, if she chose. Dennis's letter, certainly, and maybe even Ken's grand stand. It wasn't as if the whole team had turned on her, just Ken and Dennis. Two people had barked at her—three, counting Don, who had gone. This was not a defeat, just a month of skirmishes.

And yet. Judy couldn't help wondering what would happen if a copy of Dennis's indictment fell into a bishop's hands, or a papal legate's. Where would she stand then? Could she still shrug? There had to be a line somewhere that she couldn't cross without bringing the hierarchy down on her unprotected head, and Judy was unsure where that line was. "If someone in authority, such as our bishop, read that letter," Judy would attempt to explain later, "someone who didn't know the situation, wouldn't he pat the two men [Ken and Dennis] on the back and say, 'Yeah, get rid of that radical feminist who wants to call God woman. How *dare* she?'"

But surrender?

It was just, she had tired of the fight. Some people are born to take sides, others to make peace. Judy is of the second type, although perhaps if the battle had been waged in some place other than the Christian church— if she were employed by a law office, say, or a social service agency or a political party—the fighter's role might have come to her slightly more easily. The church is different. Especially in modern times, especially within the confines of a parish, church culture leans heavily against the taking of sides. Making peace, not waves, is the categorical imperative. Scrappers are tolerated, up to a point, but as an aberration. The important thing (in Christian congregations almost regardless of denominational stripe) is not to be effective, but to be, well, *nice*. It is this be-nice culture that makes it so difficult for church groups to deal creatively with conflict or even disagreement.

The results are inevitable. The few who have power generally keep it. The few who voice their anger often get their way. Direct confrontation is rare; passive-aggressive meanspirited expressions of stifled rage abound— from "forgotten" announcements to cheap apologies, from cutting public ad-libs to venomous private letters.

So the be-nice culture insures most clergy against organized opposition, while amplifying the voices of the few laity who are comfortable with aggression. Yet the be-nice culture is not easily dispensed with, because it springs from the very essence of Christian identity. For one thing, most people seek in religion not a place to get things done, but a place to find peace. For another, nonretaliation is fundamental to the Christian ethic. Jesus may have warned, from time to time, that his disciples must stand ready to battle for justice and truth, and he certainly never commanded them to "be nice," but he also never seems to have contemplated seriously the possibility that his disciples might fight *among themselves*. So he left little or no guidance for resolving disputes or voicing complaints. Certainly he never said, "Speak your mind, let it all hang out, don't take no shit from nobody." He never said, "Power to the people! Let no one tell you what to think!" He said, "Blessed are the meek," and "Love your enemies," and "Pray for those who persecute you," and "If someone strikes you on one cheek, offer the other cheek too."

By now, however, Judy had run out of cheeks. "Enough," she said again, and all the questions that had plagued her for a year suddenly seemed to have been answered in that one word. As she looked over Dennis's letter once more, it seemed almost to be a wry message from God, a neon light flashing: "Judy, what's it going to take for you to get the message?"

Dennis had it right: no more chains. Before she went to bed, Judy sat down at her own computer. With more certainty of purpose than she had mustered for what seemed a very long time, her tears suddenly tasting of freedom, she typed the letter of her dreams.

February 6, 1994

Dear Fr. Paul,

It is with great reluctance and a broken heart that I am writing this letter of resignation. It has become increasingly difficult for me to continue as Director of Adult Sacraments. I am most concerned about leaving you at this time but it is impossible for me to continue. Please know that I love and respect you and I am most grateful for the chance you have given me here at St. Paul's. May God bless you always.

In Christ's peace,
Judith Nice

Belonging

"Tough practice!"

"Yeah. Goin' out with Stacey tonight?"

"Yah, gonna hang out at my place."

"So, ya gonna screw her tonight?"

Muted giggles, with both male and female accents, tripped through the chapel-cum-meeting room of the parish center on this last Saturday before Lent, which was also the 185th birthday of Abraham Lincoln. On the chapel's dais, three teenage girls were acting out their assumptions about what boys talk about in locker rooms. They glared out at the gigglers briefly before finishing their vignette.

"I hope so, if she doesn't chicken out again."

"OK, good luck, see ya later."

The threesome picked up their feminine identities and sauntered to their seats.

"Comments?" asked Dan Killian, a volunteer teacher with the St. Paul's confirmation program. While some confirmation courses were optional, this one, Morality and Sexuality, was mandatory for all candidates. Dan, the fifty-year-old director of the North Tonawanda Public Library, looked at the group's five boys, whose assorted limbs were spread across chairs and banquet tables in one corner of the room.

"First of all, we usually don't talk about *practice*," said a tall, lean guy with neat clothes and clean-cut blond hair.

"Unless it was a really *tough* practice," allowed a burly youth in a Bills cap and generic sweatshirt, who was lounging next to his insepara- ble and equally tough-looking buddy clad, more seasonally, in Chicago Bulls garb. "*Then*, you might say, 'Boy, that was a tough prac- tice.'"

"Which is *exactly* what we said," pointed out the thin girl in loose jeans and sweatshirt who had deadpanned the S-question.

"You're right there, Candace," said Bulls, "that's a quote, 'cos I've said it before."

"But what about the rest of it?" asked Dan Killian. "You think it was realistic locker-room talk?"

"Most of it," Bills said, and Bulls agreed.

"I'd say it could happen, but *I've* never heard it happen," said the tall boy, knee up on the chair.

"Aw, what grade you in?" spat a studiously cool, dark-eyed senior who radiated hormones—a function not so much of her ironed-on Jordache jeans, low-cut sweater, deep tan, and heavy makeup as of the way she draped herself over a table edge.

"Ninth."

"OK, *freshman*," said Senior with woman-of-the-world resignation, "wait till you get up to like junior, senior." She half turned toward him, upper body pumping in the steady rhythm of a thin right calf that swung wide from her left knee. "*That's* when you'll hear it."

The boy shrugged and the next group of girls-as-boys took to the dais, debating the easiest way to turn a girl on.

"Blow in her ear?" exclaimed Bills afterward.

"Yeah, like, *c'mon*," said Bulls. But the boys' portrayals of girls' freshen- ing-up chatter evoked similar intergender scorn.

"See the stereotypes?" said Dan Killian, mild-mannered and bespecta- cled in turtleneck sweater and gray flannels. "Real girls are not Barbie; real boys are not Tom Cruise. The reality is that we all have characteristics that belong to both sexes. A man likes flowers, it doesn't mean he's feminine, it means he likes flowers. A woman likes hard physical sports, it doesn't mean she's like a man, it means she likes sports."

Bills nudged Bulls and whispered something; they chuckled while watching the tabletop intently. Senior bobbed unceasingly, her swinging leg vibrating her chair.

"Any questions?" There were none, and Dan herded the kids into the larger meeting room, where chairs were arranged in a wide horseshoe around a TV stand. Fran Pangborn, the part-time religious education coordinator in charge of confirmation training, hit a play button to run the credits of a video called "The Island Affair."

Five shipwrecked characters (played by teenage amateurs on the shores of a suburban pond) *are marooned on two islands. Two boys, Albert and Bruno, are separated by shark-infested waters from a girl named Carla, her mother Della, and an older man, Edgar. The star-crossed Albert and Carla are in love, but boatless Carla sits on her beach, staring over the water as she ponders a dilemma. Edgar has a boat, but will take her to Albert only if she first makes love to him. She consults her mother, who says it is Carla's own choice to make, but "sometimes if we do what we know is wrong to get what we want, we end up losing what we wanted." Still, Carla agrees to Edgar's deal.*

Scene change to Albert's island. After a perfunctory embrace, Carla sits cross-legged with her beloved on neatly mowed grass and tells him how she got there. He tells her that, much as he loves her, he cannot accept her having given herself to another man.

Exit Albert. Enter Bruno, who has overheard everything and tells Carla he understands that she acted out of love. Bruno and Carla walk hand in hand into the future.

The End.

Dan Killian now split the confirmation candidates into two groups. Their task: rank the video's five characters for moral virtue, using number 1 for the "best" and number 5 for "worst." It took just under three minutes for each group to achieve rough consensus.

The most moral person, the first group said, was Della, the mother. Dan wrote "D" on top of a flip chart, and asked for a reason.

"Because," said Senior, her shoulders going bump-bump-bump in time with her ever-swinging lower leg, "she gave her daughter the freedom to choose."

"OK," said Dan, "that's a value statement." He wrote the word "Freedom" across from the "D" on his chart, and turned to the other group, which said Della was morally best because she had given her daughter good advice.

"OK," said Dan, "that's another value statement." He started another column, put "D" at the top, and wrote: "Good advice." Both groups agreed that the friendly Bruno and the scrupulous Albert came next, but they disagreed as to the order—Senior arguing strongly that Bruno ranked first, "because he understood," while Candace pointed out that he could easily have been conning the girl.

Fourth, in everyone's estimation, came Carla.

"Why?"

"Oh, because she should have waited," said Senior while rolling her eyes knowingly to the ceiling.

"Why?" asked Dan again.

"Because she was selling herself."

Dan thought for a moment, then wrote: "Self-worth." Bills nudged Bulls again and their shoulders rocked silently as they sat there, heads in hands and elbows on knees, like benched defensemen.

When the reports were done, Dan stood back and examined his chart, which looked like this:

1	D	D	→	Freedom. Good advice
2	B	A	→	Tried to understand/Couldn't forgive
3	A	B	→	Understood/Conning?
4	C	C	→	Self-worth
5	E	E	→	Exploitive

"There's no really right and wrong answers," Dan said then, "but the people who put this together had a kind of trick key to figuring out the answers." He added a third column to the flip chart:

A
B
C
D
E

"Huh?" a few kids said at once.

"It's a question of actions and motivations," Dan said, and then he gave the reasons provided by "the people who put this together." Albert had "acted on what he believed. That's what morality means: acting on what you believe and living with the consequences." Carla, for example, had not. "The people who put this together said that what *she* was interested in was being popular."

Around the horseshoe, a dozen faces screwed up in scorn. "How can you be popular on an *island?*" asked Freshman.

Dan smoothed his thinning silky white hair and looked around for support.

"Well," he asked, "what do you guys think, then? What was Carla's deep motivation?"

"Oh my God," groaned Senior. "She just wanted to get to the other island!"

Similar skepticism greeted Della's low ranking, although Candace, her cautious dark eyes fixed on Dan, allowed that Della might have given her daughter a more straightforward answer. Dan shrugged. "That's just how one group ranked them, and I don't necessarily agree with them. I think the way you guys ranked them has some good aspects to it too." Getting good advice, and good information, was "an important component of making a good decision," Dan said. "But confidence in your ability to stand on your own, and confidence in what you believe—that's *essential.*"

He looked around the horseshoe, noted some blank stares, and suggested a "caffeine break." Senior, who had voluptuously arranged herself across a sofa, her sweater slipping carelessly from one shoulder to exhibit a white bra strap on tan skin, jumped up at once and announced she needed some fresh air.

"No," said Fran Pangborn, displaying a traffic cop's palm.

"I gotta," said Senior, circumnavigating the palm and heading for the stairs. Fran lowered the hand, raised an eyebrow, and said to Dan, "She's going to have a cigarette."

He shrugged. "I know it."

In the kitchen, someone at the coffee urn asked Candace why she was in the confirmation course. "My mom said I had to," she replied straightforwardly. "My dad didn't have much to say, but anyways, my mom gets her way on things like this." Having to go to confirmation class, she added, was just one dumb church rule among many. "It's like—" She waved her hand for inspiration. "Like, making annulments so hard to get. That's dumb too."

And what about Dan Killian—what was *he* doing here of a Saturday afternoon? "It was a call," he said privately later. "Whether the call was from God or not, I don't know. The older you get, the less segmented your religion gets." The approach had come, five years ago, from Dawn Riggi, the parish's former religious education coordinator. It happened that, just a week previously, Dan had learned that a young man he knew had AIDS. "He was my secretary's son. He made a point of talking to me about it," Dan says. "He told me to talk to my own kids, to make sure they knew about AIDS and that they wouldn't make any dumb decisions." So, when Dawn approached Dan about teaching the Morality and Sexuality course, he felt obliged to say yes.

This was not the first time Dan Killian had experienced a call. Half German, half Irish, the oldest of seven children brought up on rural Grand Island between Buffalo and Niagara Falls, Dan had joined a seminary program at Maryknoll College in Glen Ellyn, Illinois. In his junior year, he had changed his mind about being a priest but stayed on to finish his philosophy degree, obeying the college's no-dating rule with an un-'60s lack of protest. Upon graduation, he got drafted and was sent to Thailand, where he built roads with the Corps of Engineers. He had considered a teaching career, and still thinks of himself as a frustrated teacher, but when he came home from Thailand, librarianship seemed to offer a faster track to career and family. He met his wife, Jennifer, in library school. The Killians' first child died of lung disease; they now have two sons in college and two daughters at Kenmore West High.

Dan and Jennifer were keen members of a parish discussion program in the late '70s. In 1984, Father Paul asked Dan to take charge of a more ambitious three-year program, known as RENEW, in which all parishioners were invited to join small groups for discussion of faith and life. Dan is one of the many lay leaders at St. Paul's whose ministry can be traced to RENEW. It was at the end of this program that Dawn Riggi approached Dan about the morality course. Father Paul had asked that the course deal specifically and explicitly with sexual morality. This would require an adult with a calm demeanor, an ability to listen, and the rare mix of strongly held values with a fairly open mind. Dan, with his thoughtful manner and straightforward charm, his brow serious between silky white hair and quiet Irish smile, seemed to fit the bill.

Dan says the bottom line of the annual course is this: "Think twice before you do something stupid. Stupid, as in using drugs, or having sex in a stupid way. Or doing something selfish that hurts people. At least take some time, and get some adult input, before you decide on things with serious consequences.

"I'm trying to teach them a process of thought. And if, through all of this, some kids get the idea that really, being sexually active at their age is dumb, and if a few of them who would have died of AIDS don't die, that's good enough for me.

"Is premarital sex wrong? Is someone going to go to hell if they have it? I don't know. Sex itself is not bad or good. It can be the best thing for a couple, and it can be the worst. But I do think it's a lot better for a couple to wait for marriage."

The Morality and Sexuality course that Dan and Dawn developed (using materials mostly produced for Catholic high schools) consisted of three sessions. First came a long Sunday that ranged over the underlying concepts of maturity and self-respect; later, a weeknight covered the biological facts of life; finally, there was this Saturday session, described in the prospectus as "Morality Day."

Apart from "The Island Affair," the materials for Morality Day that year included case studies of moral dilemmas (*Vincent, failing two courses in his senior year, is offered advance copies of the tests for $40—should Vincent accept? Katie is depressed and suicidal, but has sworn her best friend Alice to silence—should Alice keep her promise or tell someone in authority?*) and a "Diagram of the Creative Problem-Solving Process." According to the latter, the first step in decision-making is to "defer judgment" while working through each of the remaining five steps, which are: "fact-finding . . . , problem-finding . . . , idea-finding . . . , solution-finding . . . ," and "acceptance-finding."

Further, there was "A Guide for Making Moral Decisions." This stated that "actions, decisions, and attitudes" were right or wrong depending, at least in part, on the results. A right action would produce "an increase in your ability to trust others . . . , greater honesty in relationships . . . , the breaking down of barriers between people . . . , [and] a greater sense of self-respect." It would also produce "a feeling of peace and joy in your life" as opposed to "a feeling that life is a bummer."

Course homework (required for credit) included a written analysis of a case study of "Nonmarital Sexual Intercourse: Mark and Sue," which described a couple who are "engaging in sexual intercourse" even though "they both believe that sexual intercourse as an expression of their intimacy for one another is wrong." The question: what should Mark and Sue do, "in light of the Christian moral values"? These values were characterized in brackets as "hopeful, loving, daring, imaginative, peaceful, forgiving."

Dan Killian's course plan carefully avoided two topics: abortion and birth control. If a candidate raised either subject, Dan was ready to discuss them frankly and without taking a strong ideological stance, but he hoped they would not come up (and indeed, that year, they did not).

Birth control, Dan explains, is just too complex an issue: "It would take weeks to build a foundation for that kind of discussion, so it's easier to focus on not being sexually active." But he concedes that it's also pragmatic for him to avoid the matter: "Like many modern Catholics in America, I don't fully agree with the church's official position," Dan says. "So I prefer not to deal with it. My wife and I make our own decisions." After Melanie Killian was born fourteen years ago, Dan and Jennifer decided, for the sake of the latter's health as well as the four kids' well-being, that enough was enough. Dan had a vasectomy.

Abortion is different. Dan says, "I agree with ninety-nine percent of the church's position. It's not a matter of the woman's freedom of choice—as my wife says, you already made your choice when you chose to have sex. Then the question becomes, are you willing to live with the consequences of that decision? If you're not ready to have a child, don't have sex. Or, if you do have sex, then you'd better be on the pill or whatever."

Where Dan differs from the magisterium is in cases where pregnancy threatens the woman's life. "I think any individual has the right to self-defense," Dan says. "That also comes in, possibly, in the case of rape, especially if the abortion is done quickly afterward. Some people in the church don't like remembering that St. Thomas Aquinas taught that abortion is not a sin if it's done in the first three months."

The reason Dan chooses not to raise abortion with the confirmation candidates is that it's a discussion that tends to go nowhere. "The whole matter seems very controversial among young girls," he says. "You can get into a very heavy discussion between the girls on each side; it's a hot topic that ends up dividing the class. So, again, you really don't have the time to build a background for a discussion like that."

Whether or not Dan has strong personal views on a subject, he prefers not to use his course as a vehicle for them. In his view, the church has too often inveighed against sex itself in a kneejerk way. He blames the exaltation of celibacy for priests and religious: "The direct result," he says, "is the baloney that some couples are taught by priests—couples with ten or more kids being told things like 'If you can't have more children, get separate rooms!' That's not the advice of a caring and loving church—it's the advice of a frustrated celibate."

When the kids returned to the meeting room, each enriched by the legal stimulant of her or his choice, Dan handed out a ditto sheet headed "Hierarchy of Human Needs." It featured the famous pyramid developed by one of Dan's guiding forces, the humanist psychologist Abraham H. Maslow:

For Dan, Maslow got it right when he described the human being as a "wanting animal," whose desires, once satisfied, are quickly replaced by higher desires until, in a few individuals, only the drive for self-actualization remains. That ultimate "meaning need" is (in the words of Killian's ditto) the desire to become "everything that we are capable of becoming, in the broadest time-and-space framework."

Moral decisions, Dan told the class, are only possible when the more basic needs—survival and security—are met, and only once a sense of community—belonging—has been found. Only in community can values be attained. "Let's take a quick poll of the room," Dan said. "What do you value?"

"Life," said a bespectacled girl in a Notre Dame sweater.

"Softball," said a scrawny girl in a white T-shirt.

"People," said Candace.

"Family," said Bulls.

"Huntin'," said Bills.

"A clean fish tank," said Freshman.

"Freedom."

"Reading a book."

"Sleeping."

"Equality."

"Cleaning my car," said Senior.

Dan wrote each offering on a fresh sheet of the flip chart, then hurriedly suggested a few more: inner peace, patience, humility, self-control, faith in God, health, and "approval of the opposite sex." The time was 4:50, and the candidates were supposed to end the day by attending the 5 P.M. Mass (required for credit).

Dan handed out a list of the Ten Commandments and briskly interpreted them in light of Maslow's hierarchy. "The point I was trying to make earlier is that morality depends on meeting our needs. Something is right if it meets our real need, and wrong if it goes against that need. Taking food away from someone, killing them, is wrong because it doesn't help a person meet their real needs. The Ten Commandments speak to some of those same issues, but from a religious point of view." Dan said that all the commandments boiled down to this: "Love the Lord your God with all your heart, and love your neighbor as yourself."

Then, having run out of time, he gave one more homework assignment (yes, required for credit) to a roomful of groans. "Write down the underlying

value of each commandment," Dan ordered, "and rephrase each commandment in modern terms." This was as close as Morality Day had come to the
classic approach, remembered by many of the parents and most of the
grandparents of those in this group; back then, kids had been required to
memorize the Ten and question nothing.

Guilt, the pedagogic principle of old, has fallen out of favor. In its place
reigns self-esteem, the watchword of the new age. And for Dan Killian, true
disciple of Abraham Maslow, the trade is a good one. "Acting as a moral
person is not a gut thing," Dan explains privately, "but a head thing. Do I
follow my impulses blindly, or am I a free human being, who acts partly out
of my head? Freedom is not letting your body go wandering around doing its
own thing. Freedom is knowing you're in control of your own behavior, as
much as you can control it." The alternative, for Dan, is life without meaning. He quotes T. S. Eliot's *Sweeney Agonistes*:

> Birth, and copulation, and death.
> That's all the facts when you come
>   to brass tacks:
> Birth, and copulation, and death.

"If that's all there is," Dan says, "then life has no meaning. But it's not
as straightforward as we were taught at Bishop Duffy High, where the priests
thought all the answers were in St. Thomas Aquinas. Morality is a matter of
doing the right thing because you know it's the right thing and you have
decided to do it."

The vital requirement for making this kind of free decision, according
to both Maslow and Killian, is self-respect. But to respect oneself, one must
first achieve belonging—a sense of being a part of (or at least part of a part
of) the human family.

Belonging: some find it at home, and with their friends and relatives;
some find it in the workplace group, the sports team, the crowd of buddies,
the party comrades, the interest group, the fatherland. Some even find it
amid the anonymous commerce of the city, during those rare times when
strangers unite behind a great cause in time of crisis. Or behind a sports
team—the Bills, for instance—in time of playoffs.

And some find it in a parish, in the universal church, in the communion of saints, in a common faith. But (if Maslow's pyramid was the right way up) *to believe, you must first belong.*

In fundamentalist religions, this truth means that people shape their beliefs and behavior to conform intricately to those of their fellow belongers. In Protestant and Jewish communities of a more liberal stripe, it means "community" comes first, and creeds are mere detail—an embarrassment, almost, and always to be interpreted broadly.

Catholicism has usually been somewhere between these poles. Belonging comes to Catholics in an unparalleled variety of forms, from Benedict's contemplative monasticism to Berrigan's activist socialism. Regarding differences in belief, the pendulum of tolerance never reaches the agnostic extreme of the most liberal Protestants; neither does it often touch the dogmatic extreme of the Holy Inquisition.

Today, in mainstream parishes like St. Paul's, the pendulum swings most freely on the side of "community," and rarely rings the dogmatic chime. During the days and nights of Lent that year at St. Paul's, as in most times and places, Catholics would find their belonging, and thus their believing, in manifold ways.

Day one: Ash Wednesday. "Remember you are dust, and to dust you shall return," Father Dick intoned as he deposited a wavy vertical black smudge on Jamie Shaner's forehead at early Mass. Jamie wore the smudge to work; no one asked her about it, but it was her silent statement of where she belonged. Back home at midday, with Tyler down for his nap, Jamie sat down for what she planned as a daily ritual through the forty penitential days ahead. She opened a little purple book, *The Lenten Labyrinth* by Edward Hays (whose book of Advent blessings the Shaners had used last fall), and read the first meditation:

> Ash Wednesday challenges us to ponder the reality we most dread to consider: our own death. The journey of the labyrinth and the way of the disciple of Christ begins with the task of seriously reflecting on one's own death, embracing it so that one can truly embrace life. May the gift of holy ashes . . . help you to realize

that only by a Christ-like death can you experience the promise of Easter's life.

Day two: Thursday morning. Seven women, all over fifty, all regulars in Father Dick's weekly Bible study group, pondered the merit of Lenten self-deprivation versus positive charitable acts. The idea of a special discipline for Lent remains a rare constant in Catholic identity; another is the debate over that discipline's ideal form. At the study group, Eleanore Speicher, a daily presence at the 8:30 A.M. Mass and a local Conservative Party stalwart, weighed in for traditional sacrifices. Mary Kay Clark, a liberal Democrat and Eleanore's ideological but amiable nemesis, argued for charity.

"Doing something is fine, social action and all," said Eleanore, "but personal sacrifice is often harder. I long for candy like an alcoholic longs for booze. I wouldn't decry the idea of giving up something."

"It's a reminder," agreed Geri Calleri, petite, trim, cheerful, alluring, and seventy. "It reminds you to pray more, to be kinder, to give more."

"I guess, for myself," Father Dick said, and stopped. "Well, I think it's a very valid part of our Catholic, or Christian, tradition, or discipline, to deny ourselves something during Lent. As Mother Teresa said, 'We create this emptiness within, this hunger that we realize can only be filled by God.' So I think it's a very valid tradition. But I myself have a very hard time with it. I used to—I haven't done it for a long time now—but I used to begin Lent by saying I'm not going to smoke my pipe so much, or I'm gonna give up peppermint candy. But I find it just doesn't work. Maybe I'm too weak-willed or something. So I've gone to what Mary Kay is talking about, looking for something to do that I wouldn't ordinarily do, and that I hope might become part of a long-term thing."

"But I think it's *good* to deny yourself," asserted Geri. "It's a great sacrifice. Like, you know, I'm a great nibbler. I love to nibble."

"So you've given up nibbling?" said Mary Kay, smiling. Geri was always good for a gentle tease.

"So, I *might* give up nibbling! Like, last night, at ten o'clock, I was so hungry, I said to myself, 'Oh my God, what'm I gonna do? I'm so *hungry*.' I couldn't believe how hungry I was for something sweet. And it was *difficult* for me to deny myself!"

"So, did you?"

Geri looked at the table for a minute, then grinned coyly and shrugged, "No." The whole table broke up. "But I just *had* to!" Geri shouted above the laughter. "I had to have a little bit of cereal. But I promised: from now on, that's it!" The laughter rolled faster. "I *am!* I'm gonna eat better in the day so I don't get hungry. I promised!"

Day three: Friday. The kindergarten class was scheduled to have an overnight in the school gymnasium, and at 3:30 P.M. the pastor wandered into the school office to find the class's agitated teacher complaining to the principal that the gym was occupied by tables and chairs for a Sodality meeting still in progress, and the janitor had gone home.

"Amy, don't worry about it," Father Paul said.

"But, Father—" the teacher began.

"Amy, I said don't worry about it."

At 4:30 P.M., the pastor started stacking chairs and tables. A few Sodality members saw what he was doing, and helped him finish the job.

Day four: Saturday. Forty-seven eucharistic ministers, lectors, musicians, ushers, and parish councillors donned "HELLO MY NAME IS" lapel stickers for a "Morning of Prayer and Reflection" with the theme "How can we recapture the sense of community at worship?"

"People coming to Mass are not looking to be judged," said the guest speaker, Monsignor James Wall, a noted local spiritual director. "But they often expect to be judged, and they feel judged. They hear, or think they hear, people saying, 'Are you divorced? Remarried? Do you have AIDS? Are you a homosexual? Then, you have no business here.' But God does not say that. He says, 'Judge not, lest ye be judged.' He says, 'Hospitality.' He says, 'Welcome the stranger.'

"If you're a eucharistic minister, look the person in the eye and offer the host with a smile that says, 'This makes you and me one: you're Christ, and you're Christ, and you're Christ, and I'm gonna treat every one of you with the reverence with which I'm gonna treat this Host.'" Rose-Ann Martin, inclined to feel the Host is treated with altogether too *little* reverence these days, shifted in her seat and sighed.

"Treat each person as if they were Christ," Wall went on. "Kids included: let them play, let them make a bit of noise: above all, make them feel welcome." Around the semicircle, some stared stonily. "And there's nothing wrong with invading the sanctuary during the passing of the Peace," Wall said. "If your wife is a eucharistic minister, why not go up there and give her a kiss?" Rose-Ann let out a terrible groan; a few others shook their heads.

Monsignor Wall just smiled, and called for discussion groups to list suggestions for improving the parish's sense of community. Rose-Ann admonished her group: "It's the divine sacrifice, not a Happy Meal. The Kiss of Peace is a time to prepare for the sacrament, not for yakkity-yakkity-yak."

Day five: the first Sunday in Lent. From around the diocese of Buffalo, 355 adult candidates for baptism and confirmation gathered at the vast amphitheater of St. Amelia's, Tonawanda, for the Rite of Election, to be enrolled formally among those seeking to belong to the communion of saints.

Those in the St. Paul's contingent, still absorbing the news of Judy's imminent departure, nonetheless enjoyed their first encounter with the stately but aging Bishop Head, whose announcement of retirement was imminent. They also enjoyed a rare glimpse of the array of cultures and races that comprise the Roman Catholic Church in most North American cities today. The candidates sang sacred songs in cadences that ranged from traditional to gospel by way of mariachi, and joined long lines of initiates moving slowly to the altar as their names were called—

. . . *Makowski, Bisonette, Anderson, Russo, Wentworth, Cheng, Aponti, Duschinski, O'Connor, Rodriguez, Russell, Ehrensberger, Merrill* . . .

—and inscribed in the Book of the Elect. In the lines of the Elect, dark old women dressed all in black stood behind fair young women in stirrup pants and men in jeans and ponytails; men wearing dark suits with closed white collars and no ties stood with men in expensive-looking sweaters and cords. Some women wore heavy makeup and elaborate dos, others no makeup and sexless nun cuts. Many of the Elect were of marrying age; many others were much older or younger; a few leaned on canes and tripods; some were enrolled as complete families. Chattering and chuckling, the Elect inched forward while a flute and piano played, and exchanged quick handshakes with the bishop, who in his homily made it clear that this day's duties were among his happiest in a troubled year. "The Catholic Church in western New York is alive, well, and growing!" he exulted. "My dear catechumens and candidates, the Lord declares you ready."

Day six: Monday. When Bernice Graff brought communion to Jo Kamuda, she found her not in her former place on the sofa but confined to a wheelchair, her head immobilized to protect it from falling over. She was, however, still able to swallow the sacrament.

Bernice told Jo she might be adjusting the communion schedule slightly next month on account of her trip to International Falls, Minnesota, to meet her new granddaughter, Therese Marian. Carolyn had briefly thought of naming the child Bernice, but that was the name she had chosen years ago for a fetus miscarried four months into an earlier pregnancy. "I already have a Bernice in heaven," Carolyn told her mother.

Day seven: Tuesday. Father Paul, feeling a sense of disarray among lay committees since the resignations of Father Don and Judy, had moved into a take-charge mode that included unusual appearances at meetings of both the Liturgy Committee and the Adult Formation committee.

In the Liturgy Committee, he vetoed an edict (announced before Father Don's departure) against baptisms during Lent: "This business has become a real pain in the butt," he said. "After Lent, we'll have such a backlog that we already have one Sunday scheduled when we'll have to do eight babies. That's an atrocity. That takes away any kind of a personal effort—it's more like taking a ticket at the meat counter. And with their ethnic backgrounds a lot of parents are still living with the idea that you can't take your baby out of the house until after baptism. So we're going to have to establish a couple of Sundays during Lent when babies will be baptized. Period." He also said this: "Liturgists be damned. We have to do what needs to be done."

At the Adult Formation meeting, he grew red-faced but held firm as people argued in favor of making pulpit announcements of "community-building" events. "We're there to pray," Father Paul said, "not to have a town crier give out the local news." He also said this: "You people think I'm a lame duck, but I'm still in charge here."

The truth was, the pastor was tired. Especially with Father Don gone, there were too many Masses, too many funerals, too many meetings. He was weary too of worrying about money. As the pastor wound down his time at St. Paul's, the coffers were declining too dramatically to ignore. A dreadful winter hadn't helped boost collections. Nor had the competition from Bills playoff games. Nor had the new rules from the U.S. bishops' conference that had made Mass attendance optional on two sometime holy days of obligation in the past few months (All Saints and Mary Mother of God) because they fell on a Monday and a Saturday.

In all, collections in November, December, and January had been $20,000 below the previous year, and trustee Walt Pangborn was predicting a deficit of $150,000 for the year—$60,000 more than budgeted—which would eat almost all the parish reserves.

And there was no solution in sight, so long as the parish continued to subsidize St. Paul's School. If only the nuns were still around: in 1967 there were twelve sisters living in the St. Paul's convent, all teaching in the school. One by one, they had retired or died, to be replaced by lay teachers earning much higher salaries, and in 1975, the year Msgr. Ring died, the parish reported a deficit for the first time. In 1986, the school gained its first lay principal, Mrs. Louise Lopardi; three years later, the convent was closed and converted into a parish center and school extension.

By then, parishioners who chose to send a child to the school were being asked to pay tuition of up to twelve dollars a week. But this was nowhere near the real cost of running the place, and the school subsidy continued to drain the general parish budget. Over the first three years of the '90s, the school's salary line alone exceeded all other parish costs, and the transformation of the parish bottom line from black to red in those years reflected neither a decline in income nor higher parish costs, but higher *school* costs.

In this, St. Paul's mirrored school parishes across America, where the waning availability of nuns has meant paying salaries that, despite remaining hopelessly uncompetitive with those in public schools, can at least hope to attract quality lay teachers. Even so, those teachers must be either extremely dedicated or somewhat desperate. At most Buffalo-area parish schools that year, a teacher with a bachelor's degree started at a salary of $11,780, compared with $26,000 for a teacher with one year's experience in Erie County public schools. Tuition, where any is charged, has been kept much lower than cost in line with the tradition of educating the poor. Nationally, school subsidies consumed more than a third of the average Sunday collection in the early '90s.

And now the teachers of St. Paul's School (and those of twenty-four other Catholic schools in the region) had petitioned for a unionization ballot. Occasionally bitter campaigning had begun and, in Father Paul's morose prediction, the vote would be too close to call.

Day eight: Wednesday. For many weeks, Lake Erie had been frozen solid as far as the eye could see, but now, the temperatures briefly reached the high 60s. Spring could not come too soon for Ruthie Hemerlein, defiant divorcée and pilgrim for Mary. For Ruthie, the idea of moving in with her son Roger's family in Atlanta, as Roger wanted, was becoming more attractive with each wintry day. As the snow fell, she worked her way through the Rosary, departing frequently from the script to muse freely and at length on Mary's mysteries. The lupus was no better and no worse, the cancer was still at bay, and yet Ruthie found her thoughts turning often toward her own death. The doctors wanted her to come in for a bone marrow test, but Ruthie figured she would let be what would be. She had had her threescore and ten; there was more to living than being kept alive. But she hoped to see one more Easter.

Day nine: Thursday. At her noon-hour assignation with Edward Hays, Jamie read this:

Traveling the maze of the way is the greatest of all adventures. . . .
Jesus is also given to you as a guide. The good news is his travelers'
information. Jesus says, "As you walk down the pathway and you
see a sign that reads, 'An eye for an eye—if someone hurts you,
hurt 'em back,' don't go that way. It's a dead end. Returning violence for violence is literally a dead end. If you see a sign that says,
'Don't feel obligated,' don't go that way. Be obligated. Be generous,
Be luxurious in your love. When you see a sign in the maze that
says, 'Love those of your own country, love your neighbors but hate
your enemies,' do not go that way either, for that law will never
take you all the way home."

Day ten: Friday. The new National Catholic Reporter carried an un-
repentant apologia from Edwina Gateley, minister to prostitutes
at Chicago's Genesis House, renowned speaker and writer on scripture and
prayer, and revered role model for countless liberal Catholic women, including both Judy Nice and Jamie Shaner. Gateley had come in for wide criticism after a previous copy of the Reporter carried a picture of her wearing a
stole, a liturgical vestment usually reserved for priests. On that occasion, an
annual gathering of progressive Catholics under the name Call to Action,
Gateley had appeared to lead the convention in a celebration of the Eucharist. After the picture appeared, some dioceses and ecclesiastical conven-
tions had canceled speaking appearances by Gateley.

In her rebuttal, Gateley wrote that she had worn the stole "as a symbol
of my Christian leadership during that conference" and that the words of
eucharistic consecration had been said together by more than 2,000 people,
including more than 200 ordained priests.

"I have never considered myself a spectator at Eucharist but always a
concelebrant," she wrote. "The only difference on this occasion was that I
wore a Hessian stole and stood on a platform. It was certainly not the first
time I wore a stole. Nor will it be the last. . . . I was first vested with a

stole as a yelling infant at my baptism. Metaphorically speaking, I have never really taken it off. It is a sign of my discipleship."

Day eleven: Saturday afternoon. As usual in Lent, slightly more penitents than usual were turning up for the weekly confessions period on Saturdays, which ran for one hour from 3:30 P.M. The women mostly knelt in a pew until a priest became available, which meant they waited longer than most of the men, who leaned against the walls in rough lines near the booths.

The sounds in church were these: Mozart on the p.a.; footsteps; doors opening; doors closing; occasionally, a cough. An elegantly groomed man in trench coat and dark suit with metal-edged shoes walked click-click-click down the center aisle, waited, entered a booth, emerged after a few minutes, clicked up the aisle, passed through the rear glass doors, and seemed to leave. Then, surprisingly, he returned, click-click-click, whispered to another man standing in line, and, when the booth opened up, went in again, came out a minute later, and clicked his way out again.

Most Catholics no longer confess weekly, or anywhere nearly so often, receiving the sacrament of Reconciliation, if at all, during communal penance services in Advent and Holy Week. Under the 1983 Code of Canon Law, only those in a state of serious sin (also known as mortal or grave sin) are required to receive sacramental Reconciliation before taking communion. Some modern priests have a name for the holdout weekly penitents who keep them stuck in musty confessionals on Saturday afternoons listening to laundry lists of usually venial and mostly predictable sins. "Scrupes," they call these penitents—the scrupulous ones. Most of the weekly penitents at St. Paul's are from nearby parishes; that way, they can drive straight from here to Mass at 4 or 4:30. That way (as Father Don used to joke), "the scrupes can be sure they're snow white" when they receive the Lord's body.

There are still some "scrupes" in the priesthood too. Helen Prejean, the Death Row nun, wrote in *Dead Man Walking* of a convicted murderer who confessed to the priest chaplain days before his execution. Afterward, the condemned man told Sister Helen that he had confessed " 'you know, the heavy-duty stuff,' and when he had finished, the priest had asked, 'Have any impure thoughts? Say any obscene words?' And it was all he could do, he says, not to hit the 'old man.' "

D ay twelve: the second Sunday in Lent. From the parish bulletin:

Let the Good Times Roll
St. Paul's Youth Ministry is sponsoring a parish
Skating Party
4:30 P.M.–7:00 P.M. Rainbow Skating Rink

D ay thirteen: Monday, February 28. On her final day in the employ of St. Paul's, Judy Nice checked her "to do" list one last time. Baptism schedules, pre-Cana rosters, and post-confirmation "Mystagogy" classes had been allocated to lay volunteers; Pat Blum had agreed to look after the rest. Judy locked her office, dropped the keys in Father Paul's mail tray, and left quietly by the kitchen door.

D ay fourteen: Tuesday. The sexual abuse lawsuit against Joseph Cardinal Bernardin was dropped without a settlement. The Washington *Post* said in an editorial that the Chicago archbishop had "demonstrated grace and largeness of spirit" after Stephen J. Cook, a thirty-four-year-old man with AIDS, announced that he no longer considered his hypnotically "recovered" memories of abuse by Bernardin reliable. The cardinal received congratulatory calls from the Pope and from Hillary Rodham Clinton. Seven weeks later, Cook would reach an out-of-court settlement in his lawsuit involving another priest and the archdiocese of Cincinnati, which, he alleged, had ignored the priest's molesting behavior in the late 1960s and early 1970s. (Bernardin was the archbishop in Cincinnati at the time.)

D ay fifteen: Wednesday. The Liturgy Committee met to plan Holy Week and evaluate the "Morning of Prayer and Reflection." Once more, Father Paul was in attendance. In advance of the meeting, Nancy

Piatkowski had mailed out the discussion groups' lists of ways to build a sense of community. About these suggestions, which ranged from a prayer hot line to a babysitting service, Father Paul said, "Surveys of all kinds are nonsense. The thing that bothers me is, these are people who are leaders in the parish, and many of these ministries they're speaking of are already in place. The question for us pastorally is, how do you communicate all that's available to people?"

Rose-Ann Martin said, "Father, I have an idea too. We should offer a pet-sitting service." It was impossible to tell if she was serious.

Day sixteen: Thursday. Respect Life hosted an information meeting at St. Paul's on the advertised topic of:

The Difference Between
a Health Care Proxy
and a Living Will

Slightly fewer than fifty of St. Paul's 5,555 adult parishioners attended.

Day seventeen: Friday. For Karen Monaco's second-grade class at St. Paul's School, the day began with the usual disembodied prayer read by the principal, an announcement that someone's aunt had died, the Pledge of Allegiance, and endless notices including the unavailability that day of "the downstairs girls' lav." A placard near the loudspeaker proclaimed MRS. MONACO'S CLASSROOM RULES, which began:

(1) Believe in yourself.
(2) Be honest.
(3) Mind your manners.

and ended:

(9) Be friends with everyone.

Mrs. Monaco, in prim pink blouse and long gray skirt, spent much of the morning patrolling work groups that solved math puzzles or painted popsicle sticks or spelled words with alphabet macaroni. She said, "Good for you!" a lot. Also: "Good question! . . . Good watching, Meghan! . . . Good learning, Corey! . . . Good *job!*" At moments of excess buzz, she challenged the children to "be the boss of your body" and quieten to the point where everyone could hear the buzz of the fluorescent tubes. "Good for *all* of you," she would beam then.

But as Friday's noon approached, such feats of self-control slowly proved less possible for the children and Mrs. Monaco's "Good for you"s were slowly buried under a pile of shushing, as in: "Shh, when is Y a vowel? Right! Excellent job, Steve! Shhh. David, I think, shhh, you've had enough time with the glue, shhh. Julie, come out of the coat closet, please, shhhh, that's not a good choice. OK, math time, shhhh, clean desks please. Corey, please put your book away now."

"But he's got *his* out."

"But *you're* in charge of?"

"Me."

"That's right. You're in charge of *you*. Shhhh. Know what? Before we break for lunch, shhhh, we're gonna try—shhhhh!"

"Mrs. Monaco, Steve stole my pencil."

"Steve, what do you owe David? What are you going to say to him?"

Steve walked around the table and looked David solemnly in the eye. David stopped crying and gazed back, waiting, and the class fell silent too. Steve slowly raised his two hands outward until the arms were parallel to the ground.

"I didn't steal your pencil," he said, and walked back to his seat while David calmly returned to his drawing. From out in the corridor came the chirping and shuffling of a line of kindergarten students, heading to the music room, and Father Paul's rich baritone: "Hi, everyone. Christine, is your granny home from the hospital? Hi, darling, how's your baby sister doing? Tell your mom I asked about her, OK? Hi, dear, cut your hair? Looks good on you. . . ."

Day eighteen: Saturday. The latest *Wanderer* reported from the Los Angeles archdiocesan Religious Education Congress that "thousands of parish catechists in search of instruction in the faith were exposed to a smorgasbord of dissent featuring process theology, New Age gnosticism, liberation theology, repudiation of magisterial authority, feminist and prohomosexual advocacy, and simple diehard liberalism."

Day nineteen: the third Sunday in Lent. Without Father Don, Lent and Holy Week were providing major unpaid work for Nancy Piatkowski, but she was putting her stamp on liturgical order. One signal: a bold-lettered placard for servers, lectors, and eucharistic ministers:

PLEASE DO NOT
REMOVE—REARRANGE—THROW OUT
ANYTHING
IN THE SACRISTIES
WITHOUT CHECKING
WITH NANCY

A smaller notice, in script with the date, noted:

I have filled the altar
candles with oil.
—Nancy

This last was taken as a personal affront by Ray Krempholtz, the head usher, who had filled the candle-shaped lamps for many years. Ray took Father Paul aside after the 8:30 Mass. "You can tell Madam Queen," Ray said, "that I won't be taking care of the candles anymore."

"Ray," said Father Paul. "I have a lot of things on my mind. Why don't *you* tell her?"

Day twenty: Monday. After dinner, Colleen Connolly's older daughter Francisca reminded her of the family's on-and-off Lenten ritual, and Maria ran to the bookshelf to bring a New Testament. From Mark's Gospel, Colleen read in her rich low voice the story of Jesus praying in Gethsemane while his disciples slept, and then shoved her chair back, an arm crooked over the back, and smiled her confident dimpled smile as the girls talked the story over. Francisca, ten, said that Jesus had been arrested "because he loved anyone who wants to love." Maria, six, wanted to know when they were going to get to the nails and the spear. They had been reading Passion stories during Lent, but Francisca loved Mary Magdalene stories best. Her favorite was when Mary perfumed Jesus' feet and he told her, "Your sins are forgiven." This was one of the first Spanish phrases that Colleen had learned from her daughters.

It was two years since Colleen, unmarried and childless at thirty-eight, had adopted the two sisters from an orphanage in El Salvador. That Lent, they were still awaiting legal clearance for their twelve-year-old sister Marta to join them in America. Meanwhile, Maria was lobbying for a spring vacation in the orphanage. "Cool idea," said Colleen, a high school English teacher, "but not *this* spring."

She wondered at the girls' fond memories of the orphanage, a place grim to Colleen's eyes with its chronic shortage of running water and the stern Italian nuns—the *Madres,* the girls called them—who did not spare the rod. But for the girls, the orphanage represented food, shelter from war, and the *Madres'* love. The girls had been begging for water on the street when United Nations workers took them to the *Madres.* When Colleen arrived to fetch them, Maria, especially, was still clinically malnourished— bones soft, teeth deformed, blood sugar low, metabolism erratic. In a motel room before leaving for America, Francisca woke her new mom in the middle of the night, and Colleen was panic-stricken: Was one of the girls sick? But all the sisters wanted was to have a second hot shower—who could imagine so much water?

More marvels followed their arrival in October 1992 at Colleen's bright two-story home on leafy Nassau Avenue, with its deep rust wall-to-wall carpeting, its neatly trimmed front lawn, the Stars and Stripes hanging from a brass eagle on the porch, and, above all, its bathroom. But first came school. They had missed six weeks of the year, and Colleen took them that same afternoon to admit them at St. Paul's.

It happened that, as she parked, Father Paul was walking over from the rectory. The girls noticed the gringo's Roman collar and raced into his arms, to be rewarded by a huge loud embrace. The pastor led them into the school lobby, where Francisca turned to Colleen with a contented smile and pointed to a statue of Jesus with the Sacred Heart exposed. "This is OK, Mom," she said in Spanish. "Jesus is here." Two days later, the girls were taking the school bus. After six months, they were beginning to forget Spanish phrases. After eighteen months, each girl had grown four inches. But some things are never forgotten. When a friend of Colleen's family died, Maria asked what heaven was. Her big sister replied, "Heaven is where no one is ever hungry."

For Colleen, daughter of St. Paul's stalwarts and scion of generations of Irish Catholics, whose parish-trustee dad and constant mother had taught her to pray to the saints when in trouble, who had despised the parish church as retrograde through her antiwar and antiestablishment twenties, and still rejects Rome's teachings on many issues, especially those regarding sex and gender, the girls have led her to a newfound respect for old traditions.

"There's a sense of belonging," Colleen says. "That's one thing the church has got right. Even the very institutionalized church that I hate so much is ironically the church that took care of my daughters." For a while, Colleen had made a point of taking the girls to the Saturday-night Spanish Mass at Holy Cross on the lower West Side, with its mariachis and tambourines and dancing. But soon they had transferred their belonging to St. Paul's—although Maria, who enjoys chattering and shuffling about during Mass (while Francisca scowls affectionately and tut-tuts "MAR-ia!"), still wonders why no one dances there.

Day twenty-one: Tuesday. Halfway through Lent, many entering the church for morning Mass still dipped into the doorway fonts and crossed themselves before noticing that their fingers were dry. The Liturgy Committee had explained in a catechesis sheet that this deprivation would, like the reduced music and lack of alleluias during Mass, "make us long even more for the cleansing and refreshing waters which we celebrate at Easter." The note added: "We hope that these endeavors will not be a matter of discontent, but, rather, a means to a greater spiritual awakening."

Day twenty-two: Wednesday. Representatives of the world's episcopal conferences were flying to Rome for secret meetings with Pope John Paul II. The subject: the Pope's plans to issue an apostolic letter declaring an end to the debate on the ordination of women. It would later be reported that the bishops only just managed to dissuade the Holy Father from describing his teaching on this matter as "irreformable," which would have been interpreted as establishing the letter among a select few papal pronouncements that claim infallibility. Instead, the Pope agreed to describe the teaching as one that must be "definitively held" by all Catholics.

Day twenty-three: Thursday. Jamie Shaner led the catechumenate in a session known formally as "Presentation of the Creed and the Our Father." In eighty minutes, the group worked its way line by line through the trinitarian dogma of the Nicene Creed and the petitions of the Lord's Prayer. Ken Monaco contributed little to the discussion, and kept his usual cordial demeanor. (Ken did not know it yet, but Judy had given instructions before her departure that he should not be allowed to lead any more sessions of the catechumenate.)

After Thursday night's session, Ken privately expressed amazement at the speedy dispatch of the Creed and the Our Father. "The Creed is the mother lode of beauty and wisdom," he said. "We could have discussed it for five weeks."

Day twenty-four: Friday. The deadline for applications for the post of parochial vicar had passed, and Father Paul had received no calls. He announced that starting Easter Monday, the 7 A.M. weekday Mass would be dropped, and invited those who preferred that time to attend at St. Andrew's or St. John's instead.

Returning from one of his frequent visits to the school, the pastor passed a line of portraits of the graduating class. Since 1988, the priests of the parish had posed with the class. In no two of those pictures was the contingent of priests identical. Back in the rectory, the pastor managed a quick pass at his mail tray before heading on to the sacristy to vest for the noon Mass. He spent the afternoon buried in paperwork, and by nightfall had made the decision he had been postponing since Christmas. The next morning, the sixty-two-year-old pastor would sit at his desk and handwrite a three-paragraph letter to Bishop Head, asking to be relieved at St. Paul's by the summer. "The demands of this large parish, some health problems, and future visioning dictate a change," he wrote. "I will serve wherever needed and put in for another assignment when I see one that I can handle till retirement."

The meaning of this last phrase was clear to Father Paul himself: someplace smaller. Almost anywhere, so long as it didn't have a school.

Day twenty-five: Saturday, 12:30 P.M. In the St. Paul's School gym, fifteen banquet tables had been laid for a Passover meal, more or less. On each mauve paper cloth sat a candle ready for ceremonial lighting, a jug of grape juice, and a miscellany of strange foods, all part of the preparation for First Eucharist. Jesus had, after all, instituted his sacramental feast at a Passover Seder roughly like this.

Sammy Forlenza and his mom had chosen a table otherwise occupied entirely by the extended family of a girl in the other second-grade class. Sammy ignored the girl but enjoyed the company of her grandfather, a burly silver-haired man with a blue sweater shoved up to his elbows, who winked at Sammy throughout the ritual meal of strange foods, each of which was accompanied by an Exodian explanation read by Mrs. Blum or by a man Sammy didn't recognize.

Sammy took four cautious sips at his plastic tumbler of grape juice, one for each ritual blessing of "wine," and consented to dip celery into salt water as "a sign that nature comes to life in springtime" and a reminder of "the sweat and tears of the Jews who were slaves for so long in Egypt." Sammy likewise tolerated matzohs and niblets of roasted lamb, and was enthusiastic over the haroses, a sweet mix of apple, nuts, and cinnamon memorializing "the mortar used by the Israelites as brick layers in their slavery." He drew the line altogether at horseradish ("how bitter is slavery and how it can be sweetened by God's redemption") and hard-boiled eggs (Sammy preferred poached). Still, he found the whole thing fairly cool, especially dessert of brownies and apple squares (no blessings or explanations attached).

Day twenty-six: the fourth Sunday in Lent. The New York *Times* carried a front-page story and pictures of the first thirty-two women to be ordained to the priesthood in the Church of England—these first thirty-two would serve in a single diocese, Bristol.

The *Western New York Catholic* available at St. Paul's that day carried a story and picture of the ordination by the Bishop of Buffalo of one deacon. The diocese would gain five priests that year, and lose twenty-eight.

Day twenty-seven: Monday, 9 A.M. At the Plaka restaurant, formerly Watson's and still the after-Mass coffee hangout of many, Eleanore Speicher was complaining about the Sodality board. She had proposed at the last general meeting that the Sodality chairwoman should write the pastor concerning the placement of the exposed Blessed Sacrament during the solemn vigil on the coming Holy Thursday. In Eleanore's view, the sacrament's former throne, central and prominent behind the high altar, was far preferable to last year's positioning of the sacrament.

"Oh, yeah," said Mary Jane Schneggenberger, recalling Father Don's and Nancy's modest waist-level placement amid flowers in the north transept. "In that dumb little *box!*"

It seemed to Eleanore that an official letter would be appropriate, seeing as how the Sodality was dedicated to the Blessed Virgin. But the Sodality board had responded that Eleanore's motion represented a "personal preference," which she should take up with the chair of the Liturgy Committee, Nancy Piatkowski.

"Oh, sure," said Mary Jane. "Her Majesty."

"So, Eleanore, you gonna talk to her?" asked Mary Kay Clark with an innocent smile.

"I don't think so. You know, I don't even know what she looks like."

Day twenty-eight: Tuesday. Sammy Forlenza's mother, Mary Ann—who was, along with her husband, Sam, as fascinated as their son with the intricate challenges of Nintendo's SuperMario—discovered a hitherto unnoticed pipeline from the Chocolate Island. The pipeline led to a subterranean area infested with baseball-throwing sharks—the ninety-fifth and final secret SuperMario world. The game was conquered, and Mary Ann's triumph was celebrated for several days by the entire Forlenza family.

Mary Ann had been musing recently upon a question posed by an acquaintance who lived in another city. The question: why would a couple with so little interest in religion put their son and themselves through the bother of First Reconciliation and now First Eucharist? Feeling her snap answer of the time less than adequate, Mary Ann wrote a letter, which said, in part:

> *If you take away everything around a child (say Sammy)—his home, his church & sacraments, his school, his family, his community— he would be less sure of who he is and why he exists. As you add each of these things to a child's life, he has more faith in who he is, and more self-confidence.*
>
> *Children who are surrounded with all these things, I believe, flourish more as individuals. . . . Therefore, I feel (and Sam feels) that it's beneficial to have religion in a child's life.*

Day twenty-nine: Wednesday. In the reading room, the latest *Commonweal* featured as its cover story a wrenching memoir, "Giving Up the Gift: One Woman's Abortion Decision," by a pseudonymous mother of three who had felt forced by depression and health complications to abort her latest pregnancy. "Nearly three years later," she wrote, "I am still appalled by what I have done. I still mourn my baby and my former idea of who I was. My grief is compounded by my estrangement from my church."

The writer's journal illustrated how agonizingly her abortion decision had been made, after much prayer and many tears. It was also a testament to profound shame:

August 19, 1991: My due date. I have a private burial ceremony in the backyard for the child whose name is known by no one but me. Under a lilac bush I bury the only concrete evidence that this being existed—the blue-tipped plastic stick, indicating a positive result, from my home pregnancy test. I lay a withered carnation on the ground. . . . Had I been Mary, Jesus would never have been born.

I remain depressed through autumn and winter.

Afterward, in a state of mortal sin and yet feeling unable to approach a priest for counseling or confession, she had watched herself "digging myself in a continually deeper hole toward hell by continuing to participate in the Eucharist. But without God, without my community, I would die spiritually." Her conclusion:

I do not ask the church to change its position on abortion. I am not trying to justify my action or exonerate myself. But I do ask the church for a more open invitation to counseling and reconciliation, as well as reassurance to women that they will not be shamed or condemned. . . .

Day thirty: St. Patrick's Day. Shamrocks decorated most St. Paul's School windows, and a large "Top o' the Morning" appeared on the Spanish teacher's door. Conversely, the "Bienvenidos" plaque on Colleen Connolly's front door had a big shamrock hanging from it. Duncan, the tiny noisy dog belonging to Rose and Bill McKenna, sported a green bandanna. Ruthie Hemerlein's fellow tenants held a St. Pat's party in the common room. They gathered at four o'clock, drank half a keg of beer and nibbled snacks, sat down for a dinner of corned beef and cabbage, which, Ruthie says, "everyone thinks is Irish but really isn't, but never mind," and then went to bed. Except for Ruthie and a few others, who sat drinking vodka and tonic until the late hour of ten. "It's a terrible thing to live in an old folk's home," Ruthie shrugs.

Day thirty-one: Friday. Pope John Paul II met with the secretary-general of the United Nations Conference on Population to express his "disturbing surprise" over a draft consensus document that, among other things, affirmed that "all individuals have a basic right to choose when and if they will have any children," and appeared to include abortion among legitimate methods of family planning.

Day thirty-two was St. Joseph's Day, a bigger deal in Kenmore than St. Pat's since Italians outnumber the Irish hereabouts. Many with Sicilian blood celebrated the feast by inviting neighbors and strangers to partake at "St. Joseph's Tables," a spread of meatless dishes; various local Italian restaurants did likewise, accepting donations for charity. For years, parishioner Rita Sears had provided a table, with the traditional statue of the Blessed Virgin's consort as its centerpiece, in the St. Paul's School cafeteria. Since the feast fell on Saturday this year, it was the public school students in Religion classes that dug into her fried codfish fingers, breaded vegetables, pastries, pasta, and desserts in honor of the saint who (according to a blue typed sheet she handed out) had once provided prayerful Sicilian fishers with a huge catch of sardines in a time of famine.

Day thirty-three: On the evening of the fifth Sunday in Lent, Barb and Tony Cribbs settled into their worn den sofa with smokes and drinks to watch a much-hyped TV documentary called *Ancient Prophecies*. Narrator David McCallum solemnly reported millennial and miscellaneous predictions from Nostradamus to Edward Cayce—and the apparitions of Mary at Fatima, whose secret "last message" is allegedly known only to an aged nun and Pope John Paul II. Barb and Tony found the film one long giggle, starting with the careful disclaimer, scrolling slowly in white text on a black screen—

The following is not a news program or documentary. The people ap-pearing on camera are not necessarily experts and are expressing personal opinions only. Although significant opposing viewpoints exist, they are not included. . . .

—and through the scenes of Nostradamus at work with quill in hand (the footage scrupulously labeled "Dramatization") to the final apocalyptic images of earthquakes, AIDS, and other late-century terrors.

Next morning in the cosmetics department, Barb was astonished to find her co-workers discussing quite seriously whether the end of the world was nigh. But then, as a committed unbeliever, she finds faith, in general, simply mystifying—including the faith of her sister, Judy Nice. The puzzlement is mutual.

"How *could* I believe?" Barb asks. She names, one by one, the disasters that life has laid at her door: a son born without a urethra who later developed a serious drug problem; a husband too disabled to work. "How could I believe," she asks, "when these things happen?"

Yet Judy points to the same evidence. "If I'd been through what Barb has been through," she says, "how could I survive without believing?"

Day thirty-four: Monday. Jamie read in Hays's *The Lenten Labyrinth:*

To live life fully, you must confront the reality of a death, which, regardless of your age, always comes too soon. When teenagers die, there is the great lament: "Oh, (s)he was so young. Death came too soon." What age is too soon: 18, 28, 38, or even 88? Is not each of these ages too soon to die? You may say, "Well, I am a Christian. I believe in Christ, and Christ has promised life to all who believe in him!" True, but you are still going to die! . . . If today you had to meet, face to face, the flesh-eating beast at the center of the maze, could you die without regrets?

Day thirty-five: Tuesday. The latest *Time* magazine reported a Vatican response to a startling move by four German bishops, including the president and vice president of the national bishops' conference.

The four had announced six months ago that where parishioners were "convinced in conscience of the invalidity of their first marriage but are not able to prove it at church tribunals," parish priests should help a person "arrive at a personal decision in conscience [about restoration to communion] which must be respected by the church and the parish." After a long silence from Rome, Joseph Cardinal Ratzinger, prefect of the Congregation for the Doctrine of the Faith, had now confirmed that there were "some problems" with the four bishops' new policy and a "dialogue" was in progress on the matter.

Day thirty-six: Wednesday. Halfway through Catholic Charities Week, teams of canvassers headed by Ken Monaco were working their way through lists of St. Paul's parishioners who might make large donations. The parish's target for this year was $65,000.

Day thirty-seven: Thursday. The last surviving RENEW group at St. Paul's held its monthly Bible study at Barb Sutton's house. The group of seven parishioners and a Presbyterian friend had stubbornly clung to life long after the diocese stopped supplying study material, and now found its study guides in Christian bookstores. The current guide, on John's Gospel, was published by the conservatively inclined Protestant house InterVarsity Press.

Today's passage was from the Gospel's eighth chapter, a series of dialogues between Jesus and the Pharisees. Polite goodwill reigned as the women (whose ages ranged between sixty and seventy-six) worked their way through the discussion questions.

Question: *Have you ever tried to talk about Christ with a family member or co-worker who was hostile to your message? How did you try to penetrate that person's spiritual barriers?* Barb mentioned her brother-in-law, a Jehovah's Witness. Dorothy Braunscheidel cited her Jewish son-in-law. The group's consensus was that other people's beliefs should be respected and penetrating someone's "spiritual barriers" was not a good trick to try at home.

Question: *It seems as if Jesus is deliberately provoking the Jews by what he says. Why do you think he is being so blunt?* Here, the group's sympathies clearly lay with the rude Nazarene's critics. "If some thirty-year-old man came in here today to try to change our beliefs, we'd try to get him out of here," someone pointed out.

Day thirty-eight: Friday, the last day before the first Mass of Holy Week. On a side altar, today and every day through the year, an intercession book was available for written petitions. Some recent entries:

Please find work for John.
Please pray that my husband and I unite soon.
Thank you Lord Jesus Christ for your Love in today's Mass. I try to think, act, more like the Saint you would have me be. Amen.
GOD, THE FATHER—YOU KNOW WHAT I NEED!
Thank you Jesus. Please: a healthy baby.
HI GOD—THANK YOU! PLEASE GIVE ME GUIDANCE!
Dear God, please take away my anger.
Happy Birthday Mom!
Thanks for another day.
Dear God, I'm sorry for my short temper. I am so ashamed that I can't get my point across without screaming like a fool. I love you so much. I pray to be more patient & loving like you.
Please keep R—— away from me. No more.
God hold you C—— in the palm of his hand until we meet again.
Please, Lord, I know it seems a bit late but help my parents to be able to keep their house and not have to sell it.
Please Pray for My Big Grama.

Christ in Nikes

"Edelweiss," Mike Merrill growled, with a slight wrinkling of his nose, as he saw the song sheet. The growl was muffled, but Mike's grumpy mood had assumed a shade of despair as he took his place in a ragged lunchtime circle and despairingly recognized the clumsy meter of the rewritten lyrics:

> *Bless our friends, bless our food*
> *Come, O Lord, and sit with us. . . .*

It was Saturday, the fortieth day of Lent. The catechumenate of the diocese had been invited to the St. Columban Center at Derby-on-the-Lake for a pre-sacraments retreat for the beginning of Holy Week. Thankfully, given Mike's present mood, the retreat was now half over. Derby-on-the-Lake, a strange old world of stately homes where gentry once rode with hounds after foxes, sat serenely on Lake Erie, a twenty-minute drive from downtown. One of Derby's most splendid pseudo-Grecian mansions was now the diocese's retreat center; its three floors and sideways extension just accommodated eighty candidates and ten team members. A wide staircase climbed to a "quiet room" where two red armchairs looked silently out over the ice. Downstairs, Mike added his voice mid-chorus in a hoarse whisper:

> . . . *May our talk glow with peace,*
> *Bring your love to surround us.*
> *Friendship and peace, may it bloom and grow,*
> *Bloom and grow forever.* . . .

Michael the Ambivalent had been out of sorts for the past few weeks, and this retreat was turning into the last straw. The childlike songs, the bright smiles, the ceaselessly strumming guitar, the exhortations to "journey" and "share," the lantern-lit opening worship last night, the children's stories with titles such as *Peppe the Lamplighter*—it was all too much. The adult in Mike, the man of reason at war with the seeker of faith, rebelled.

It hadn't helped that his roommate had kept him awake most of the night with snoring, nor that this morning's advertised "hot-seat session" had turned out to be something akin to a revival meeting. The group had been seated in three concentric circles in a warm paneled meeting room. A lit oil lamp shared a small white-clad table with a purple stole and a basket of napkins, for use in case of tears. An empty armchair, the "hot seat," had been placed near the table. Each of the chair's successive occupants was asked to "share" her or his "story" and then to select a new victim.

Little Janet Ehrensberger was among the first, chosen at random by the stranger before her. Her voice shook slightly but she carried her head in her usual perky way as she began a discourse much shorter, at ninety seconds or so, than those of any who preceded or followed her and, unlike them, lacking both details and tears.

"Hi, I'm Janet Ehrensberger," she said simply. "I'm from St. Paul's, Kenmore. I'd been attending a support group at St. Paul's when Sister Mary Jude, who ran the group, told me about the RCIA Inquiry group. . . . I kept going to RCIA but I don't know why. Some Thursdays, I'd had a bad day at work and when I got home I decided not to go that night, but then seven o'clock rolled around and I'd be saying to myself, 'Oh, I'd better be going.' And I've been going ever since. And I'll be baptized next Saturday. Any questions?"

Someone asked what her former religion was. "Agnostic," Janet answered, "with a lukewarm Protestant background."

Someone else asked what kept her in the catechumenate. "I'm still not sure." She shrugged. "Being baptized is something I know I want to do, but why? I don't know yet."

Without so much as a glance at the basket of napkins, Janet got up and chose a young woman with a ready giggle and curly ginger hair falling over bony shoulders. Like many here, this young woman wore an engagement ring. She reached into the napkin basket three times—first when describing the breakup of her parents' marriage long ago, then as she told how her Catholic fiancé and his parents had become "my family," and finally when she said to this large group of near-strangers, "And now, *you're* all my family."

Next up was a thirtyish brunette in shoulder-padded checked jacket over a white chiffon blouse and tight new jeans, her dark Mediterranean hair neatly trimmed. She seemed poised, even slightly sardonic, as she looked around and announced, "OK, a little about me and my walk with the Lord." But soon she too was digging into the napkins as she told how she had married an alcoholic who "had perversions"; how he left her "devastated"; how a colleague at the hospital where she worked had "brought me to the Lord: that was the day of my salvation." And then came the time when she had woken in the middle of the night feeling engulfed in heat, and her colleague had helped her see that she had been filled with the Holy Spirit. Since then, God had looked after her every step. He had sent her an unsolicited charge card. Now he had called her to go to Haiti, where he needed people in the medical line.

A team member cut off the stream of words and tears with a request that everyone stand and rub their neighbors' backs. But the hot seat was soon filled by a paunchy male catechumen who only wished his mother, rendered incommunicado by a stroke, could understand what he was doing. Plus, his marriage had been on the rocks but, "thanks to the Lord, we're renewing our vows next Monday." (Gasps and applause.)

Mike Merrill, sitting in the back row at an angle sufficiently acute, he hoped, to avoid the attention of those making hot-seat selections, clapped with just enough vigor to keep him anonymous and then returned to his accustomed still posture, eyes resolutely on the floor. There was more applause for the tearful young woman from a broken irreligious home, whose grandmother had called yesterday to say she would be coming to the baptism; more still for the blind former Baptist who had been attending Mass since marrying a Catholic man years ago and now, at age seventy-three, had decided she wanted to receive the sacraments herself. "The Lord has helped me through so many times of crisis," she sobbed. "When I went blind ten years ago, I called upon him, 'Dear Lord, help me,' and he did." Janet Ehrensberger, sitting nearby with her hands in her lap and head cocked, rose to pass the old woman a napkin.

With lunch approaching, a single mom volunteered herself for the hot seat. "I feel like I've been searching all my life and now I've found my way, because, like, I'm going to school, and I've had so many good things happen to me that I feel like it's God watching over me." Another young woman followed. She had been raped by her stepfather and spent the next six years on the road in a frantic attempt to put distance between herself and her past, until one night she heard a voice saying, "You are human. These are feelings. Deal with them." She picked up the phone, called the nearest church, "and here I am." (Applause.)

Mike was wearing the rough wool gray sweater that Melanie liked to wear around the house. He missed Melanie, and hated all this free-flowing emotion. But that wasn't all. His current ill humor had been with him for most of Lent, but he doubted Lent had much to do with it either. He couldn't entirely place the source of his gloom. Certainly, with the end of his first year of med school looming, study was sapping his energy. But equally certainly, Judy Nice's resignation had been a blow to the spirit. When Melanie had got home from work that winter day, Mike was in the kitchen doing the dishes, and when he looked up and said, "I've had bad news," Melanie's heart had gone out to him because his face reminded her of the day he had got a letter from New Hampshire saying an old friend had died.

Judy's decision had struck at the heart of Mike's own ambivalence about joining the Catholic Church. When he had started in RCIA, in search of "religious coherence" for his family and of a remedy for his own sense of spiritual aloneness, he had known he would have difficulty living with the "crazy aunt" of church dogma. Slowly, he had grown comfortably familiar with the catechumenate's ethos of toleration. Now he could see the wall.

At the Rite of Sending, a ceremony at the ten o'clock Mass on the first

Sunday in Lent, the parish had been formally introduced to the catechu-mens and candidates who, that same afternoon, would be declared "ready" by the bishop and received as Elect. Jamie Shaner, stepping into Dennis Hurley's shoes as Mike's parish sponsor, had said this:

> *Mike didn't approach this process wide-eyed and full of eager anticipa-tion. He came into it pretty skeptical of what it would be. Mike told us he expected rote memorization and documented dogma, he said he ex-pected judgment, and he even expected intolerance. In spite of these expectations, he was prepared to continue, and he found that he was willing to be as "hypocritical" as he needed to be to get through this process to become a Catholic. So you have to wonder, why would any-one want to be a part of something that had such negative connotations? Mike said he sensed an essence of our church, something deep in its roots that is rich with a tradition so many of us take for granted . . . and thankfully, Mike found that he didn't have to be hypocritical. . . . He found acceptance and openness, found faith in God, and found a sharing process that he could genuinely look forward to allowing himself into. . . .*

Even as he listened to these upbeat words, Mike had been wondering anew how "hypocritical" he would have to be to go through with the conversion. Judy had represented for him the best of what he had encoun-tered in Catholicism—an independent thinker, a free spirit, down-to-earth but caring. "A holy person," he had called her once. Therefore, her loss of heart had left him feeling abandoned, forced to second-guess his own per-ceptiveness. All those hours spent in the group. How could he have failed to note how everyone skirted the most troubling questions? How could he have failed to see the significance of Judy's obvious nervousness? How could he have got Ken, and Dennis, so wrong? Ken's orthodox outburst from the blue, plus the fact that Dennis had had to write his views in a letter rather than expressing them in the group, had told Mike that even in the RCIA's discrete zone of toleration, there was no arena for diversity or debate. And if so, how could this really be the church for him?

Still, Mike did not blame Ken, or Dennis, or Judy, for his low mood— he supposed his Jesuit friend Father Marty Moleski would call it a period of "desolation," as opposed to the "consolation" of religious highs. Mike blamed himself, for "intellectual pride, or maybe I mean intellectual snobbery." At the Rite of Sending, Marty Moleski, present in his capacity as Mike's sacramental sponsor, had told the congregation:

Mike has a quicksilver personality: he goes from mood to mood very rapidly. Besides his Eastern strain, the meditation spirituality, he's a scientist, training to be a medical doctor. And so, he wants proof and certitude; he wants to know for certain what's right. And frequently, Jesus, when he meets people like that, turns his back and walks across the lake. For some reason, Jesus just does not give us all the proof and certitude that we want. The scientist says, "Prove it to me and I'll believe." Jesus says, "Trust me and I'll prove it to you." And I think today Mike is making a fundamental decision to trust Jesus. . . .

Maybe so, but the scientist was not lying down to defeat. Lately, Mike had found himself unable to pray or even meditate, and as the countdown to his entry into the Catholic Church proceeded, his mood deepened. At Derby-on-the-Lake, just seven days before Easter, surrounded by enthusiasm and faith in nauseating quantity, he wondered anew what on earth he was doing to himself.

Mike started, and then looked relieved, when a finger from the hot seat was pointed at . . . no, not at him, but at a black man sitting right next to him. "My name is John," the confident young man said. "I'm being sponsored by St. Matthew's Parish, and we gotta stop with all these napkins." (Applause.) So John offered a "story" of a different kind. A rich woman wanted her dog buried in the Catholic cemetery. Her pastor advised, "Try the Methodists. They'll bury anything." But when the pet lover promised a $10,000 gift, the priest admonished, "Why didn't you tell me your dog was Catholic?"

And so to Edelweiss, and the lunch buffet. Mike stood in line behind a fellow candidate with some serious things to say about the offered food. "Macaroni and cheese," this candidate muttered to Mike. "That's carbohydrate and dairy, a bad combination. Very bad for you." Slapping Swiss cheese and lettuce onto rye, she protested also at the "dark" flavor of most of the morning's hot-seat stories. "I mean, I have some troubles too," she said, "but I get up thankfully every morning."

Mike abstractedly speared a slice of turkey. "This may cheer me up," he said. "Turkey stimulates the production of the antidepressant neurotransmitter serotonin." Then, after his usual pause for second thoughts: "Or rather, serotonin is *affected* by antidepressants, anyway."

Over the meal, a few of the candidates compared confirmation names. Janet's was Elizabeth, for her great-grandmother. Mike had chosen Thomas, for St. Thomas More, of whom he had never taken note until, faced with the name-choosing task, he picked up a book of saints' lives. Why the sixteenth-century statesman and martyr? "I like the fact that he stood up to King Henry," Mike told the lunch table. "And I like that he was a writer, because I like to write. I like that he was married. And I like that he adjusted his beard before they cut off his head—he had a sense of humor." He reconsidered his flippancy: "Well, it's not *really* because of the beard."

Despite his desolation, or maybe because of it, Mike still hoped to get "something important" out of the retreat. "Something," he repeated, sipping coffee, "though I don't know what. Some Thing. The ineffable Thing." His tone was . . . what? Sardonic? Self-effacing? It was often hard to tell with Mike. Since arriving yesterday evening, he had been at war with himself, his questioning side and his searching side duking it out, one ever-doubting, the other wanting to believe, the tension between the two making him—as he was very shortly to begin to understand—a natural Catholic.

So far, it was proving difficult for either version of Mike to get with the program. Back in the meeting room after lunch, the opening song was "Give Me Oil in My Lamp," which Mike remembered with dismay from his high school youth group. He removed his hands from his pockets to clap desultorily in blues time—*Jesus is the rock and he rolls my blues away, bop a-shoo-bop, a-shoo-bop, woo*—and reluctantly turned to his neighbor to "share" a memory of being "in the dark" and then finding "the light." And then everyone watched a subtitled Greek movie about a peasant boy who brought home the Holy Light from the paschal candle on Easter night. Accosted by bullies on the way, the boy managed to safeguard the Light but was scolded by his mother for ruining his Easter suit and white shoes. When she discovered the truth about his heroic act, she begged her son's forgiveness.

"Very touching," said Mike when the movie ended, and it was, as usual, impossible to gauge the level of his irony. Thankfully, there would now be an hour's break. Maybe a snooze would help. With any luck, his roommate would go for a walk.

By the frozen waters of Erie, Janet Ehrensberger and her sponsor, Marianne Parry, went walking. Spring was near, sort of—the grass muddy olive, the sun brave in a pale blue sky. Out of sight on the broad Niagara, a few boats were already out, but the wind was brisk and the lake itself remained hard and closed.

Some retreatants were in sweaters and Marianne wore a lightweight parka, but Janet huddled in her long beige winter coat, mitts, and knitted tuque. As they walked, Janet and Marianne talked about the past. Neither woman being what you would call loquacious, the conversation consisted mainly of short questions from Marianne, short answers from Janet, and spaces between, during which the two seemed content to stroll the retreat center's grounds in silence.

Marianne asked, Had the Catholic Church seemed strange to Janet at first? Not really; the United Church of Christ, "or whatever it was called when I was little," had not, so far as Janet could remember, been much different from the Catholicism she now knew.

Marianne asked, How come Janet had been married at Town Hall? Well, Janet had been willing to marry in the Catholic Church, but her late husband hadn't wanted to go through the pre-Cana rigmarole. Michael had said, "You work days, I work nights. When would we find the time?"

Marianne said, "OK, that's just not where he was on his journey," and she and Janet fell into one of their silences as they ambled along a slightly muddy path now dotted with Stations of the Cross on poles. They passed the blind ex-Baptist woman and her companion, who were genuflecting before a Station and murmuring, "Hail Mary, full of grace . . ." A few paces later, Janet volunteered that her sister was a born-again Baptist, married to a lapsed Catholic who was angry that the church had dropped Latin.

This astonished Marianne, whose way of expressing astonishment was to slightly raise the pitch of her arms and adjust her eyebrows a bit. "But," Marianne said, "no one ever knew what was going on. I mean, Jewish people teach their kids Hebrew; OK, teach me Latin, and then maybe I'll know what's happening."

Marianne then asked about Janet's new job. Janet said, "Well, it's OK." She mainly interviewed people trying to get off welfare, and of her current caseload of twenty-four people, at least twenty-one had histories of alcohol or substance abuse. "I have a hard time with that," she said.

"Uh-uh," said Marianne.

"The more I find out about life," said Janet, "the less I know about it." They nodded to a young couple walking quietly hand in hand and, a few paces onward, joined up with a small group of fellow St. Paul's parishioners.

"Have you written on your sheet yet?" someone asked, referring to a paper that each candidate had been given earlier that day. Each sheet contained the heading "Christ give me light to . . ." The idea was to write some specific petition on the sheet—some need or desire, some special grace yearned for at this special time.

Janet's sheet was in the deep right pocket of her coat, blank but for the title. To her questioner, she shook her head and, in explanation, shrugged. "I don't know yet."

Marianne, noting this was at least the second time Janet had used that phrase that day, suggested that if she were writing a book about Janet, the title of the book could be *I Don't Know Yet.* Janet bobbed her head and emitted a cozy chuckle.

Mike Merrill had not written anything on his yellow sheet either. He fingered it absently in his pants pocket as he walked into the meeting room, which had been arranged with circles of six or seven chairs, and chose the last chair in a circle of people he didn't know. The lights were low as the guitar strummer and another woman sang a new song:

> In this very room, there's quite enough love
> for all the world . . .
> and there's quite enough hope
> quite enough power
> to chase away every gloom,

for Jesus, Lord Jesus,
is in this very room . . .

As the guitar strummed, a team member named Sue moved from circle to circle, choosing one person, seemingly at random, from each group. The chosen one was quietly asked to go into the next room. Mike was picked from his group, and he walked, mystified, through the door to find a larger circle of chairs, which were quickly filled by four men and six women.

"You're all so willing to do this, so trusting, thank you," said Sue as she followed the chosen. As if they had any choice.

"Let's pray," Sue said. "Lord, thank you for these people's willingness to say yes to the unknown." Still with no explanation as to why they were here, she asked the group, "If Jesus were to walk into this house, how would he be?"

Answers came readily:

"He would be gentle."

"He would be peaceful."

"Graceful—no quick sharp movements."

"Very understanding."

"Loving."

"His voice would be soothing, very melodic."

"Mike?"

Mike looked at the floor for a moment, then met Sue's eye. "I think no one would understand him."

"Pardon me?"

"Because nobody understood him back then, so why would we understand him now?"

"Well, they may not have understood where he was going, but they understood his presence, didn't they?"

"Understood his presence," Mike repeated, then nodded once. "OK, maybe they did." He hesitated, seemingly fighting a need to argue this point, then gave up. "OK, sure, I agree. Peaceful, gentle, and so on."

"OK," Sue said, looking around at the group. "And what would he say to people if he were here in this house? How would he communicate?"

Jesus would, the group quickly agreed, be encouraging, understanding, patient, empathic. He would make eye contact with each person. He would listen more than he talked.

"He would," disclosed a young woman in a tight floral blouse and long blond curls, "be open to different people having answers."

Mike silently watched the floor in front of Sue's feet.

"What," said Sue, "if I asked you to be Jesus?"

Mike's head shot up.

"What," Sue continued, "would you do if you were to go back into your group and be Jesus for the people in that group?"

Mike stared, waiting (as he explained later) for Sue to confirm that her question was hypothetical. When she did not, Mike's shoulders sagged.

"I'd have to know a lot more about him," said a dark athletic man with black handlebar mustache, Bills sweatshirt, and work jeans.

"I'd have to let him work through me," suggested the girl in the floral blouse, who seemed intrigued by the idea.

"Mike, what would *you* have to do?"

Mike met her eyes, his voice calm but his gaze angry. "What would I have to do? I have no idea. Maybe go fasting in the desert for forty days." To himself, he was saying: *This is crazy; maybe heresy too,* although the latter was of less concern to him than the former.

"Well," says Sue, "you don't have time for that, because we're going to ask you to go into that group and be Jesus for them. Your group is being prepared to receive you." Mike closed his eyes, wiped a hand roughly over his forehead, and then pulled his hands into his lap as Sue and the other chosen ones batted the new task around. He was on the verge of telling Sue, *Sorry, you'll have to find another Jesus for my group,* but he didn't want to be a pest. How would she manage, the time for this advent being so near?

"We'll need to be very encouraging," someone was saying.

"Listen a lot."

"Be gentle."

"Make eye contact."

"One thing: this is *not* a role-play," Sue said, either not noticing or choosing to ignore Mike's staring at the roof in open stupefaction. "You're not role-playing, you're getting a chance to *really be* Jesus for these people, and letting them *really* experience the presence of Jesus."

Nevertheless, not everything about this encounter was to be left to divine discernment. Sue handed out a list of questions that the ten Christs "might want" to ask their groups of disciples.

The first was: *What is your name?*

The second was: *Are you happy you came today?*

The third was: *What would you like me to do for you, for your family and friends?*

Mike showed no sign of being comforted by the script. His mouth held a tight straight line while a taut finger, parallel to the ground, supported his nose.

"You don't need to think out everything you say," Sue offered. "You may not get beyond the first two questions and that's OK." Then she said, "Don't be surprised if they really accept you as Jesus, in a very open and loving way. Any questions?"

"Do we ask one by one or as a group?" asked a lanky Christ in dirty loose-laced running shoes.

"What do you think Jesus would do?" Sue asked back.

"One by one."

"Right on."

"Do we go around in a circle or pick people at random?" asked the blond Christ in the floral blouse.

"What do you think Jesus would do . . . ?"

Mike asked nothing, merely clutching his sheet of questions and stretching his body out in an apparent attempt to press it through the chair into the floor. All the Christs stood and held hands. "Name the feeling you want to let go of," said Sue. "I'm scared to death," said Mike, loudly, at once, and others took up his theme. "Lord," prayed Sue—while Mike clasped the hands of the man and woman on either side of him in a death grip even while he stood six inches back from the circumference—"with you here we can do anything—bear light, bear joy, bear peace. Come, Holy Spirit . . ."

The circle broke up and its members started sauntering into the bigger room—Jesus in blouse and stirrup pants, Jesus in Bills sweatshirt and work jeans, Jesus in mohair cardigan, Jesus in a striped blue-and-green rugby shirt, Jesus in pleated cords and Nikes. Mike, however, sat down, then started to stand up, then sat down again, breathing rapidly, then stood up, stretched his fingers, and walked stiffly to his waiting group.

But when he reached them, it was as if he had conjured out of nowhere a professional Christ's bedside manner. He smiled, looked around with quiet confidence, and shook hands all around. "When I was last here," he began, "two thousand years ago—no, actually, one thousand nine hundred and fifty years ago, more or less . . ." He made eye contact; he listened calmly; he smiled encouragingly; he nodded a lot. The whole encounter was carried through with quiet gentility.

A woman in the group said that what she wanted was to be able to trust in God. Mike, as Jesus, said cryptically: "Trust in God, but tie your camel." He did not explain that this was a quotation he once heard, from, he thought, the Koran. Repeating the aphorism to himself, he decided it was a good choice—nice and authentic, pithy, thoroughly in period. But then he remembered this was the twentieth century, so he expanded: "I mean, when you're driving down the freeway you don't close your eyes and trust God to keep you between the white lines. You need to do your own spade-work."

A few minutes later, looking at his script, he lost his place, gulped, and confessed, pointing to his chest: "This human here is very nervous. I'm sorry I can't get all my words together, because this person doesn't know very much." At another point, he forgot whether a particular group member had answered the question currently doing the round, and openly confessed his lapse. "Forgive me," he said. "When you get to my age, your memory gets bad." The disciples smiled understandingly: their messiah had never been a stranger to human frailty.

There was just one openly emotional moment, and even that was some-what restrained. A woman in the group asked "Jesus" to help her brother. She said her brother had been driving a tractor-trailer down a hill toward a small town when the brakes failed, and he had intentionally driven it into a ditch so that his load of propane wouldn't endanger the town. The man was paralyzed. His sister dabbed at her eyes and "Jesus" got up for a moment to pat her back awkwardly, promising to help and be with her brother. Mostly, however, he just listened as people talked quietly to him, mirroring his smiles and nods.

A few yards away, Janet Ehrensberger's all-female group was having a more freighted time. This Jesus—she of the floral blouse and blond curls—had glided into the room, eyes shining, and cast her unblinking gaze on her disciples. As she moved around the circle asking her questions, she clutched each pair of hands in her own and sank to her haunches to REALLY LIS-TEN. Each disciple, in turn, broke into sobs, including Janet, after she had confided in "Jesus" that this week was the anniversary of her husband Michael's death. Tears flowed without end for half an hour.

The floral-blouse "Jesus" ended the close encounter and walked off pale and taut. Back in the Christs' clubhouse, she slumped into a chair and stared at the ceiling, letting her tears flow. Meanwhile, one of her disciples sobbed uncontrollably on a team member's shoulder in the lobby for five minutes before sobs turned to giggles and then laughter.

By now, the kindergarten teacher was walking through the room strumming her guitar, and Mike Merrill's group had gotten as far as the fourth question (*Do you know my Father, and have my followers done a good job of explaining him?*). But not all the disciples had had a crack at it when "Jesus," as instructed, skipped ahead to: *I seem to have a problem making friends in the world—why do you think that is?*

Finally, the group got up, and "Jesus" hugged each one and asked, as directed, *Will you be my friend?* He secured six nods or yeses and left the room to join a shaken bunch of fellow messiahs in the outer room, where Sue greeted each one with a hug and a chance to wind down silently before comparing notes.

"*Everyone* cried!" announced the floral-blouse Jesus through her own tears.

Another Jesus, equally blond, equally thin, and equally moved, also said, "*Everyone* cried!"

The athletic mustached Jesus worried: "One woman got angry at me because I took away her husband and her father. I didn't know what to say."

"What *did* you say?"

"I told her I took them to a better place. I said she shouldn't be angry; it wasn't that I took them away but that I brought them to me. It seemed to help." He sighed. "It's a tough job."

"When I hugged them, they pulled me back, wouldn't let me go," said floral-blouse.

"Me too, the same thing happened to me," said her echo.

Mike sat silently, his finger again horizontal under the weight of his nose, as another Jesus, Swedish-looking with hair in a loose bun, told with alternating dejection and exasperation about a female disciple who could do nothing but chatter about how wonderful her boyfriend was. "Every time anyone said anything she was, like, 'My boyfriend, da-da, da-da, da-da,' and I couldn't get her to stop. When I asked that question six—*Do you know anyone who lives the way I want them to live?*—she went, 'Oh, sure, my boyfriend, he's so wonderful, da-da, da-da, da-da.' I mean, yech." The Swedish Jesus pressed herself hard into the back of her chair.

"I feel so tired," said the floral-blouse Jesus.

"Right," said the echo-effect Jesus. "Utterly drained."

"There was so much *energy* in there."

"Such *warmth*."

"You really *felt* what they were feeling."

"You could see right into their *heads*."

Mike sighed slightly.

"Mike?" said Sue.

Without cynicism, Mike fixed his cool blue eyes on Sue and said, "I wished I had had those forty days of fasting. I couldn't open my heart and let all that divine empathy through. It's not part of my personality." He paused, and shrugged. "And yet, at the same time, I realized it's not actually so hard a thing to do. To be Jesus, I mean. To listen. To care. To be a vessel of the Spirit, or whatever you want to call it." He paused again. "It gave me an idea how . . . I mean, I've always wondered how it's possible to be a good Christian. It gave me an idea how to live my life." He paused again, shrugged again. "Sort of thing."

Mike had found his Ineffable Thing, a fundamental truth about being Christian in general and Catholic in particular. Being Jesus, even in play action, had broken down a barrier—the barrier between what God could do and what people could do, the line between who God was and who Mike was.

"It's really *not* a role-play, to be Jesus," Mike said later that evening, wonderingly. "It is not impossibly hard." It figured, anyway. Mike didn't believe in drawing lines generally—between mind and body, for instance. "I am this flower, in a Buddhist way. I am this table. But up to now, that has had limits. It has been 'I am not God.' It's been, like, 'I'm just this guy. So how can I possibly live a Christian life?' This afternoon has given me permission to just go ahead and be Christ. Once I had accepted that this was what I was going to do, once I walked into that room, I was calm. I just said to myself, 'I'll just be as nice and *human* as I can be.'

"And as a result, I felt I really could see for the first time where people were coming from spiritually, when they came to Jesus: some came from crisis or trouble, some from spiritual hunger, some had just been brought up with it, and had fallen away, and had returned naturally."

I am human; I am God. Broken barriers are, in a way, the defining characteristic of Catholic Christianity. The line between body and soul is erased; the line between earth and heaven is erased. God meets humanity in a place that is earthly and heavenly at the same time. In this place, bread is bread, but is also—or rather, *and* is also—the divine body. The bread *is God*, as generations of catechism teachers have insisted—"is," rather than merely "is a symbol of."

This gigantic "is," a stumbling block to Protestants and sheer voodoo to non-Christians, has long been fundamental for Catholics, whether or not all Catholics understand it. The wine is real grape alcohol, and it is—*is*—the divine lifeblood. The water of baptism is plain tap water, *and* it is holy, the miraculous remover of all sin. Marriage is a covenant made by a man and a woman, *and* it is the sealing act of God. The absolution of a human priest *is* the absolution of the divine High Priest. The human priest himself *is* Christ when he offers Christ's sacrifice—"this *is* my body . . ."—at the altar. Jesus was—*is*—human, the son of Mary, and also the Son of God. Therefore, Mike Merrill too *is* the son of God when he ministers on God's behalf. *Is*, really; it's not just playacting.

"But I also felt the inadequacy of my human love," Mike said, replaying the afternoon's work in his mind. "There have been times in my life when I could have opened up and flooded them with love. But not today. Although the desolation faded somewhat, you know, as it went on. Maybe it was the turkey."

He considered. "No, I don't really mean that, about the turkey. I think it's like the prayer of St. Francis says: 'It is in giving that we receive.' Most of the time in my life, in most places I go, I feel like I'm giving out more than I get back. So my cup runs dry a lot. My cup—the reservoir of the substance of life in my heart. That moment, when I was Jesus, was one of a few when I felt the flow was equal in each direction. The nourishment." Giving *is* receiving: it's only natural, to a natural Catholic.

Mike considered again, and wrinkled his nose. "Although, you know, I'm still not sure I really fit in. Not completely." Ah, yes, *that* line—the battle line between Mike's questioning intellect and his searching spirit, between the sardonic and the intuitive, between reason and faith. Eventually, Mike may learn to erase that line too.

True, the instinct for reason begins with doubt, and doubt is not faith. But to doubt is to be human; reason is the way humans cope with doubt. When reason fails to make sense of a confusing world, as it inevitably does, faith offers a finishing line, a place to end the innate endlessness of doubt. Doubt untempered by faith is a road to insanity. But the same is true of faith untempered by doubt. In every century, those whose certainties have been all-encompassing have been those who, wholly out of touch with what others call reality, take up arms against those who differ, or take poison against themselves.

Faith and reason: for the true Catholic, no line is more suitable for erasing. In liberal religions, reason rules; in fundamentalism (including the fundamentalist phases and forms of Catholicism), faith rules. But in classic Catholicism, with its highest scholarly and mystical traditions living in perpetual tension, reason and faith are Siamese twins. On the fortieth day of Lent, Mike Merrill, skeptic and pilgrim, natural Catholic, had come home.

But he had not realized all of this yet as the sun began to glow on the windows of the Christs' clubhouse. The emotional volume slowly faded as the Christs descended from their high plains to compare the answers they had got to the final question, as to why Jesus had trouble making friends: "You're too powerful to make friends with," someone had said. "It's not your fault," someone else had said, "it's ours. We're too distracted by things in the world." And so to prayer, again in a circle, and this time Mike did not stand back from the scrum. Each Jesus offered a thanksgiving. Mike said, without elaboration, "Thank you for filling my cup."

In the bigger room, the strumming and singing had begun again: . . . *for Jesus, Lord Jesus, is in this very room* . . . As others left for dinner, Janet sat silent and alone in her corner, her cheeks still stained. Someone—her questioner from the muddy path earlier that afternoon—approached hesitantly and asked if she was OK. Janet nodded.

And had she decided yet what she was looking for? Janet nodded again. "Peace, I think."

Easter

Light

Saturday night: While the city plays, Dick Shaner reads words of God, of hope, in the still-darkened church. . . . *For a brief moment I abandoned you, but with great tenderness I will take you back. In an outburst of wrath, for a moment, I hid my face from you, but with enduring love I take pity on you. . . .*

For Dick, this vigil is a good way to end a spectacular spring day, which he has celebrated with some of his favorite spring activities—washing the car under a cloudless sky, lunching with his dad on Limburger cheese sandwiches, playing eighteen holes on suddenly green fairways, cheered on by songbirds. He and his wife, Jamie, have consumed this Holy Week voraciously, from the Palm Sunday procession to tonight's conclusion of the Triduum rites of Holy Thursday, Good Friday, and Easter Vigil. They both made sacramental confessions—Dick in a few minutes during the parish penance service on Monday, Jamie in an hour and a half of private soul-searching with Father Dick Sowinski on Wednesday afternoon, during which she says she tackled sins both venial and mortal and after which she emerged feeling, for the first time ever, truly "cleansed." On Thursday night, Dick Shaner's was one of twelve right feet (seven men's, five women's) washed at Mass by Father Paul; as the pastor knelt creakingly at Dick's feet, he looked up, winked, and muttered: "Jesus was a lot younger when he did this."

Both Shaners worked on Good Friday and therefore skipped the afternoon Liturgy of the Passion, and instead of the evening Stations of the Cross, they stayed home with Scotty and Tyler to decorate Easter eggs. But this morning, while Dick attacked the car with hose and sponge, Jamie and Scotty shopped for a hamper of food for the St. Vincent de Paul Society to pass on to an underprivileged family. At the 11 A.M. blessing of Easter baskets, the Shaners' vacuum-packed ham, powdered soup, Kraft dinner, and Bisquick sat prosaically among lavishly painted eggs, speckled Polish sausage, twisted breads, and cakes on the altar step. Hours from now, the Shaners will return home to hide gifts from the Easter Bunny. But here in the dark church, Easter has nothing at all to do with chocolates or rabbits. Here, Easter means an empty Palestinian tomb.

A bell chimes as Dick sits down and the next reader announces more words from the prophet Isaiah. Immediately, the sound of running water bounces off the cold stone walls as a three-bowl fountain springs to life alongside the great candle and (all at a carefully timed and rehearsed flip of sacristy switches by Nancy Piatkowski) soft lights appear amid the lilies, azaleas, hyacinths, and tulips that surround it. The relief from silent darkness extracts a low "aah" from the congregation as the reading proceeds: *All you who are thirsty, come to the water! You who have no money, come, receive grain and eat. . . . Seek the Lord while he may be found. Call him while he is near. . . . For my thoughts are not your thoughts. . . .*

Father Paul, sitting straight-backed in the deacon's seat, hands immobile on his knees in the disciplined way he was taught in seminary, peers through the colored watery light and spots ghostly faces from twelve years of births and passions and deaths. Here's a former altar boy now planning his baby's baptism; here's a woman whose husband and children he buried after a car accident. Here's a man with whom the pastor watched the endless cancerous death of his wife, and a couple who have finally got their marriage sorted out, and numerous men and women who haven't. Here's old Charlie Rider, the former trustee who welcomed Father Paul when he arrived to take over here, and Rose-Ann Martin, who has been at Mass almost every day of every week for those twelve years, and the Shaners, whose little Cory he buried, and the Monacos, anxiously awaiting news of their adoption from India.

Here, arrayed with their families in the eight pews immediately before him, are a record number of adults waiting to be received into the church—the Elect. Out of sight backstage, Nancy Piatkowski is no doubt busy checking sound dials and light switches, or checking off items on her clipboard, or chastising an altar server. All's right with the parish. The next pastor of St. Paul's will be met by people ready to share responsibility, Father Paul thinks; he hopes the new man will be willing to share it.

Nancy is satisfied so far with the first Holy Week she ever choreographed solo. As the ritual flows on in the nave and sanctuary, Nancy—who has spent much of the past three days in the church supervising the changing decor with her Liturgy Committee colleagues and trying not to lose her temper with resident nitpicker Rose-Ann Martin—tiptoes in and out of the sacristy, inspecting sacred vessels and oils and liturgical props from charcoal incense lighters to chiming altar bells. Her feet ache, but all told, it has gone smoothly, even if Father Dick flatly refused to wear the heavy best gold chasuble she had laid out tonight, and the guest celebrant of the Passion Rite on Good Friday unaccountably read the intercession for the Elect twice and that for the Pope not at all. If that was the worst glitch of the Triduum, Nancy figures she should be pleased.

A note from the organ cues the young cantor, who chants, in a golden soprano, the response: *You will draw water jo-o-oy-fully from the springs of salvation.* Young Michelle Pangborn, whose trip to see the Pope in Denver last summer remains the dominant memory of her senior year, sits stolidly, full lips pouting slightly, next to her religious educator mom, Fran, as her parish trustee father, Walt, walks to the lectern and announces a reading from the prophet Baruch: . . . *You have forsaken the fountain of wisdom! Had you walked in the way of God, you would have dwelt in enduring peace.* . . .

On Holy Thursday night, after the Mass of the Lord's Supper, Michelle and a few other Senior Youth Group members gathered near the back of the church and knelt for a while to survey, at a distance, the garden of repose where Christ's sacramental body awaited the terrible hour of betrayal and arrest. Except for the garden, the church had been stripped of finery, and the group of kids seemed beset by the sadness for, oh, maybe two minutes before reciting a hurried Lord's Prayer and departing in three carloads for the traditional tour of the altars of repose at seven churches. The expedition manifested an essentially Catholic mix of sacred and profane—in the churches, quiet brief moments of reverence among candles and incense; in the cars, loud chatter about college plans, Janet Jackson on the radio, arguments about directions, and, for one pair of seniors, romantic whispers and touches.

It also offered a glimpse of the variety of Catholic religious culture. The gold monstrance stark in candlelight among Easter lilies at Annunciation in the working-class upper West Side; the yellow and white banners against dark wood at Assumption in the Polish area of Amherst Street; the marble columns, gargoyles, and gilded tabernacle of St. Joseph's Cathedral. At the Italian-turning-Hispanic Holy Cross parish church downtown, the traditional tabernacle stood austerely between candles and two brass vases containing what looked like dried grass, under a blue ceiling with the Stations of the Cross painted right on it. At always avant-garde St. Joe's next door to the university, brown papier-mâché angels hung eerily against a shimmer of candles behind white netting.

A rust-colored moon was rising over the Kenmore rooftops as Michelle was dropped off at her house. When pressed for a reaction beyond "nice" to the night's ritual, Michelle said it left her feeling "kind of peaceful, perhaps." Most of the kids in the cars took religion less seriously than Michelle. But they—admittedly fewer than a dozen of the approximately 650 teenagers in this parish—will, like their parents, retain Catholic rituals and stories in their adult memories. Church, for them, may continue to represent home, a place to belong.

In this night between death and life, Father Dick prays after Walt Pangborn finishes reading, *we cling to you alone, God, wisdom, light to our path. Teach us the way of peace. . . .* Nancy moves to the light panel, and waits, pencil torch gripped between her teeth, for the first note of the *Gloria.*

Glory to God in the highest! Nancy hits the switches, all of them, fast: BANG! BANG! BANG! BANG! Suddenly, the church is bathed in light. *And peace to his people on earth!* Revealed to hundreds of eyes acclimated to Lenten austerity is a startling abundance of flowers and banners, gold and white cloths everywhere. Also revealed, to Nancy's fury, is a growing puddle of water under the fountain. *Alleluia! Alleluia! Alleluia! Give thanks to the Lord, for he is good!* While Father Dick proclaims the Gospel of the empty tomb, Nancy and two acolytes grovel with blue towels to dam the flood, keeping their heads low enough to go unnoticed by all but those in the foremost pews.

This is the first time Father Dick has played the role of chief celebrant at an Easter Vigil, the most complex rite of the year. The job should have gone to Father Don, but the former liturgist is spending a quiet romantic weekend in the nation's capital with the man he met there in January. Later, he will recall looking at his watch around 8 P.M. and thinking: "They're starting the vigil at St. Paul's. Well, it's not my problem now." Around now, he is trying, unsuccessfully, to persuade his lover to accompany him to the Basilica for Mass tomorrow morning.

"At Easter," Father Dick says in his homily, "we are called to become new people. . . . The Gospels indicate that those who came to the empty tomb were fearful—confused, bewildered with the news that the Lord was risen, changed, made different. They would see and experience him in a new way. And so the challenge to them too was to become new people. How does all of that happen? Maybe in the end we become Easter people, new people, by developing new habits. Trying to make changes by bits and pieces in our lives. Developing different attitudes. Taking a risk and trying on some new behaviors. Instead of our old habits of clutching on to resentments and bitterness toward others, we could try good habits of pardon and reconciliation. . . ."

Among the Elect, three pews from the fountain, Mike Merrill tries to concentrate on the homily but does not succeed. To the Ambivalent One's surprise, he will not be merely confirmed tonight but baptized—again. Before Monday night's penance service, he was sitting quietly with his wife, Melanie, steeling himself for his first confession while Melanie teased that with all the sins thus far accumulated he would have to say a whole Rosary on his knees. Then Jamie Shaner had appeared at his shoulder with the news that someone from the parish had called up the Congregational church of his boyhood to check on the form of his baptism: did they baptize in the name of the Father, Son, and Holy Spirit down there? The person who answered the phone wasn't entirely sure, so Mike would have to be baptized "conditionally," which, Jamie explained, was the word used when celebrating the rite just in case it has not been done properly before. Was that OK with him? Mike supposed so. When Jamie added that this meant he shouldn't confess, since baptism would wipe out all his sin, Melanie got peeved in her amiable way. "Thirty years of sins gone, without confession!" she sputtered. But later that week, she wandered into the Catholic Store on Colvin and there, among right-to-life booklets, Baltimore Catechisms, and bumper stickers shouting "I ♥ THE OLD LATIN MASS," bought Mike's confirmation present—a moonstone Rosary.

Tonight, Mike looks dapper in charcoal suit and white boutonniere. ("Am I the groom or the bride?" he asked his Jesuit friend and sponsor, Marty Moleski, when Jamie handed him the flower. "The bride," Marty answered with authority.) Throughout this Holy Week, Mike has been struck by new and highly esoteric insights into the Passion. After the endless Stations of the Cross devotion on Good Friday night, Mike noted in his journal that joining the church would mean being "cemented to a great Unity, a spiritual essence. Not sure how or where the death of Christ comes into this, but it seems to be the way he gathered people into himself—making a spectacle of sorts in order to get their attention." Tonight, it strikes him, apparently out of nowhere, that the death of Christ is not as sad as the sacrifice of being *alive*. "It's much easier to be dead," Mike will write in his journal later. "It's much more painful to be alive. Maybe that's heretical. So it's both sad and joyful that he came back to life." Right now, he is waiting with some anxiety for the moment when the priest will ask, *Do you believe and profess all that the holy Catholic Church believes, teaches, and proclaims to be revealed by God?*

So sweeping a question strikes him as "a bit of Catch-22," as he will later explain. "I do accept the Creed, though perhaps not in the most strict, dogmatic sense in which it is interpreted by some. But do I accept everything and not think for myself? If I did, then I wouldn't have a conscience. And having a conscience is part of what the church teaches. So there's no way I could answer 'Yes' to that question unless I kind of fudged it and used what I call my nonsense filter.

"I mean, there's nonsense everywhere. So to get what you want, sometimes you have to put up with, and filter out, a certain kind of nonsense. Who will tell me there's none of it in the Catholic Church?

"OK, now, why should religious nonsense offend me more than other kinds of nonsense? It makes sense that if one is struggling with powerful and fundamental issues, one will make powerful and fundamental mistakes. Does this mean one should not struggle with those issues? No, it does not.

"In the same way, I am proud to be a citizen of my country, even though elements of it have done some incredibly evil things. Overall, it's a better thing for me to be an American than not to be an American. In that way, overall, it is a better thing for me to be Catholic than not to be Catholic. And I have held nothing back in this process; these people, people I take to be representatives of the church, accept me for what I am, with those peculiar characteristics of mine that they may see as imperfections or strengths. So my becoming Catholic is both a compromise and an act of honesty. They know what I am, and they can deal with it. I know what they are, and I can deal with it.

"I accept the power structure of the church too. I accept it as an interesting and imperfect exercise in attempting to create a world organization based on spiritual truths. But I do not think that Catholic dogma has a monopoly on truth. I think these people try to be—and I think they have done a decent job at being—an embodiment of the highest good that they can be."

In fact, the dreaded *revealed by God* question will be asked only of those confirmation candidates who were baptized before tonight. This quirk of liturgy effects a peculiar twist on the normal approach to religious initiation. Mike Merrill has trained his critical microscope on the church's teaching, judged some of it wanting, and decided, tolerantly, that he can live with that. But the beliefs of the initiate himself are subjected to no critical examination at all.

Mary and Joseph," the cantor sings; "—pray for us," the congregation responds. "Michael and all Angels—pray for us; Anna and Elizabeth . . ." For many in the congregation and even among the Elect, this, rather than the sacraments which follow, is the night's most haunting moment. Those awaiting baptism stand with their godparents facing the congregation while the Litany of Saints is chanted, the golden-voiced soprano's bidding met, again and again, by the congregation's response, three short words, one unwavering note, hanging in the air as if carried on an angel's wings:

> *. . . pray for us*
> *Isaac, Sarah, Abraham,* **pray for us**
> *Jacob, Joseph, Samuel,* **pray for us**
> *David and Solomon,* **pray for us**
> *Isaiah, Jeremiah,* **pray for us**
> **All you holy men and women pray for us.**
>
> *Peter, Paul, and Andrew,* **pray for us**
> *James, John, and all Apostles,* **pray for us**
> *Mary Magdalene, Veronica,* **pray for us** *. . .*

Standing in the sanctuary awaiting baptism, Mike has a visceral sense of hundreds of dead people—Mary and Joseph and Michael and all the angels and all the saints and prophets—crowding their way into the church, filling it to the rafters. A few yards away, Dave Taylor, despite his Baptist roots, is filled with the same sensation, as he always has been on hearing the great Litany ever since his own confirmation, when he stood fighting tears as the names rolled on. Even Judy Nice's husband, Rick, who is not an especially religious man but who has occasionally dreamed of angels and on at least one occasion felt certain of a supernatural presence in his bedroom, spies a spectral face on the white cloth over the tabernacle. It might, he thinks, be St. Joseph.

> *. . . Felicity, Perpetua,* **pray for us**
> *Cosmas and Damian,* **pray for us**
> *John Chrysostom and Justin,* **pray for us**

This Holy Week, in the wake of her crisis of belonging, Judy Nice has been reexamining her entire faith. On Thursday night, she wrote a strange kind of creed in her journal: "Right now, I know only this: I believe in a loving, passionate Creator 'God.' I believe in Jesus the Christ, the anointed one, 'God become Man.' I believe in Spirit & Grace and her presence in all of time and humanity. After this, I just don't know. So what is it I commemorate tonight? The body of Christ!" But she could more easily skip her own birthday party than skip a Triduum celebration. She was back in church yesterday, Good Friday, for the celebration of the Passion, standing in line for the ritual adoration of the cross and smiling down as a small boy straddled the foot of the big wooden cross to kiss it, the two altar boys holding the cross's arms seeming not to notice the extra weight. Something had changed inside Judy—she was unable to feel as sad, this Holy Week, as she expected to. "I am letting go of my feeling of unworthiness," she wrote in her journal last night. "In the Passion reading, I couldn't shout 'Crucify him!' with the rest of the congregation. Because that is nowhere near where I am right now. Yet those are the things—unworthiness, guilt—that I have always identified most strongly with."

> *. . . Lucy, Agatha, and Agnes,* **pray for us**
> **All you holy men and women, pray for us.**

> *Jerome and Eusebius,* **pray for us**
> *Scholastica and Benedict,* **pray for us . . .**

Over to Judy's right, Dennis Hurley's shoulders are hunched beneath a new gray suit and his eyes seem closed. He made a surprising appearance in the sacristy on Holy Thursday night, coming up to greet Dave Taylor as he stood with Coty-Ann Henk awaiting a briefing on the protocol of having one's feet washed.

"How's it going at the . . . ," Dennis asked, and waved a hand vaguely southward.

"Bank?"

"No, the . . ." Dennis pointed more specifically, to the corridor into the rectory.

"RCIA? Pretty good. In some ways it's better; we have to pull together more now."

"I miss it," Dennis murmured.

Dave, for once, was nonplussed. But Coty-Ann said, matter-of-fact, "We miss you too."

"Well," Dennis said after a short silence, "I wouldn't want people to feel awkward."

"I don't think they would."

"Well . . ."

"I don't know anyone who would feel that way," Coty-Ann said. "Do you, Dave?"

"No, I really don't," Dave said. "You should come."

> . . . *Ambrose, Monica, and Augustine,* **pray for us**
> *Martin and Gregory,* **pray for us**
> *Clare, Francis, and Dominic,* **pray for us** . . .

Even Rose-Ann Martin, the daily Mass-goer, former nun and liturgical bulldog, finds little to criticize in this vigil. The feel of it is "simple," she will say later, which is her highest praise for a liturgy. It certainly comes as a relief after Good Friday's rites, especially "that damned adoration of the cross, which took forever," and the evening's Stations, which was, to Rose-Ann's mind, more a "concert" than a devotion. By the fifth Station, her thoughts had become so murderous toward organist and choir that, for the first time in her life, she walked out of church and went home.

> . . . *Francis Xavier, Ignatius,* **pray for us**
> *Elizabeth and Catherine,* **pray for us**
> *Louis and Wenceslas,* **pray for us** . . .

Although the pews are almost full tonight, thousands of parishioners give the vigil a miss. For many, it's a question of the rite's length (two hours and forty minutes); for others, the vigil (unlike morning Mass on Easter Day) has no resonance in family tradition. Falling in the latter group is the ever-faithful Rose McKenna, she who once defied church law by receiving communion before her husband Bill's annulment. Rose and Bill are spending the evening at home, Bill watching TV from his wheelchair and Rose, leaning alternately on cane and stovetop, cooking a potato-and-vegetable casserole for her ailing parents' Easter dinner. There won't be a family gathering this year because of Rose's mom's frailty, but Rose wants her parents to have a good meal anyway.

Like the McKennas, Colleen Connolly will wait for morning to make her Easter communion. She and her daughters Francisca and Maria spent much of Holy Thursday packing up outgrown clothes and shoes to send as an Easter gift to the San Salvador orphanage that had rescued the two girls from the streets. For conversation while packing, Colleen asked, "What do people need to live?"

"Love," said the older and more theologically sophisticated Francisca. But Maria said, "First food, then shoes . . ." The next morning, Good Friday, while the girls and their mom packed Easter baskets for poor families, Maria pondered the necessity for all this good work and drew a conclusion. "You know, Mom," she said, "the Easter Bunny doesn't know where you are when you're poor."

And so, tonight, when Colleen tucks Maria into bed, the six-year-old asks her mother, "Can you go downstairs and write the Easter Bunny a note?" Certainly. "Put it on the front door," Maria instructs, "and write this: 'Maria and Francisca Ayala Lopez Connolly live here and they're not poor anymore. So please don't pass our house—stop and visit us.' "

Sammy Forlenza is likewise in bed by now. Today, Sammy went with his parents to Premier Cheese to do some grocery shopping, and then to the cemetery to visit Grandpa's Sam's grave and leave some flowers. Sammy is hoping the Easter Bunny will give him a Hardy Boys book. But nothing can beat yesterday. Good Friday was, Sammy says, "the most awesome day of my life," because his buddy Brandon's birthday party was held at Lasertron. Sammy was on the green team, which won all three rounds of play with the laser guns.

*. . . **All you holy men and women, pray for us.***

*Lord be merciful, **save your people***
*From all evil, **save your people***
*From every sin, **save your people***
*From everlasting death, **save your people** . . .*

Bernice Graff sits with her fellow eucharistic ministers, remembering an Easter not so long ago when her son Paul, then in the novitiate, got a ride home from Baltimore with two friars. Bernice can still see him bounding up the front stairs of Ray's house, his three small nieces grabbing and hugging him. Bob was home that year too—Bob was always home for the holidays.

Yesterday, Bernice took holy communion to her shut-ins, including the now almost totally immobilized Jo Kamuda. This time, Bernice could barely hear or understand anything Jo said. "Poor Mary," Bernice wrote in a Holy Week journal, "having to watch her son being tortured and crucified! I can *kind of* feel her pain today, but hers of course was much worse."

Similarly, Ken Monaco will later say of this Holy Week, "Karen and I really identified with crying in the garden and carrying the cross." This refers not to an actual death but to the death-resurrection-death-resurrection of the Monacos' adoption effort. In March, the Monacos demanded a refund of their fees for the canceled placement of the eight-year-old boy who had turned out to have incurable hepatitis B. Wednesday of Holy Week brought a faxed refusal from the agency in Washington implying—to the Monacos' minds—a threat to the prospects of adopting six-year-old girl Manjula (or Maria, as the Monacos thought of her). Feeling powerless, Karen handwrote a fax of apology; Holy Thursday brought an equally conciliatory phone call from Washington. Ken went to work on Good Friday more cheerful than the season dictated—it was, after all, the anniversary of his and Karen's engagement ("Great Friday," they had called it ever since). His mood improved still more when he and his office colleagues weighed in for the results of their five-week weight-loss contest. Ken won with a twenty-three-pound reduction, thanks to his Lenten fast, which had included bread-and-water Fridays.

For the vigil, Ken has a seat in the front pew, in his role as the long-suffering Jeff Tredo's sponsor. It is two years now, almost exactly, since Jeff walked into Judy's office seeking baptism. Tonight, his first marriage annulled at last, Jeff stands in the sanctuary, among the Elect.

> . . . *Send your spirit* (**hear our prayer**)
> *in its fullness* (**hear our prayer**)
> *on your sons and daughters* (**hear our prayer**)
> *who believe and profess you* (**hear our prayer**)

> **Christ hear us, Lord Jesus hear our prayer**

Finally the moment comes when Mike Merrill, Janet Ehrensberger, and the others are ready to become new through the waters of baptism. *Do you reject sin so as to live in the freedom of God's children? Father Dick asks. Do you reject the glamor of evil . . . ?* Michael the Ambivalent is first to kneel at the fountain. As he walks away poking at his head with a towel, feeling the cold water seeping into his suit and noticing how Father Paul is standing by to retrieve the towel, he suddenly catches himself thinking, "I guess it's OK for me to die now." He whispers this thought to his Jesuit sponsor, who replies, "Only if you don't sin between now and then."

Now Janet Ehrensberger steps forward, wearing a collarless white elbow-length blouse, floral vest, and knee-length beige skirt, all bought at AM&A's on Monday. Because she is shorter than Mike, Janet merely bends her head over the fountain. *Janet Elizabeth, I baptize you in the name of the Father, and of the Son, and of the Holy Spirit.* Marianne Parry dabs at the back of Janet's neck, but the water drips down into her blouse. If this water brings the "peace, I think," that Janet hoped for, it does not take effect immediately. Janet's main feeling as she returns to her place is relief that it's over.

Judy Nice, who would have been there in the sanctuary with them, watches from her pew, leaning forward, hands in lap, smile tight, big tears falling down her cheeks. Unknown to her, Rick has spotted another angel—male or female, he doesn't know—sitting on the beam of the crucifix above the altar. The angel, Rick notices, leans forward slightly to watch as each of the Elect goes under the water.

Half an hour later, in the quiet moments after communion, Ruthie Hemerlein sits serene, eyes closed, head back, chin resting immobile on a bent finger. She sits this way for the longest time before opening her eyes for the final prayer and dismissal. Ruthie made her confession last Saturday, and as usual the two main things she talked about, the things she most wanted to change in her life, were her fear of being alone and her waves of self-pity. But tonight, Ruthie's mind is filled with death, with memories of her saintly stepmother, and with contentment. "I don't want to end my life," she will write to a friend before this Easter season ends, "but I know it's bound to be getting closer now. The aloneness of it really gets to me—I know there's nobody going to help me die when the time comes. But there's a lot of people waiting for me at the other end."

Tomorrow morning, there will be three or four inches of snow on the ground, which will conspire with the annual standing-room Easter turnout, the change to daylight saving time, and a longish homily to cause chaos in the parking lot after the eight-thirty Mass and before the ten o'clock. But soon flags will appear again on Kenmore's porches, Victoria Boulevard's bare maples will turn bright with spring green, and boat-sized chunks of ice will break off the lake and proceed in state down the Niagara. Gathering speed, they will glide past the former glory of the Erie Canal and the solid waste-land of Love Canal, thawing as they tumble over the falls into the warmer waters of Ontario, the St. Lawrence, and the Atlantic. On the first day of May, the fifth Sunday of Easter, at 10:48 A.M., the name of Samuel Thomas Forlenza will be called and a boy will stand at the altar step with palms high and straight. His new gray cotton suit hanging loose over his tiny shoulders, he will pry the wafer out of his left hand and carefully insert it into his mouth. He will wait for both his parents to do likewise, and then walk solemnly over to sip at the chalice. He will neither screw up his nose nor wipe at his face. Hands flattened vertically into each other before his chest, he will return to his father and mother, a member, with them, of the Communion of Saints.

Afterword

This book is the true story of what I saw, heard, and learned in St. Paul's Parish, Kenmore, between May 1993 and May 1994. I chose this parish after spending a short time in the diocese of Buffalo seeking a fairly ordinary, middle-of-the-road, heterogeneous parish where the pastor and staff would be comfortable with this kind of research. Father Paul Whitney was enthusiastic; asked what, if anything, he expected of me or the book, he said, "I expect to be surprised, and challenged." For the twelve months that followed, I conducted more than 150 hours of taped interviews with members of the parish, attended liturgical, educational, and social gatherings, and talked informally with Catholic people both within the parish and elsewhere. I was given free access to rectory records and all parish events, and neither the pastor nor any staff member ever refused to provide requested information.

All the names are real except those of "Claire and Dave," who asked that their names (but no other details) be altered for the sake of Claire's parents, and that of "Tony," the reticent catechumen. I was allowed to sit in on catechumenate sessions (I attended eleven of these sessions plus most of the weekend retreat) on condition that I would respect the choice of those candidates who declined to be identified. For this reason, I changed some background details about "Tony."

Every other fact in this book is, to the best of my knowledge, accurate. While I personally witnessed many of the events described here, I sometimes had to rely on the memories of others. In these cases, I made special efforts to check the facts with at least two participants—more, where points of view or memories conflicted. As well, I read or showed pages of manuscript to those whose stories are told therein, with the understanding that they would help me correct facts without attempting to censor the stories. Twenty parishioners also agreed to write, and allowed me to read, detailed personal journals and reflections during Holy Week 1994; these journals informed much of the first and last chapters.

The "present" time in this book is Easter 1994. Water has flowed down the Niagara since then, and there have been some changes in Kenmore.

Father Paul Whitney left St. Paul's as advertised in the summer of 1994, and is now the pastor of St. Mary's church in the village of Medina, New York, exactly 1.6 miles from the first tee of his favorite golf course. The parish has no school. He was succeeded in Kenmore by Father Paul Nogaro, a more distant man whose weekly "Heart to Heart" column in the parish bulletin tends to focus on finance and fund-raising, and whose early liturgical innovations included restoring the sale of vigil candles in the sanctuary.

Looking back on the year described in this book, Judy Nice sometimes wonders if the process of talking to me so regularly, of actually giving voice to her doubts, might have crystallized them and forced her to confront them earlier than she might otherwise have done. A few months after resigning her position at St. Paul's, Judy, to her own surprise, accepted another church position—catechumenate director at St. Joseph's University parish. She found it hard to explain why she did so: a friend had asked her help; she was feeling a loss of identity as a "housewife"; it was an opportunity to prove that she could, after all, do a good job ("that I was still valid, in what I did"). The following spring, she quit that job, too, with a feeling that she had been affirmed both in her competency as an educator and in her discomfort with what she was supposed to teach. The last time I saw her, drinking pink lemonade in her newly redecorated living room, she seemed relaxed, happy and confident in her ability to discover a new niche after completing the last two semesters of her B.A. studies. "I read John's Gospel in the original Greek," she exclaimed of one course. "It was like, Wow! He really never said, 'Man.' He said, 'Humankind.' " Judy and her family go to Mass at St. Joe's every Sunday, but not Holy Days. "I still feel part of the Catholic Church," she says. "But a *different* part of it."

Ken Monaco has not returned to the catechumenate team. He says he needed time to devote to his family after his and Karen's adoption dream came true on September 8, 1994, the feast of the birth of the Blessed Virgin Mary. On that day, a six-year-old girl soon to be renamed Maria Monaco boarded an Air India flight to New York. On meeting her new family at JFK Airport, she was stony-faced and utterly silent; as soon as the car pulled out of the airport lot, she fell asleep. Awakening thirteen hours later, she consented to sit on Ken's lap, but remained grim-faced and voiceless. Ken took from around his neck the holy scapular that he always wears, and pointed out its tiny laminated picture of the blessed Mother. "Maria," the little girl said, and smiled. A year later, starting second grade at St. Paul's School, a keen swimmer, soccer player, and devotee of her big brother Chris, she seems to smile a great deal.

Dick Shaner's term on the Parish Council ended shortly after the events recorded here. His wife, Jamie, was one of ten candidates standing for election to the next council—she was not elected, but gained a seat when a successful candidate withdrew. Jamie ended her involvement in the catechumenate soon after Easter, and the following winter the Shaners moved to suburban Williamsville and joined a parish a few miles closer to their new home.

In July, 1995, Mike Merrill and his wife, Melanie, had a son, Michael Asa. Mike Senior, ever ambivalent, now attends Mass about once every two weeks. "I don't get a big spiritual experience out of going to church," he says, "but plugging myself into this, this outward ritual, reminds me of the important things in life, the things that do not change, and makes me feel less like a human outcast than I used to. It reminds me to try to bring myself into line with the will of God, to use Catholic language. Or, to use Buddhist language, to stay on the path, to work toward the liberation of all sentient beings." He pauses to shift the baby in his arms, and considers. "But it's not as though being baptized was the defining event of my life, or anything like that."

Michelle Pangborn achieved a perfect 4.0 grade-point average in her second semester of engineering studies at Cornell University, and spent much of the following summer helping out with research into ceramic crystal growth. She attends Mass weekly at the school's Catholic center, but is not otherwise active in religious affairs. Two years after World Youth Day, Michelle says that thinking about her time in Denver, and humming the theme song (*We are one body . . .*) still gives her an odd feeling of peacefulness.

Sammy Forlenza is now in the fourth grade, and in the past year has won, among other awards, special recognition for multiplication skills, for reading five hundred books, and for helping fellow students with special needs. SuperMario World has been largely supplanted by Mortal Kombat II; Sammy wears braces on his teeth, but has otherwise not changed much physically, which frustrates him enough to have inspired a poem (which was selected for the Kenmore-Tonawanda school district's anthology), entitled "Being Small." The central stanza reads:

> *My dad says,*
> *"You know you're strong."*
> *But I don't care;*
> *I'd rather be long.*

After receiving his first communion, Sammy and his mom stopped going to Mass every week, but continue to show up at St. Paul's at Easter and Christmas.

"Claire and Dave" now have a baby son; both sets of grandparents are equally devoted. The couple plays a leading role in the St. Paul's catechumenate, which endured a lull after the departure of Judy Nice. No one was baptized or confirmed at Easter 1995, although a woman who had been attending Inquiry was initiated the following summer, before moving to Rochester.

Dennis Hurley has not returned to the catechumenate, and, other than regular attendance at Mass, has not become active in other parish affairs. He says he is concentrating on his family commitments.

I bought Rose-Ann Martin breakfast at Denny's after the ten o'clock Mass one recent Sunday, and showed her the pages of manuscript based on interviews with her. As she read, her usual glower was replaced by a rueful smile frequently transformed into hearty chortles. "Bulldog!" she exclaimed over the nickname I had given her; she shook her head as her shoulders heaved. But Rose-Ann had had a hard summer, a desperate financial struggle having combined with the loss of her closest friend (and of one of her two dogs) to send her into a depression. Catholic Charities provided free counseling, which helped somewhat, as did an appointment to teach two writing courses at Niagara U., the acquisition of a new dog whom she named Princess Jenny the First, and a newfound habit of saying the Rosary every day.

When Nancy Piatkowski read her pages, we were sitting in a somewhat less cluttered front room than the one described in these pages. Nancy's 128-page thesis on "St. Joseph's tables" earned her a master's degree in humanities, after which she performed an impressive mess-control operation at home before launching a job hunt. Nancy resigned as chair of the Liturgy Committee at St. Paul's a few months after Father Nogaro's arrival; she and her husband Dennis are now members of the Cathedral parish, and serve on the diocesan Liturgical Commission.

Nothing much changed in the lives of Rose and Bill McKenna in the year and a half after Easter 1994, except that Rose now has her master's degree in social work, and Bill (who seems slightly weaker as he wrestles his unruly body from wheelchair to dining-room chair but declines, as always, to talk about his health) has returned to politics, helping a friend campaign for the county legislature. They have seldom missed the ten o'clock Mass at St. Paul's, apart from six weeks last summer while the disability ramp was being overhauled as part of the centenary renovations.

Colleen Connolly is now engaged to marry Paul Culligan, a forty-six-year-old divorced father and practicing Catholic, pending word from the Tribunal regarding an annulment. Paul plans to adopt Colleen's Salvadorean daughters, Maria and Francisca. The girls have not given up hope for a reunion with their sister, Marta, but that hope has become slim. According to Colleen, a relative "coerced" Marta to escape from the El Salvador orphanage and start domestic work for a local family, rendering the pending adoption application moot.

Bernice Graff, who now has twenty-one grandchildren, takes communion to Jo Kamuda every second Friday, but no longer can offer a glass of water after the sacrament since Jo, now confined to her bed, is fed entirely by tubes.

The teachers of St. Paul's School voted to unionize, and the new pastor negotiated a four-year contract that promised to narrow the gap between them and teachers in public schools. Father Nogaro also succeeded in establishing a parish school board, achieving one of his predecessor's longtime goals. At fiscal-year end last August, Father Nogaro announced that the parish had staved off deficit spending, helped by "Booster Fund" raffle tickets that showed a $6,632 profit and a "One Time Gift" appeal that raised over $16,000. The parish launched a long-distance sales campaign with Allied Telecom, and when its application for a bingo permit failed, began investigating the idea of getting a pro-bingo ordinance on Kenmore's electoral ballot.

Bishop Edward D. Head's resignation having been accepted by Pope John Paul II, the Most Rev. Henry J. Mansell took canonical possession of the diocese of Buffalo in June 1995.

Father Don, who asked me to withhold his last name, says he has no intention of returning to pastoral work. He lives in Baltimore with a man he met through a gay-lesbian computer bulletin board, and has a management job in the hospitality industry. The two men attend a downtown Presbyterian church that they describe as "gay-friendly." Father Don says he still considers himself a Catholic but has not received a Catholic sacrament since August 1994.

Last winter, during several hours of interviews in his new home, I sensed a subtle but profound change in Father Don. He seemed mellower, happier, slower to sarcasm, less angry at his core. Most surprisingly, I saw a tender side to his personality at which I would never have guessed. "Sweetie," he called his partner, Steve, laying a hand softly on his shoulder as they passed each other between kitchen and dining room. I asked whether he considered himself to be living in a state of mortal sin. He shook his head, smiled, and said: "I'm in a stable loving relationship. I believe it was God who brought Steve and me together. God did not create us to be unhappy, to be miserable, to be heroes. We were created to love, to be social creatures. That's what it means to be human. I think my relationship is making me a better person, and bringing out a side of me that was ignored for a very long time. It's bringing out more ability to compromise, more of the loving, compassionate side. And it certainly has taken away the loneliness. I feel more alive, more fulfilled. I feel whole."

Three days after that Easter, Ruthie Hemerlein started to hemorrhage and landed in the hospital. When I last visited her, Ruthie had been back in the hospital five times in as many months, but sat straight-backed as ever in her armchair as leaves started yellowing far below; she steepled her hands on her belly in her placid way and we compared stories of my tiny son and her tiny grandson. I mentioned that my visits with her had represented a rare constant during the sometimes turbulent year I had spent at St. Paul's. She said: "You're looking at me as if you think that's a plus. Well, I tell ya, I'm bored." She made me promise to sign a copy of this book for her, and I suppose we both silently wondered if she would live to see it.

In the cause of fairness, I asked Judy Nice, Ken Monaco, and Father Paul Whitney to read and comment on the entire manuscript before publication. All three pointed out several factual inaccuracies (which have been corrected in the final text), but Ken's critique was more far-reaching. He felt that a preponderance of liberals in this book represented a bias against the few interviewees who were loyal to the Pope. The effect was to present a caricature of orthodox people as hard-hearted, simpleminded, and "robotic," and to degrade the church's magisterium and priesthood. He wrote me a lengthy note in which he said that the RCIA group at St. Paul's had served as "an excellent tool for creating internal apostates, wherein the church itself becomes a trivialization." In this regard, Ken wrote: "I remember reading in the past five to six years that at least 40 percent of American Catholics prefer only a symbolic union with Rome." Instead of helping to correct this problem, the St. Paul's RCIA had aggravated it, Ken wrote, by placing too much emphasis on the human conscience, thus failing to achieve "a true and balanced sense of what it means to be unfaithful to God."

Ken wrote: "I believe that restoring a proper sense of what is sinful is the first step that should be taken in squarely facing the spiritual crisis in

America today. I think of the analogy of an 'eclipse' of the sun or moon in relation to the *eclipse of the conscience*, as in both instances there is a great dimming of light."

While the reporting and reflections in *What God Allows*—including any biases—are entirely my own, I do owe profound debts to a legion of people, many unknown to each other, who made it possible. Most vitally, my thanks go to those who entrusted me with their thoughts and memories, sometimes of an intimate kind, and allowed me to observe them as they lived their lives. The courage, candor, and reflectiveness of Paul Whitney and Judy Nice, especially, made this book possible, as did the trust, generosity, and hospitality of Ken and Karen Monaco, Jamie and Dick Shaner, Sam and Mary Ann Forlenza and their son Sammy, Rose-Ann Martin, Janet Ehrensberger, Bernice Graff, Ruthie Hemerlein, Dennis Hurley, Rose and Bill McKenna, Mike Merrill and Melanie Graban, Nancy Piatkowski, "Claire and Dave," Father Don and Steve, Dan Killian, Michelle and Fran Pangborn, Pat (Blum) Sciandra, Eleanore Speicher, Barb and Tony Cribbs, Colleen Connolly and her daughters Francisca and Maria, Father Dick Sowinski, Father Daniel Liderbach, S.J., Sister Mary Jude Rindfuss, S.S.M.N., Father Sam Faiola, Barbara Miller, and Jeff and Jennifer Tredo, among many others.

Thanks are due also to the following copyright holders of quoted works: Jaime Rickert for his song, "Is Your God So Small" (copyright © 1989 by Jaime Rickert, Parish Mission Team, 38 Montebello Road, Suffern, NY); Word Inc. for "Be Careful Little Hands" in the album *The Bill Gaithier Trio: Especially for Children of All Ages* (copyright © 1973 by The Bill Gaithier Trio); Jack Miffleton for his song "Willa-Mena Amphisbena" (copyright © 1987 by Jack Miffleton).

I owe special gratitude to Tom Cahill, who commissioned this work for Doubleday and lavished his blunt and thoughtful critique on the first draft; to Casey Fuetsch, who edited the final draft with loving care; to Christian Schoenberg, Trace Murphy, Katherine Trager, M. K. Moore, and countless others at Doubleday, consummate professionals all; to my tireless agent, Ed Novak, for his faith, persistence, and encouragement; to Mildred Istona, Rona Maynard, and my other colleagues at *Chatelaine* magazine in Toronto for their flexibility, patience, and enthusiastic support; to Sister Regina Murphy, S.S.M.N., for invaluable guidance and information from this project's inception; and to Sister Sandra Makowski, S.S.M.N., for background on canon law and procedure.

Less tangible but still substantial debts are owed to John Fraser, Ernest Hillen, Brenda and Joe Berger, and my parents, Max and Queenie Shapiro, all of whom provided encouragement, sometimes without knowing it, at times when this work had almost defeated me, and to my son, David, who was born as this book was in its final stages and tolerated its completion. Finally, I thank two women who profoundly affected the book—one who had nothing whatever to do with its production and one who lived through every painful step. Barbara Moon, editor-at-large of *Saturday Night* magazine, an intolerably demanding task-driver and brilliant reader (who will, no doubt, be less than satisfied with this work), taught me over the course of some years as my editor that writing, when done properly, has less to do with big words than with clear thoughts, sharp eyes and ears, and an open heart. And Louise Paul, my wife, conquered her ingrained suspicion of things religious to bolster me and endure me through months of research and writing, to do a lot more than her fair share of caring for baby David when I was rewriting and editing, to read the manuscript with a gently critical eye, and, throughout, to delight in what this work meant to me, even when it separated us and forced sacrifices on us. Let love be praised.

TORONTO, FALL 1995